D1549552

SERMONS.

(FOURTH SERIES.)

SERMONS

PREACHED AT BRIGHTON.

BY THE LATE

EV. FREDERICK W. ROBERTSON,

THE INCUMBENT OF TRINITY CHAPEL.

FOURTH SERIES.

NEW EDITION.

HENRY S. KING & CO.
65 CORNHILL & 12 PATERNOSTER ROW, LONDON.
1875.

TO

THE CONGREGATION

WORSHIPPING IN

TRINITY CHAPEL, BRIGHTON,

FROM AUGUST 15, 1847, TO AUGUST 15, 1853,

THESE

RECOLLECTIONS OF SERMONS

PREACHED BY THEIR LATE PASTOR,

ARE DEDICATED.

PREFACE TO THE FOURTH SERIES.

It is proposed shortly to issue a volume entitled "Pulpit Notes," which will consist of the skeleton or outline which Mr. Robertson prepared before delivering his Sermons. In some cases only a line or a single word is given to indicate a division of his subject; in others he has written out a *whole* thought, to be further amplified and completed in course of preaching.

The Editor believes that such a volume will be of service in two ways—first, as offering suggestions to preachers in the preparation or consideration of their addresses; and, secondly, as being sufficiently complete for purposes of home reading where it is the custom at family prayers, or on Sundays, to read a short discourse, occupying but a few minutes.

With reference to the first of these, it seems to be felt very generally that the pulpit is not what it was originally intended to be. There is a wide-spread opinion that it was designed for the edification of the mind as well as the heart; and it may be that one great cause of the indifference with which men are said to listen to preachers arises from the fact that for the most part their addresses are far below the intelligence of their audience, who are wearied with the

trite repetitions of platitudes that neither instruct nor inform.
These Sermons and "Pulpit Notes" evidence the character
of a teaching, not only earnestly listened to, but also most
influential. Perhaps the contrast between these and the
sermons usually preached, may suggest a means of re-
awakening an interest now almost dormant in the minds
of listeners. In this view, a volume will shortly be issued,
and if it be found successful another will be put to press.

The Editor appends a portion of a letter from a friend
on the subject of preaching, because it serves to show that
the indifference he has adverted to springs from other causes
than mere irreligiousness.

MY DEAR ——,

I THINK one great need in our pulpit ministrations is naturalness ;
by which I mean an exact recognition of the facts of our daily life. The
phrase "the dignity of the pulpit" has given a fatally artificial character
to the mass of sermons. Mr. Spurgeon and his vulgar slang is a violent
reaction from the cold unfelt conventionalities with which men have
grown so familiar ; and his success is due to the fact that he recognises
the men and women before him as flesh and blood—sinning, suffering,
tempted, falling, struggling, rising. Like all extreme reactions, it
shocks a great many by its levity, its irreverence, and its vulgarity.

But it is in this direction must come our pulpit reform. We come
day after day to God's house, and the most careless one of us there, is
still one who, if he could really hear a word from God to his own soul,
would listen to it—ay, and be thankful for it. No heart can tell out to
another what waves of temptation have been struggled through during
the week past—with what doubtful success. How, after the soul has
been beaten down and defiled, with what bitter anguish of spirit it has
awoke to a knowledge of its backslidings and its bondage to sin :—not
to this or that sin merely, but to a general sense of sinfulness pervading
the whole man, so that Redemption would be indeed a joyful sound.

Many are miserable in their inmost hearts, who are light-hearted and
gay before the world. They feel that no heart understands theirs, or
can help them. Now, suppose the preacher goes down into the depths

of his own being, and has the courage and fidelity to carry all he finds there, first to God in confession and prayer, and then to his flock as some part of the general experience of Humanity, do you not feel that he must be touching close upon some brother-man's sorrows and wants? "Be ye as I am, for I am as ye are." Many a weary and heavy-laden soul has taken his burden to the Saviour, because he has found some man of "like passions with himself," who has suffered as he has, and found relief. I think a bold faithful experimental preaching rarely fails to hit some mark, and oftentimes God's Spirit witnesses to the truth of what is said, by rousing this and that man to the feeling, "Why I, too, have been agonizing, and falling, and crying for just such help as this. Ah, this man has indeed something to say to me."

*   *   *   *   *   *

I may be wrong in my opinion, but it is one of deep conviction, gained long ago, that no amount of external evidence in the way of proof of the truth of Christianity is worth anything in the way of saving a human soul.

There is always as much to be said on one side as the other, because, just as Archimedes could not move the earth without a fulcrum, so there must be something taken for granted in all external evidence, which a rigid logician might fairly demur to granting. But when, as with the Spirit of God, the voice of a man reaches his fellow-man— telling him of his inner aspirations and failures, his temptations, his sins, his weakness—not in generals, but in details—of light that has come and has been extinguished ; of hopes born, yet not nourished ; of fears which have grown stronger and stronger, and which refuse altogether to be silent, even in the midst of the engagements or pleasures of life—does not the man feel that here is a revelation of God's truth as real and fresh as if he had stood in the streets of Jerusalem, and heard the Saviour's very voice ? The man feels that, in this word, which has, so to speak, "told him all that ever he did," there must be a divine life. "One touch of nature makes the whole word kin."

*   *   *   *   *   *

I think that a ministry which should work mightily amongst a people would be one in which very rarely is heard any development of the *modus operandi* or "*plan* of salvation ;" in which *proof* of the divine mission of Christ, or of God's revelation, was never attempted, but in which the great facts themselves were set forth as the alone solution of the wants, sorrows, and sins of the hearers; in which the fact of Adam's fall, and any consequences it had on the human race, were only touched upon incidentally; but in which the individual man's fall was pressed home upon him from his own certain convictions. Not because Adam fell, and the race fell in him, but because *you* have fallen —*therefore you* need a Saviour, and divine life and light are indispensable.

The man who quietly slumbers under Adam's sin and its tremendous consequences—his relation to which consequences, how is it possible for a poor uneducated person to comprehend ?—may be aroused to a sense of his connection with the fact of a fall in himself, and a need of such a restorer as Christ. I am sure I don't know whether this is orthodox or not ; but I doubt whether orthodox creeds and confessions of doctrine have ever turned one soul from the error of his ways, or brought him in real earnest to Christ.

        *   *   *   *   *   *

Let us look at this boldly. Seventeen thousand pulpits echo in our land every Sunday, to what each preacher considers the soundest form of Christ's Gospel. Is it God's word that is preached ? Has He changed His purpose ? Has He ceased to care for man ?—and does He no longer intend that " His word shall not return to Him void ?" Yet where is the divine evidence that it is His word which is preached, as shown in hearts quickened and aroused, "about their Father's business ?"

        *   *   *   *   *   *

CONTENTS.

SERMON XX.
RECONCILIATION BY CHRIST.

Preached February 2, 1851.

SERMON XXI.
THE PRE-EMINENCE OF CHARITY.

Preached March 13, 1853.

SERMON XXII.
THE UNJUST STEWARD.

Preached January 8, 1849.

SERMON XXIII.
THE ORPHANAGE OF MOSES.

(A SERMON PREACHED ON BEHALF OF THE ORPHAN SOCIETY.)

Preached February 16, 1851.

CONTENTS.

SERMONS.

I.

THE CHARACTER OF ELI.

"And the child Samuel ministered unto the Lord before Eli. And the word of the Lord was precious in those days; *there was* no open vision."—1 Sam. iii. 1.

IT is impossible to read this chapter without perceiving that it draws a marked contrast between the two persons of whom it speaks—Eli and Samuel.

1. They are contrasted in point of years: for the one is a boy, the other a grey-headed old man; and if it were for only this, the chapter would be one of deep interest. For it is interesting always to see a friendship between the old and the young. It is striking to see the aged one retaining so much of freshness and simplicity as not to repel the sympathies of boyhood. It is surprising to see the younger one so advanced and thoughtful, as not to find dull the society of one who has outlived excitability and passion. This is the picture presented in this chapter. A pair of friends—childhood and old age standing to each other in

the relationship, not of teacher and pupil, but of friend and friend.

2. They are contrasted again in point of office. Both are judges of Israel. But Eli is a judge rendering up his trust, and closing his public career. Samuel is a judge entering upon his office : and the outgoing ruler, Eli, is placed under very novel and painful circumstances in reference to his successor. He receives God's sentence of doom from the lips of the child he has taught, and the friend he has loved. The venerable judge of forty years is sentenced by the judge elect.

3. Still more striking is the contrast in point of character. A difference of character we expect when ages are so different. But here the difference of inferiority is on the wrong side. It is the young who is counselling, supporting, admonishing the old. It is not the ivy clinging for its own sake to the immovable wall, to be held up : but it is the badly built, mouldering wall held together by the ivy, and only by the ivy kept from falling piecemeal into ruin.

4. Once more, we have here the contrast between a judge by office and a judge by Divine call. In the first days of the judges of Israel we find them raised up separately by God, one by one, one for each emergency. So that if war threatened the coasts of Israel, no man knew whence the help would come, or who would be Israel's deliverer. It always did come : there was always one, qualified by God, found ready for the day of need, equal to the need ; one whose fitness to be a leader no one had before suspected. But when he did appear, he proved himself to be Israel's acknowledged greatest—greatest by the qualities he displayed, qualities given unto him by God. Therefore men rightly said he was a judge raised up by God.

But it seems that in later days judges were appointed by hereditary succession. When danger was always near, men became afraid of trusting to God to raise up a defender for them, and making no preparations for danger of invasion ; therefore, in the absence of any special qualification marking out the man, the judge's son became judge at his father's death ; or the office devolved on the high priest. This was Eli's qualification, it would seem. Eli was high priest, and therefore he was judge. He appears not to have had a single ruling quality. He was only a judge because he was born to the dignity.

There is an earthly wisdom in such an arrangement— nay, such an arrangement is indispensable. It is wise after an earthly sort to have an appointed succession. Hereditary judges, hereditary nobles, hereditary sovereigns : without them, human life would run into inextricable confusion. Nevertheless, such earthly arrangements only *represent* the heavenly order. The Divine order of government is the rule of the Wise and Good. The earthly arbitrary arrange- ment—hereditary succession, or any other—stands for this, representing it, more or less fulfils it, but never is it perfectly. And from time to time God sets aside and quashes the arbitrary arrangement, in order to declare that it is only a representation of the true and Divine one. From time to time, one who has qualifications direct from God is made, in Scripture, to stand side by side with one who has his qualifi- cations only from office or earthly appointment ; and then the contrast is marvellous indeed. Thus Saul, the king appointed by universal suffrage of the nation, is set aside for David, the man after God's own heart : and thus the Jews, the world's hereditary nobles, descended from the blood and stock of Abraham, are set aside for the true spiritual succession, the Christian Church—inheritors by Divine right, not of Abraham's blood, but of Abraham's faith. Thus the hereditary high priests in the genuine line of Aaron, priests by lawful succession, representing priestly powers, are set aside at once, so soon as the real High Priest of God, Jesus Christ, whose priestly powers are real and personal, appears on earth.

And thus by the side of Eli, the judge by office, stands Samuel, the judge by Divine call : qualified by wisdom, insight, will, resting on obedience, to guide and judge God's people Israel. Very instructive are the contrasts of this chapter :—We will consider,—

I. Eli's character.
II. Eli's doom.

Eli's character has two sides ; we will take the bright side first. The first point remarkable in him is the absence of envy. Eli furthers Samuel's advancement, and assists it to his own detriment. Very mortifying was that trial. Eli was the one in Israel to whom, naturally, a revelation should have come. God's priest and God's judge, to whom so fitly as to him could God send a message ? But another is preferred : the inspiration comes to Samuel, and Eli is superseded and disgraced. Besides this, every conceivable circumstance of bitterness is added to his humiliation— God's message for all Israel comes to a boy : to one who had been Eli's pupil, to one beneath him, who had performed for him servile offices. This was the bitter cup put into his hand to drink.

And yet Eli *assists* him to attain this dignity. He perceives that God has called the child. He does not say in petulance—" Then, let this favoured child find out for himself all he has to do, I will leave him to himself." Eli meekly tells him to go back to his place, instructs him how he is to accept the revelation, and appropriate it : "Go, lie down : and it shall be, if He call thee, that thou shalt say, Speak, Lord ; for thy servant heareth." He conducts his rival to the presence chamber, which by himself he cannot find, and leaves him there with the King, to be invested with the order which has been stripped off himself.

Consider how difficult this conduct of Eli's was. Remember how difficult it is to be surpassed by a younger brother, and bear it with temper ; how hard it is even to be set right, with meekness ; to have our faults pointed out to us : especially by persons who in rank, age, or standing, are our inferiors. Recollect how in our experience of life, in all professions, merit is kept down, shaded by jealousies. Recollect how rare generous enthusiasm is, or even fairness ; how men depreciate their rivals by coldness, or by sneering at those whom they dare not openly attack.

It is hard to give information which we have collected with pains, but which we cannot use, to another who can make use of it. Consider again, how much of our English reserve is but another name for jealousy. Men often meet in society with a consciousness of rivalry ; and conversation flags because they fear to impart information, lest others should make use of it, and they should thus lose the credit of being original.

One soldier we have heard of who gave up the post of honour and the chance of high distinction to cover an early failure of that great warrior whom England has lately lost, and to give him a fresh chance of retrieving honour. He did what Eli did : assisted his rival to rise above him. But where is the man of trade who will throw in a rival's way the

custom which he cannot use himself? Where is the professional man, secular or clerical, who will so speak of another
of the same profession, while struggling with him in honourable rivalry, or so assist him, as to ensure that the brightest
lustre shall shine upon what he really is? Whoever will
ponder these things will feel that Eli's was no common act.

Now, for almost all of us, there are one or two persons
in life who cross our path, whose rise will be our eclipse,
whose success will abridge ours, whose fair career will thwart
ours, darken our prospects, cross our affections. Those one
or two form our trial; they are the test and proof of our
justice. How we feel and act to them, proves whether we
are just or not. It was easy for Eli to have instructed any
one else how to approach God. But the difficulty was how
to instruct Samuel. Samuel alone, in all Israel, crossed his
path. And yet Eli stood the test. He was unswervingly
just. He threw no petty hindrances in his way. He
removed all. He gave a clear, fair, honourable field.
That act of Eli's is fair and beautiful to gaze upon.

2. Remark the absence of all priestly pretensions.

Eli might with ease have assumed the priestly tone.
When Samuel came with his strange story that he had heard
a voice calling to him in the dark, Eli might have fixed upon
him a clear, cold, unsympathizing eye, and said, "This is
excitement—mere enthusiasm. I am the appointed channel
of God's communications; I am the priest. Hear the
Church. Unordained, unanointed with priestly oil, a boy,
a child, it is presumption for you to pretend to communications from Jehovah! A layman has no right to hear
Voices; it is fanaticism." Eli might have done this; he
would have only done what ordained men have done a
thousand times when they have frowned irregular enthusiasm .

into dissent. And then Samuel would have become a mystic, or a self-relying enthusiast. For he could not have been made to think that the Voice was a delusion. *That* Voice no priest's frown could prevent his hearing. On the other hand, Eli might have given his own authoritative interpretation to Samuel, of that word of God which he had heard. But suppose that interpretation had been wrong?

Eli did neither of these things. He sent Samuel to God. He taught him to inquire for himself. He did not tell him to reject as fanaticism the belief that an inner Voice was speaking to him, a boy; nor did he try to force his own interpretation on that Voice. His great care was to put Samuel in direct communication with God; to make him listen to God; nay, and that independently of him, Eli. Not to rule him; not to *direct* his feelings and belief; not to keep him in the leading-strings of spiritual childhood, but to teach him to walk alone.

There are two sorts of men who exercise influence. The first are those who perpetuate their own opinions, bequeath their own names, form a sect, gather a party round them who speak their words, believe their belief. Such men were the ancient Rabbis. And of such men, in and out of the Church, we have abundance now. It is the influence most aimed at and most loved. The second class is composed of those who stir up faith, conscience, thought, to do their own work. They are not anxious that those they teach should think as they do, but that they should *think*. Nor that they should take this or that rule of right and wrong, but that they should be conscientious. Nor that they should adopt their own views of God, but that faith in God should be roused in earnest. Such men propagate not many *views;* but they propagate Life itself in inquiring minds and earnest hearts.

Now this is God's real best work. Men do not think so. They like to be guided. They ask, what am I to think? and what am I to believe? and what am I to feel? Make it easy for me. Save me the trouble of reflecting and the anguish of inquiring. It is very easy to do this for them; but from what minds, and from what books, do we really gain most of that which we can really call our own? From those that are suggestive, from those that can kindle life within us, and set us thinking, and call conscience into action—not from those that exhaust a subject and seem to leave it threadbare, but from those that make us feel there is a vast deal more in that subject yet, and send us, as Eli sent Samuel, into the dark Infinite to listen for ourselves.

And this is the Ministry and its work—not to drill hearts, and minds, and consciences, into right forms of thought and mental postures, but to guide to the Living God who speaks. It is a thankless work; for as I have said, men love to have all their religion done out for them. They want something definite, and sharp, and clear—words—not the life of God in the soul : and indeed, it is far more flattering to our vanity to have men take our views, represent us, be led by us. Rule is dear to all. To rule men's spirits is the dearest rule of all ; but it is the work of every *true* priest of God to lead men to think and feel for themselves—to open their ears that God may speak. Eli did this part of his work in a true spirit. He guided Samuel, trained his character. But " God's spirit !" Eli says, " I cannot give that. God's voice ! I am not God's voice. I am only God's witness, erring, listening for myself. I am here, God's witness, to say—God speaks. I may err—let God be true. Let me be a liar if you will. My mission is done when your ear is opened for God to whisper into." Very true, Eli was superseded. Very true, his work was done. A new set of views, not his, respecting Israel's policy and national life, were to be propagated by his successor; but it was Eli that had guided that successor to God who gave the views: and Eli had not lived in vain.

My brethren, if any man or any body of men stand between us and the living God, saying, " Only through us— the Church—can you approach God; only through my consecrated touch can you receive grace; only through my ordained teaching can you hear God's voice; and the voice which speaks in your soul in the still moments of existence is no revelation from God, but a delusion and a fanaticism " —that man is a false priest. To bring the soul face to face with God, and supersede ourselves, that is the work of the Christian ministry.

3. There was in Eli a resolve to know the whole truth. "What is the thing that the Lord hath said unto thee? I pray thee hide it not from me: God do so to thee, and more also, if thou hide any thing from me of all the things that He said unto thee." Eli asked in earnest to know the worst.

It would be a blessed thing to know what God thinks of us. But next best to this would be to see ourselves in the light in which we appear to others: other men's opinion is a mirror in which we learn to see ourselves. It keeps us humble when bad and good alike are known to us. The worst slander has in it some truth from which we may learn a lesson, which may make us wiser when the first smart is passed.

Therefore it is a blessing to have a friend like Samuel, who can dare to tell us truth, judicious, candid, wise; one to whom we can say, " Now tell me what I am, and what I seem; hide nothing, but tell me the worst." But observe, we are not to beg praise or invite censure — that were weak. We are not to ask for every malicious criticism or tormenting report—that were hypochondria, ever suspecting, and ever self-tormenting; and to that diseased sensibility it would be no man's duty to minister. True friendship will not retail tormenting trifles; but what we want is one friend at least, who will extenuate nothing, but with discretion tell the worst, using unflinchingly the sharp knife which is to cut away the fault.

4. There was pious acquiescence in the declared Will of God. When Samuel had told him every whit, Eli replied, "It is the Lord." The highest religion could say no more. What more can there be than surrender to the Will of God? In that one brave sentence you forget all Eli's vacillation. Free from envy, free from priestcraft, earnest, humbly submissive—that is the bright side of Eli's character, and the side least known or thought of.

There is another side to Eli's character. He was a wavering, feeble, powerless man, with excellent intentions, but an utter want of will; and if we look at it deeply, it is *will* that makes the difference between man and man; not knowledge, not opinions, not devoutness, not feeling, but will—the power to be. Let us look at the causes of this feebleness.

There are apparently two. 1. A recluse life—he lived in the temple. Praying and sacrificing, perhaps, were the substance of his life; all that unfitted him for the world; he knew nothing of life; he knew nothing of character. When Hannah came before him in an agony of prayer, he misjudged her. He mistook the tremulousness of her lip for the trembling of intoxication. He could not rule his own household; he could not rule the Church of God—a shy, solitary, amiable ecclesiastic and recluse—that was Eli.

And such are the really fatal men in the work of life, those who look out on human life from a cloister, or who know nothing of men except through books. Religious persons dread worldliness. They will not mix in politics. They keep aloof from life. Doubtless there is a danger in knowing too much of the world. But, beyond all comparison, of the two extremes the worst is knowing too little of life. A priesthood severed from human sympathies, separated from men, cut off from human affections, and then meddling fatally with questions of human life—that is the Romish priesthood. And just as fatal, when they come to meddle with public questions, is the interference of men as good as Eli, as devout, and as incompetent, who have spent existence in a narrow religious party which they mistake for the World.

2. That feebleness arose out of original temperament. Eli's feelings were all good: his acts were all wrong. In sentiment Eli might be always trusted: in action he was for ever false, because he was a weak, vacillating man.

Therefore his virtues were all of a negative character. He was forgiving to his sons, because unable to feel strongly the viciousness of sin; free from jealousy, because he had no keen affections; submissive, because too indolent to feel rebellious. Before we praise a man for his excellences, we must be quite sure that they do not rise out of so many defects. No thanks to a proud man that he is not vain. No credit to a man without love that he is not jealous: he has not strength enough for passion.

All history overrates such men. Men like Eli ruin families by instability, produce revolutions, die well when only passive courage is wanted, and are reckoned martyrs. They live like children, and die like heroes. Deeply true to nature, Brethren, and exceedingly instructive, is this history of Eli. It is quite natural that such men should suffer well. For if only their minds are made up for them by inevitable circumstances, they can submit. When people come to Eli and say, " You should reprove your sons," he can do it after a fashion ; when it is said to him, " You must die," he can make up his mind to die : but this is not *taking* up the cross. Let us look at the result of such a character.

1. It had no influence. Eli was despised by his own sons. He was not respected by the nation. One only of all he lived with, kept cleaving to him till the last—Samuel ; but that was in a kind of mournful pity. The secret of influence is will—not goodness ; not badness—both bad and good may have it. But will. And you cannot coun- terfeit will if you have it not. Men speak strongly and vehemently when most conscious of their own vacillation. They commit themselves to hasty resolutions, but the resolve is not kept ; and so, with strong feelings and good feelings, they lose influence day by day.

2. It manifested incorrigibility. Eli was twice warned ; once by a prophet, once by Samuel. Both times he answered submissively. He used strong, nay, passionate expressions of penitence. Both times you would have thought an entire reformation and change of life was at hand. Both times he was warned in vain.

There are persons who go through life sinning and sorrowing—sorrowing and sinning. No experience teaches them. Torrents of tears flow from their eyes. They are full of eloquent regrets. You cannot find it in your heart to condemn them, for their sorrow is so graceful and touching, so full of penitence and self-condemnation. But tears, heart-breaks, repentance, warnings, are all in vain. Where they did wrong once, they do wrong again. What are such persons to be in the next life? Where will the Elis of this world be? God only knows. But Christ has said, " Not every one that saith unto me, Lord, Lord, shall enter into the kingdom of heaven."

3. It resulted in misery to others.

Recollect what this weakness caused. Those young men, Eli's sons, grew up to be their country's plague. They sapped the moral standard of their countrymen and countrywomen. They degraded the ministry. " Men abhorred the offering of the Lord." The armies of Israel, without faith in God, and without leadership of man, fled before the enemy. All that was Eli's doing. A weak man with good feelings makes more misery than a determined bad man. Under a tyranny men are at least at rest, for they know the worst. But when subjects or children know that by entreaty, or persistence, or intimidation, they can obtain what they want, then a family or a nation is cursed with restlessness. Better to live under bad laws which are firmly administered, than under good ones where there is a misgiving whether they may not be changed. There is no wretchedness like the wretchedness caused by an undetermined will to those who serve under it.

II

THE APPOINTMENT OF THE FIRST KING IN ISRAEL.

"And Samuel said unto all Israel, Behold, I have hearkened unto your voice in all that ye said unto me, and have made a king over you."
—1 Sam. xii. 1.

OUR subject to-day is the selection of the first King of Israel.

We have arrived at that crisis in Israel's history when the first shock occurred in her national life. That shock was bereft of part of its violence by the wisdom of a single man. By the lustre of his personal character, by his institutions, and by his timely concessions, Samuel won that highest of all privileges which can be given to a mortal—the power of saving his country. He did not achieve the best conceivable; but he secured the best possible. The conceivable best was, that there should have been no shock at all, that Israel's elders should have calmly insisted on a reformation of abuses: that they should have come to Samuel, and demanded reparation for the insulted majesty of Hebrew law in the persons of the young judges, his sons, who had dared to dishonour it. This would have been the first best. The second best was the best practicable—that the shock should be made as light as possible; that Samuel should still control the destinies of his country, select the new king, and modify the turbulence of excess. So that Israel was in the position of a boat which has been borne down a swift stream into the very suction of the rapids. The best would be that she should be put back ; but if it be too late for this, then the best is that there should be in her a strong arm and a steady eye to keep her head straight. And thus it was with Israel. She plunged down the fall madly, rashly, wickedly; but under Samuel's control, steadily. This part of the chapter we arrange in two branches :—

I. Samuel's conduct after the mortification of his own rejection.

II. The selection of the first monarch of Israel.

I. The tenth chapter broke off in a moment of suspense. The people having accepted Saul as their king, had been dismissed, and Samuel was left alone, but his feelings were very different from those which he had in that other moment of solitude, when he had dismissed the delegates of the people. That struggle was past. He was now calm. The first moment was a terrible one. It was one of those periods in human life when the whole meaning of life is perplexed, its aims and hopes frustrated; when a man is down upon his face and gust after gust sweeps desolately over his spirit. Samuel was there to feel all the ideas that naturally suggest themselves in such hours—the instability of human affection —the nothingness of the highest earthly aims. But by degrees, two thoughts calmed him. The first was the feeling of identification with God's cause. " They have not rejected thee, but they have rejected Me." Had it been mere wounded pride, or pique, or family aggrandisement arrested, or ambition disappointed, it would have been a cureless sorrow. But Samuel had God's cause at heart, and this gave a loftier character to his sadness. There was no envenomed feeling, no resentment, no smarting scornfulness. To be part of a great Divine Cause which has failed, is an elevating as well as a saddening sensation. A conviction mingles with it that the cause of God will one day be the conquering side.

The other element of consolation was the Divine sympathy. If they had been rebellious to their ruler, they had also been disloyal to Jehovah. An unruly subject has had a poor school in which to learn reverence for things heavenly. Atheism and revolution here, as elsewhere, went hand-in-hand. We do not know how this sentence was impressed by the Infinite Mind on Samuel's mind ; all we know is, he had a conviction that God was a fellow sufferer. This, however, was inferior in point of clearness, to *our* knowledge of the Divine sympathy : Jehovah, the unnameable and awful, was a very different conception from "God manifested in the flesh." To the Jew, His dwelling was the peak round which the cloud had wreathed its solemn form, and the thunders spent themselves ; but the glory of the Life of Jesus to us is, that it is full of the Human. The many-coloured phases of human feeling all find themselves reflected in the lights and shadows of ever-varying sensitiveness which the different sentences of His conversation exhibit. Be your tone of feeling what it may, whether you are poor or rich, gay or sad—in society or alone—adored, loved, betrayed, misunderstood, despised—weigh well His words first, by thinking what they mean, and you will become aware that one heart in space throbs in conscious harmony with yours. In its degree, that was Samuel's support.

Next, Samuel's cheerful way of submitting to his fate is to be observed. Another prophet, when his prediction was nullified, built himself a booth and sat beneath it, fretting in sullen pride, to see the end of Nineveh. Samuel might have done this; he might have withdrawn himself in offended dignity from public life, watched the impotent attempts of the people to guide themselves, and seen dynasty after dynasty fall with secret pleasure. Very different is his conduct. He addresses himself like a man to the exigencies of the moment. His great scheme is frustrated. Well, he will not despair of God's cause yet. Bad as things are, he will try to make the best of them.

Now remark in all this, the healthy, vigorous tone of Samuel's religion. This man, the greatest and wisest then alive, thought this the great thing to live for—to establish a kingdom of God on earth—to transform his own country into a kingdom of God. It is worth while to see how he set about it. From first to last, it was in a practical, real way—by activity in every department of life. We recollect his early childhood, his duty then was to open the gates of the temple of the Lord, and he did that regularly, with scrupulous fidelity, in the midst of very exciting scenes. He was turning that narrow circumscribed sphere of his into a kingdom of God. Afterwards he became ruler. His spirituality then consisted in establishing courts of justice, founding academies, looking into everything himself. Now he is deposed : but he has duties still. He has a king to look for, public festivals to superintend, a public feast to preside over ; and later on we shall find him becoming the teacher of a school. All this was a religion for life. His spirituality was no fanciful, shadowy thing ; the kingdom of God to him was to be in this world, and we know no surer sign of enfeebled religion than the disposition to separate religion from life and life-duties.

Listen: what is secularity or worldliness? Meddling with worldly things? or meddling with a worldly spirit? We brand political existence and thought with the name "worldly"—we stigmatize first one department of life and then another as secular; and so religion becomes a pale, unreal thing, which must end, if we are only true to our principles, in the cloister. Spirituality becomes the exclusive property of a few amiable mystics; men of thought and men of action draw off; religion becomes feeble, and the world, deserted and proscribed, becomes infidel.

II. Samuel's treatment of his successor, after his own rejection, is remarkable. It was characterized by two things —courtesy and generosity. When he saw the man who was to be his successor, he invited him to the entertainment; he gave him precedence, bidding him go up before him; placed him as a stranger at the post of honour, and set before him the choice portion. This is politeness; what we allude to is a very different thing however, from that mere system of etiquette and conventionalisms in which small minds find their very being, to observe which accurately is life, and to transgress which is a sin.

Courtesy is not confined to the high-bred; often theirs is but the artistic imitation of courtesy. The peasant who rises to put before you his only chair, while he sits upon the oaken chest, is a polite man. Motive determines everything. If we are courteous merely to substantiate our claims to mix in good society, or exhibit good manners chiefly to show that we have been in it, this is a thing indeed to smile at; contemptible, if it were not rather pitiable. But that politeness which springs spontaneously from the heart, the desire to put others at their ease, to save the stranger from a sensa-

tion of awkwardness, to soothe the feeling of inferiority—
that, ennobled as it is by love, mounts to the high character
of a heavenly grace.

Something still more beautiful marks Samuel's generosity.
The man who stood before him was a successful rival. One
who had been his inferior now was to supersede him. And
Samuel lends him a helping hand—gracefully assists him to
rise above him, entertains him, recommends him to the
people. It is very touching.

Curiously enough, Samuel had twice in life to do a
similar thing. Once he had to depose Eli, by telling him
God's doom. Now he has to depose himself. The first he
shrank from, and only did it at last when urged. That was
delicate. On the present occasion, with a large and liberal
fulness of heart, he elevates Saul above himself. And that
we call the true, high Gospel spirit. Samuel and the people
did the same thing—they made Saul king. But the people
did it by drawing down Samuel nearer to themselves.
Samuel did it by elevating Saul above himself. One was
the spirit of revolution, the other was the spirit of the
Gospel.

In our own day it specially behoves us to try the spirits,
whether they be of God. The reality and the counterfeit,
as in this case, are singularly like each other. Three spirits
make their voices heard, in a cry for Freedom, for Brotherhood, for human Equality. And we must not forget, these
are names hallowed by the very Gospel itself. They are
inscribed on its forehead. Unless we realise them, we have
no Gospel kingdom. Distinguish however, well the reality
from the baser alloy. The spirit which longs for freedom
puts forth a righteous claim; for it is written, "If the Son
shall make you free, ye shall be free indeed." Brotherhood

—the Gospel promises brotherhood also—"One is your master, even Christ; and all ye are brethren." Equality— Yes. "There is neither Jew nor Greek, circumcision nor uncircumcision, barbarian, Scythian, bond, nor free." This is the grand Federation, Brotherhood, Emancipation of the human race.

Now the world's spirit aims at bringing all this about by drawing others down to the level on which each one stands. The Christian spirit secures equality by raising up. The man that is less wise, less good than I,—I am to raise up to my level in these things. Yes, and in social position too, if he be fit for it. I am to be glad to see him rise above me, as generously as Samuel saw Saul. And those that are above me, better than I, wiser than I, I have a right to expect to elevate me, if they can, to be as wise and good as themselves. This is the only levelling the Gospel knows. What was the mission of the Redeemer but this? To raise the lower to the higher, to make men partakers of the Divine Nature—His Nature, standing on His ground; to descend to the roots of society, reclaiming the outcasts, elevating the degraded, ennobling the low, and reminding, in the thunder of reiterated "Woes," those who had left their inferiors in the dark, and those who stood aloof in the titled superiority of Rabbi—of the account to be rendered by them yet.

And if we could but all work in this generous rivalry, our rent and bleeding country, sick at heart, gangrened with an exclusiveness, which narrows our sympathies and corrupts our hearts, might be all that the most patriotic love would have her. Brethren in Christ, I earnestly urge again the lesson of last Sunday. Not by pulling down those that are above us, not by the still more un-Christlike plan of keeping down those that are beneath us, can we make this country of ours a kingdom of Christ. If we cannot practise, nor bear to have impressed upon us, more condescension, more tenderness, and the duty of unlearning much, very much of that galling, insulting spirit of demarcation with which we sever ourselves from the sympathies of the class immediately beneath us, those tears may have to flow again which were shed over the City which would not know the day of her visitation : lulled into an insane security even at the moment when the judgment eagles were gathered together, and plunging for their prey.

Once more there is suggested to us the thought that Samuel was now growing old. It seems, by the eleventh and thirteenth chapters, in connection with the text, that the cause which hastened the demand of the elders for a king was the danger of invasion. The Ammonites and Philistines were sharpening their swords for war. And men felt that Samuel was too old for such a crisis. Only a few Sundays ago we were considering Samuel's childhood, his weaning, education, and call. Now he is old : his hair is grey, and men beginning to feel that he is no longer what he was. A high, great life ; and a few chapters sum it all up. And such is all life.

To-day we baptize a child ; in a period of time startlingly short, the minister is called upon to prepare the young man for confirmation. A little interval, and the chimes are ringing a merry wedding peal. One more pause, and the winds are blowing their waves of shadow over the long grass that grows rankly on his grave. The font, the altar, and the sepulchre, and but a single step between. Now we do not dwell on this. It is familiar—a tale that is told.

But what we mention this for is, to observe that though

Samuel's life was fast going, Samuel's work was permanent.
Evidence of this lies in the chapter before us. When Saul
came to the city and inquired for the Seer's house, some
young maidens, on their way to draw water, replied; and their
reply contained an accurate account, even to details, of the
religious service which was about to take place. The judge
had arrived; there was to be a sacrifice, the people would
not eat till he came, he would pronounce a blessing, after
that there would be a select feast. Now, compare the state
of things in Israel when Samuel became judge. Had a man
come to a city in Israel then, there would have been no
sacrifice going on, or if there had, no one would have been
found so accurately familiar with the whole service; for then
" men abhorred the offering of the Lord." But now, the
first chance passer-by could run through it all, as a thing
habitual—as a Church of England worshipper would tell
you the hours of service, and the order of its performance.
So that they might forget Samuel—they might crowd round
his successor—but Samuel's work could not be forgotten :
years after he was quiet and silent under ground, his courts
in Bethel and Mizpeh would form the precedents and the
germs of the national jurisprudence.

A very pregnant lesson. Life passes, work is permanent.
It is all going—fleeting and withering. Youth goes. Mind
decays. That which is done remains. Through ages,
through eternity, what you have done for God, that, and
only that, you are. Ye that are workers, and count it the
soul's worst disgrace to feel life passing in idleness and uselessness, take courage. Deeds never die.

III.

PRAYER.

"And he went a little farther, and fell on his face, and prayed, saying, O my father, if it be possible, let this cup pass from me : nevertheless not as I will, but as thou *wilt*."—Matt. xxvi. 39.

NO one will refuse to identify holiness with prayer. To say that a man is religious, is to say the same thing as to say he prays. For what is prayer? To connect every thought with the thought of God. To look on everything as His work and His appointment. To submit every thought, wish, and resolve to Him. To feel His presence, so that it shall restrain us even in our wildest joy. That is prayer. And what we are now, surely we are by prayer. If we have attained any measure of goodness, if we have resisted temptations, if we have any self-command, or if we live with aspirations and desires beyond the common, we shall not hesitate to ascribe all to prayer.

There is therefore, no question among Christians about the efficacy of prayer; but that granted generally, then questionings and diversities of view begin. What is prayer? What is the efficacy of prayer? Is prayer necessarily words in form and sequence; or is there a real prayer that never can be syllabled? Does prayer change the outward universe, or does it alter our inward being? Does it work on God, or does it work on us?

To all these questions, I believe a full and sufficient answer is returned in the text. Let us examine it calmly, and without prejudice or prepossession. If we do, it cannot be but that we shall obtain a conclusion in which we may rest with peace, be it what it eventually may. We will consider—

   I. The right of petition.
  II. Erroneous views of what prayer is.
 III. The true efficacy of prayer.

I. The right of petition. " Let this cup pass from me." We infer it to be a *right*. 1. Because it is a necessity of our human nature.

The Son of Man feels the hour at hand : shrinks from it, seeks solitude, flies from human society,—feels the need of it again, and goes back to his disciples. Here is that need of sympathy which forces us to feel for congenial thought among relations ; and here is that recoil from cold unsympathizing natures, which forces us back to our loneliness again. In such an hour, they who have before forgotten prayer betake themselves to God : and in such an hour, even the most resigned are not without the wish, " Let this cup pass." Christ Himself has a separate wish—one human wish.

Prayer then, is a necessity of our Humanity, rather than a duty. To force it as a duty is dangerous. Christ did not ; never commanded it, never taught it till asked. This necessity is twofold. First, the necessity of sympathy. We touch other human spirits only at a point or two. In the deepest departments of thought and feeling we are alone ; and the desire to escape that loneliness finds for itself a voice in prayer.

Next, the necessity of escaping the sense of a crushing Fate. The feeling that all things are fixed and unalterable, that we are surrounded by necessities which we cannot break through, is intolerable whenever it is realized. Our egotism cries against it; our innocent egotism, and the practical reconciliation * between our innocent egotism and hideous fatalism is Prayer, which realizes a living Person ruling all things with a Will.

2. Again, we base this right on our privilege as children. " My Father "—that sonship Christ shares with us reveals the human race as a family in which God is a Father, and Himself the elder brother. It would be a strange family, where the child's will dictates; but it would be also strange where a child may not, as a child, express its foolish wish, if it be only to have the impossibility of gratifying it explained.

3. Christ used it as a right, therefore we may.

There is many a case in life, where to act seems useless —many a truth which at times appears incredible. Then we throw ourselves on Him—He did it, He believed it, that is enough. He was wise, where I am foolish. He was holy, where I am evil. He must know. He must be right. I rely on Him. Bring what arguments you may: say that prayer cannot change God's will. I know it. Say that prayer ten thousand times comes back like a stone. Yes, but Christ prayed, therefore I may and I will pray. Not only so, but I *must* pray; the wish felt and not uttered before God, is a prayer. Speak, if your heart prompts, in articulate words, but there is an unsyllabled wish, which is also prayer. You cannot help praying, if God's spirit is in yours.

* Mesothesis.

Do not say I must wait till this tumult has subsided and I am calm. The worst storm of spirit is the time for prayer: the Agony was the hour of petition. Do not stop to calculate improbabilities. Prayer is truest when there is most of instinct and least of reason. Say, " My Father, thus I fear and thus I wish. Hear thy foolish, erring child —Let this cup pass from me."

II. Erroneous notions of what prayer is. They are contained in that conception which He negatived, " As I will."

A common popular conception of prayer is, that it is the means by which the wish of man determines the Will of God. This conception finds an exact parallel in those anecdotes with which Oriental history abounds, wherein a sovereign gives to his favourite some token, on the presentation of which every request must be granted. As when Ahasuerus promised Queen Esther that her petition should be granted, even to the half of his kingdom. As when Herod swore to Herodias' daughter that he would do whatever she should require. It will scarcely be said that this is a misrepresentation of a very common doctrine, for they who hold it would state it thus, and would consider the mercifulness and privilege of prayer to consist in this, that by faith we can obtain all that we want.

Now in the text it is said distinctly this is not the aim of prayer, nor its meaning. "*Not* as I will." The wish of man does not determine the Will of God.

Try this conception by four tests.

1. By its incompatibility with the fact that this universe is a system of laws. Things are thus, rather than thus. Such an event is invariably followed by such a consequence. This we call a law. All is one vast chain, from which if

you strike a single link, you break the whole. It has been truly said that to heave a pebble on the sea-shore one yard higher up would change all antecedents from the creation, and all consequents to the end of time. For it would have required a greater force in the wave that threw it there— and that would have required a different degree of strength in the storm—that again, a change of temperature all over the globe—and that again, a corresponding difference in the temperaments and characters of the men inhabiting the different countries.

So that when a child wishes a fine day for his morrow's excursion, and hopes to have it by an alteration of what would have been without his wish, he desires nothing less than a whole new universe.

It is difficult to state this in all its force except to men who are professionally concerned with the daily observation of the uniformity of the Divine laws. But when the Astro-nomer descends from his serene gaze upon the moving heavens, and the Chemist rises from contemplating those marvellous affinities, the proportions of which are never altered, realising the fact that every atom and element has its own mystic number in the universe to the end of time; or when the Economist has studied the laws of wealth, and seen how fixed they are and sure : then to hear that it is expected that, to comply with a mortal's convenience or plans, God shall place this whole harmonious system at the disposal of selfish Humanity, seems little else than impiety against the Lord of Law and Order.

2. Try it next by fact.

Ask those of spiritual experience. We do not ask whether prayer has been efficacious—of course it has. It is God's ordinance. Without prayer the soul dies.

But what we ask is, whether the good derived has been exactly this, that prayer brought them the very thing they wished for? For instance, did the plague come and go according to the laws of prayer or according to the laws of health? Did it come because men neglected prayer, or because they disobeyed those rules which His wisdom has revealed as the conditions of salubrity? And when it departed was it because a nation lay prostrate in sackcloth and ashes, or because it arose and girded up its loins and removed those causes and those obstructions which, by everlasting Law, are causes and obstructions? Did the catarrh or the consumption go from him who prayed, sooner than from him who humbly bore it in silence? Try it by the case of Christ—Christ's prayer did not succeed. He prayed that the cup might pass from Him. It did not so pass.

Now lay down the irrefragable principle, "The disciple is not above his master, nor the servant above his lord. It is enough for the disciple that he be as his master, and the servant as his lord." What Christ's prayer was not efficacious to do, that ours is not certain to effect. If the object of petition be to obtain, then Christ's prayer failed; if the refusal of His position did not show the absence of the favour of His Father, then neither does the refusal of ours.

Nor can you meet this by saying, "His prayer could not succeed, because it was decreed that Christ should die; but ours may, because nothing hangs on our fate, and we know of no decree that is against our wish."

Do you mean that some things are decreed and some are left to chance? That would make a strange, disconnected universe. The death of a worm, your death, its hour and moment, are all fixed, as much as His was. Fortuity, chance, contingency, are only words which express our ignorance of causes.

3. Try it by the prejudicial results of such a belief.

To think that prayer changes God's will, gives unworthy ideas of God. It supposes our will to be better than His, the Unchangeable, the Unsearchable, the All-Wise. Can you see the All of things—the consequences and secret connections of the event you wish? and if not, would you really desire the terrible power of infallibly securing it?

Consider also the danger of vanity and supineness resulting from the fulfilment of our desires as a necessity. Who does not recollect such cases in childhood, when some curious coincidences with our wishes were taken for direct replies to prayer, and made us fancy ourselves favourites of Heaven, in possession of a secret spell. These coincidences did not make us more earnest, more holy, but rather the reverse. Careless and vain, we fancied we had a power which superseded exertion, we looked down contemptuously on others. Those were startling and wholesome lessons which came when our prayer failed, and threw our whole childish theory into confusion. It is recorded that a favourite once received from his sovereign a ring as a mark of her regard, with a promise that whenever he presented that ring to her she would grant his request. He entered on rebellion, from a vain confidence in the favour of his sovereign. The ring which he sent was kept back by his messenger, and he was executed. So would we rebel if prayer were efficacious to change God's will and to secure His pardon.

4. It would be most dangerous too, as a criterion of our spiritual state. If we think that answered prayer is

a proof of grace, we shall be unreasonably depressed and unreasonably elated—depressed when we do not get what we wish, elated when we do ; besides, we shall judge uncharitably of other men.

Two farmers pray, the one whose farm is on light land, for rain ; the other, whose contiguous farm is on heavy soil, for fine weather; plainly one or the other must come, and that which is good for one may be injurious to the other. If this be the right view of prayer, then the one who does not obtain his wish must mourn, doubting God's favour, or believing that he did not pray in faith. Two Christian armies meet for battle—Christian men on both sides pray for success to their own arms. Now if victory be given to prayer, independent of other considerations, we are driven to the pernicious principle, that success is the test of Right.

From all which the history of this prayer of Christ delivers us. It is a precious lesson of the Cross, that apparent failure is Eternal victory. It is a precious lesson of this prayer, that the object of prayer is not the success of its petition ; nor is its rejection a proof of failure. Christ's petition was not gratified, yet He was the One well-beloved of His Father.

III. The true efficacy of prayer—"As Thou wilt."

All prayer is to change the will human into submission to the will Divine. Trace the steps in this history by which the mind of the Son of Man arrived at this result. First, we find the human wish almost unmodified, that "That cup might pass from him." Then he goes to the disciples, and it would appear that the sight of those disciples, cold, unsympathetic, asleep, chilled His spirit, and set that train of thought in motion which suggested the idea that perhaps the passing of that cup was not His Father's will. At all events He goes back with this perhaps, "*If* this cup may not pass from me except I drink it, Thy will be done." He goes back again, and the words become more strong: "Nevertheless not as I will, but as Thou wilt." The last time He comes, all hesitancy is gone. Not one trace of the human wish remains; strong in submission, He goes to meet His doom—"Rise, let us be going: behold he is at hand that doth betray me." This then, is the true course and history of prayer. Hence we conclude,—

1. That prayer which does not succeed in moderating our wish, in changing the passionate desire into still submission, the anxious, tumultuous expectation into silent surrender, is no true prayer, and proves that we have not the spirit of true prayer.

Hence too, we learn—

2. That life is most holy in which there is least of petition and desire, and most of waiting upon God: that in which petition most often passes into thanksgiving. In the prayer taught by Christ there is only one petition for personal good, and that a singularly simple and modest one, "Give us this day our daily bread," and even that expresses dependence far rather than anxiety or desire.

From this we understand the spirit of that retirement for prayer, into lonely tops of mountains and deep shades of night, of which we read so often in His life. It was not so much to secure any definite event as from the need of holy communion with His Father—prayer without any definite wish; for we must distinguish two things which are often confounded. Prayer for specific blessings is a very different thing from communion with God. Prayer is one thing, petition is quite another. Indeed, hints are given us which make it seem that a time will come when spirituality shall be so complete, and acquiescence in the Will of God so entire, that petition shall be superseded. " In that day ye shall ask me nothing." " Again I say not I will pray the Father for you, for the Father Himself loveth you." And to the same purpose are all those passages in which He discountenances the Heathen idea of prayer, which consists in urging, prevailing upon God. " They think that they shall be heard for their much speaking. Be not ye therefore like unto them : for your Father knoweth what things ye have need of before ye ask Him."

Practically then, I say, Pray as He did, till prayer makes you cease to pray. Pray till prayer makes you forget your own wish, and leave it or merge it in God's Will. The Divine wisdom has given us prayer, not as a means whereby to obtain the good things of earth, but as a means whereby we learn to do without them ; not as a means whereby we escape evil, but as a means whereby we become strong to meet it. " There appeared an angel unto Him from heaven, strengthening Him." That was the true reply to His prayer.

And so, in the expectation of impending danger, our prayer has won the victory, not when we have warded off the trial, but when like Him, we have learned to say, " Arise, let us go to meet the evil."

Now contrast the moral consequences of this view of prayer with those which, as we saw, arise from the other view. Hence comes that mistrust of our own understanding which will not suffer us to dictate to God. Hence, that benevolence which, contemplating the good of the whole rather than self-interest, dreads to secure what is pleasing to self at the possible expense of the general weal. Hence, that humility which looks on ourselves as atoms, links in a mysterious chain, and shrinks from the dangerous wish to break the chain. Hence, lastly, the certainty that the All-wise is the All-good, and that "all things work together for good," for the individual as well as for the whole. Then, the selfish cry of egotism being silenced, we obtain Job's sublime spirit, "Shall we receive good at the hand of God, and shall we not receive evil?"

There is one objection may be made to this. It may be said, if this be prayer, I have lost all I prized. It is sad and depressing to think that prayer will alter nothing, and bring nothing that I wish. All that was precious in prayer is struck away from me.

But one word in reply. You have lost the certainty of getting your own wish; you have got instead the compensation of knowing that the best possible, best for you, best for all, will be accomplished. Is that nothing? and will you dare to say that prayer is no boon at all unless you can reverse the spirit of your Master's prayer, and say, "Not as *Thou* wilt, but as *I* will?"

IV

PERVERSION AS SHOWN IN THE CHARACTER OF BALAAM.

"And Balaam said unto the angel of the Lord, I have sinned ; for I knew not that thou stoodest in the way against me : now therefore, if it displease thee, I will get me back again.—And the angel of the Lord said unto Balaam, Go with the men : but only the word that I shall speak unto thee, that thou shalt speak. So Balaam went with the princes of Balak."—Numbers xxii. 34, 35.

THE judgment which we form on the character of Balaam is one of unmitigated condemnation. We know and say that he was a false prophet and a bad man. This is however, doubtless, because we come to the consideration of his history having already prejudged his case.

St. Peter, St. Jude, and St. John have passed sentence upon him. "Having eyes full of adultery, and that cannot cease from sin ; beguiling unstable souls : an heart they have exercised with covetous practices ; cursed children : which have forsaken the right way, and are gone astray, following the way of Balaam the son of Bosor, who loved the wages of unrighteousness, but was rebuked for his iniquity : the dumb ass speaking with man's voice forbad the madness of the prophet." "Woe unto them ! for they have gone in the way of Cain, and ran greedily after the error of Balaam for reward, and perished in the gainsaying of Core." "But I have a few things against thee, because thou hast there them that hold the doctrine of Balaam, who taught Balak to cast a stumbling-block before the children of Israel, to eat things sacrificed unto idols, and to commit fornication." And so we read the history of Balaam familiar with these passages, and colouring all with them.

But assuredly this is not the sentence we should have pronounced if we had been left to ourselves, but one much less severe. Repulsive as Balaam's character is when it is seen at a distance, when it is seen near it has much in it that is human, like ourselves, inviting compassion—even admiration : there are traits of firmness, conscientiousness, nobleness.

For example, in the text, he offers to retrace his steps as soon as he perceives that he is doing wrong. He asks guidance of God before he will undertake a journey : "And he said unto them, Lodge here this night, and I will bring you word again, as the Lord shall speak unto me." He professes—and in earnest—"If Balak would give me his house full of silver and gold, I cannot go beyond the word of the Lord my God, to do less or more." He prays to "die the death of the righteous, and that his last end may be like his." Yet the inspired judgment of his character as a whole, stands recorded as one of unmeasured severity.

And accordingly one of the main lessons in Balaam's history must ever be, to trace how it is that men, who to the world appear respectable, conscientious, honourable, gifted, religious, may be in the sight of God accursed, and heirs of perdition. Our subject then to-day is Perversion :

I. Perversion of great gifts.
II. Perversion of the conscience.

I. Of great gifts. The history tells of Balak sending to Pethor for Balaam to curse the Israelites. This was a common occurrence in ancient history. There was a class of men regularly set apart to bless and curse, to spell-bind the winds and foretell events. Balaam was such an one.

Now the ordinary account would be that such men were impostors, or endued with political sagacity, or had secret dealings with the devil. But the Bible says Balaam's inspiration was from God.

It did not arise from diabolical agency, or from merely political sagacity :—that magnificent ode of sublime poetry, given in chap. xxiv., is from God.

The Bible refers the inspiration of the poet, of the prophet, of the worker in cunning workmanship, to God. It makes no mention of our modern distinction between that inspiration enjoyed by the sacred writers and that enjoyed by ordinary men, except so far as the use is concerned. God's prophets glorified Him. The wicked prophets glorified themselves; but their inspiration was real, and came from God, and these divine powers were perverted—

1. By turning them to purposes of self-aggrandisement.

Now, remember how the true prophets of Jehovah spoke. Simply, with no affectation of mystery, no claims to mystical illumination. They delighted to share their power with their fellows; they said "the heart of the Lord was with them that fear Him ; " that the Lord "dwelt with a humble and contrite heart." They represented themselves as inspired, not because greater or wiser than their brethren, but because more weak, more humble, and dependent upon God.

Contrast Balaam's conduct. Everything is done to show the difference between him and others—to fix men's attention upon himself—the wonderful, mysterious man who is in communication with heaven. He builds altars, and uses enchant-ments. These were a priest's manœuvres, not a prophet's.

He was the solitary self-seeker—alone, isolated, loving to be separated from all other men ; admired, feared, and sought.

Balak struck the key-note of his character when he said, "Am I not able to promote thee unto honour?" Herein then, lies the first perversion of glorious gifts : that Balaam sought not God's honour but his own.

2. By making those gifts subservient to his own greed.

It is evident that Balaam half suspected his own failing. Otherwise what mean those vaunts, "If Balak would give me his house full of silver and gold?" Brave men do not vaunt their courage, nor honourable men their honesty, nor do the truly noble boast of high birth. All who understand the human heart perceive a secret sense of weakness in these loud boasts of immaculate purity. Silver and gold, these were the things he loved, and so, not content with communion with God, with the possession of sublime gifts, he thought these only valuable so far as they were means of putting himself in possession of riches. Thus spiritual powers were degraded to make himself a vulgar man of wealth.

There are two opposite motives which sway men. Some, like Simon Magus, will give gold to be admired and wondered at ; some will barter honour for gold. In some, the two are blended, as in Balaam, we see the desire for honour and wealth ; wealth, perhaps, as being another means of ensuring reputation. And so have we seen many begin and end in our own day—begin with a high-minded courage which flatters none ; speaks truth, even unpalatable truth ; but when this advocacy of truth brings men, as it brought to

Balaam, to consult them, and they rise in the world, or in a court, and become men of consideration, then by degrees the plain truth is sacrificed to a feverish love of notoriety, the love of truth is superseded, and passes into a love of influence.

Or they begin with a generous indifference to wealth— simple, austere; by degrees they find the society of the rich leading them from extravagance to extravagance, till at last, high intellectual and high spiritual powers become the servile instruments of appropriating gold. The world sees the sad spectacle of the man of science and the man of God waiting at the doors of princes, or cringing before the public for promotion and admiration.

II. Perversion of Conscience.

1. The first intimation we have of the fact that Balaam was tampering with his conscience, is in his second appeal to God. On the first occasion God said, " Thou shalt not go with them ; thou shalt not curse the people ; for they are blessed." Then more honourable messengers were sent from Balak, with larger bribes. Balaam asks permission of God again. Here is the evidence of a secret hollowness in his heart, however fair the outside seemed. In worldly matters, " think twice ; " but in duty, it has been well said, " first thoughts are best ; " they are more fresh, more pure, have more of God in them. There is nothing like the first glance we get at duty, before there has been any special pleading of our affections or inclinations. Duty is never uncertain at first. It is only after we have got involved in the mazes and sophistries of wishing that things were otherwise than they are that it seems indistinct. Considering a duty, is often only explaining

it away. Deliberation is often only dishonesty. God's guidance is plain, when we are true.

Let us understand in what Balaam's hollowness consisted. He wanted to please himself without displeasing God. The problem was how to go to Balak, and yet not to offend God. He would have given worlds to get rid of his duty ; and he went to God to get his duty altered, not to learn what his duty was. All this rested upon an idea that the Will of God *makes* right, instead of *being* right—as if it were a caprice which can be altered, instead of the Law of the universe, which cannot alter.

How deeply this principle is ingrained in human nature you may see from the Roman Catholic practice of indulgences. The Romish Church permits transgressions for a consideration, and pardons them for the same. Such a doctrine never could have succeeded if the desire and belief were not in man already. What Balaam was doing in this prayer was simply purchasing an indulgence to sin.

2. The second stage is a state of hideous contradictions : God permits Balaam to go, and then is angry with him for going. There is nothing here which cannot be interpreted by bitter experience. We must not explain it away by saying that these were only the alternations of Balaam's own mind. They were; but they were the alternations of a mind with which God was expostulating, and to which God appeared differently at different times; the horrible mazes and inconsistencies of a spirit which contradicts itself, and strives to disobey the God whom yet it feels and acknowledges. To such a state of mind God becomes a contradiction. "With the froward"—oh, how true !—"thou wilt show thyself froward." God speaks once, and if that voice be not heard, but is wilfully silenced, the second time

it utters a terrible permission. God says, "Go," and then is angry. Experience will tell us how God has sent us to reap the fruit of our own wilfulness.

3. We notice next the evidences in him of a disordered mind and heart.

We come now to the most difficult portion of the story : "The dumb ass, speaking with man's voice, forbade the madness of the prophet." One of the most profound and pious of modern commentators on this passage, has not scrupled to represent the whole transaction as occurring in a vision. Others have thought that Balaam's own heart, smiting him for his cruelty, put, as it were, words into the ass's mouth. We care not. Let the caviller cavil if he will. There is too much profound truth throughout this narrative for us to care much about either the literal or the figurative interpretation. One thing however, is clear. Balaam did only what men so entangled always do. The real fault is in themselves. They have committed themselves to a false position, and when obstacles stand in their way, they lay the blame on circumstances. They smite the dumb innocent occasion of their perplexity as if it were the cause. And the passionateness—the " madness " of the act is but an indication that all is going wrong within. There was a canker at the heart of Balaam's life, and his equanimity was gone ; his temper vented itself on brute things. Who has not seen the like—a grown man, unreasoning as a child, furious beyond the occasion ? If you knew the whole, you would see *that* was not the thing which had moved him so terribly ; you would see that all was wrong inwardly.

It is a strange, sad picture this. The first man in the land, gifted beyond most others, conscious of great mental power, going on to splendid prospects, yet with hopelessness and misery working at his heart. Who would have envied Balaam if he could have seen all—the hell that was working at his heart?

Lastly, let us consider the impossibility under such circumstances of going back. Balaam offers to go back. The angel says, "Go on." There was yet one hope for him, to be true, to utter God's words careless of the consequences; but he who had been false so long, how should he be true? It was too late. In the ardour of youth you have made perhaps a wrong choice, or chosen an unfit profession, or suffered yourself weakly and passively to be drifted into a false course of action, and now, in spite of yourself, you feel there is no going back. To many minds, such a lot comes as with the mysterious force of a destiny. They see themselves driven, and forget that they put themselves in the way of the stream that drives them. They excuse their own acts as if they were coerced. They struggle now and then faintly, as Balaam did—try to go back—cannot—and at last sink passively in the mighty current that floats them on to wrong.

And thenceforth to them all God's intimations will come *unnaturally.* His voice will sound as that of an angel against them in the way. Spectral lights will gleam, only to show a quagmire from which there is no path of extrication. The heavenliest things and the meanest will forbid the madness of the prophet : and yet at the same time seem to say to the weak and vacillating self-seeker, "You have done wrong, and you must do more wrong." Then deepens down a hideous, unnatural, spectral state—the incubus as of a dream of hell, mixed with bitter reminiscences of heaven.

Your secret faults will come out in your life. Therefore, we say to you—be true.

V.

SELFISHNESS, AS SHOWN IN BALAAM'S CHARACTER.

"Who can count the dust of Jacob, and the number of the fourth *part* of Israel? Let me die the death of the righteous, and let my last end be like his!"—Numbers xxiii. 10.

WE acquainted ourselves with the earlier part of Balaam's history last Sunday. We saw how great gifts in him were perverted by ambition and avarice — ambition making them subservient to the admiration of himself; avarice transforming them into mere instruments for accumulating wealth. And we saw how his conscience was gradually perverted by insincerity, till his mind became the place of hideous contradictions, and even God Himself had become to him a lie; with his heart disordered, until the bitterness of all going wrong within, vented itself on innocent circumstances, and he found himself so entangled in a false course that to go back was impossible.

Now we come to the second stage. He has been with Balak : he has built his altars, offered his sacrifices, and tried his enchantments, to ascertain whether Jehovah will permit him to curse Israel. And the Voice in his heart, through all, says "Israel is blest." He looks down from the hill-top, and sees the fair camp of Israel afar off, in beautiful array, their white tents gleaming "as the trees of lign aloes which the Lord hath planted." He feels the solitary grandeur of a nation unlike all other nations—people which " shall dwell alone, and shall not be reckoned among the nations." A nation too numberless to give Balak any hope of success in the coming war. " Who can count the dust of Jacob, and the number of the fourth part of Israel?" A nation too strong in righteousness for idolaters and enchanters to cope with. " Surely there is no enchantment against Jacob, neither is there any divination against Israel?" Then follows a personal ejaculation:—" Let me die the death of the righteous, and let my last end be like his!"

Now to prevent the possibility of misconception, or any supposition that Balaam was expressing words whose full significance he did not understand — that when he was speaking of righteousness, he had only a heathen notion of it—we refer to the sixth chapter of Micah, from the fifth verse. We will next refer to Numbers xxxi. 8, and Joshua xiii. 22, from whence it appears that he who desired to die the death of the righteous, died the death of the ungodly, and fell, not on the side of the Lord, but fighting against the Lord's cause. The first thing we find in this history of Balaam is an attempt to change the Will of God.

Let us clearly understand what was the meaning of all those reiterated sacrifices.

1. Balaam wanted to please himself without displeasing God. The problem was how to go to Balak, and yet not offend God. He would have given worlds to get rid of his duties, and he sacrificed, not to learn what his duty was, but to get his duty altered. Now see the feeling that lay at the root of all this—that God is mutable. Yet of all men one would have thought that Balaam knew better, for had he not said, " God is not a man, that He should lie;

neither the son of man, that He should repent : hath He
said, and shall He not do it ? " But when we look upon it,
we see Balaam had scarcely any feeling higher than this—
God is more inflexible than man. Probably had he expressed
the exact shade of feeling, he would have said, more obstinate. He thought that God had set His heart upon Israel,
and that it was hard, yet not impossible, to alter this partiality. Hence he tries sacrifices to bribe, and prayers to
coax, God.

How deeply rooted this feeling is in human nature—
this belief in God's mutability—you may see from the
Romish doctrine of indulgences and atonements. The
Romish Church permits crime for certain considerations.
For certain considerations it teaches that God will forgive
crimes. Atonements after, and indulgences before sin, are
the same. But this Romish doctrine never could have
succeeded, if the belief in God's mutability and the *desire*
that He should be mutable, were not in man already.

What Balaam was doing in these parables, and enchant-
ments, and sacrifices, was simply purchasing an indulgence
to sin ; in other words, it was an attempt to make the
Eternal Mind change. What was wanting for Balaam to
feel was this—God *cannot* change. What he did feel was
this—God *will* not change. There are many writers who
teach that this and that is right because God has willed it.
All discussion is cut short by the reply, God has determined
it, therefore it is right. Now there is exceeding danger in
this mode of thought, for a thing is not right because God
has willed it, but God wills it because it is right. It is in
this tone the Bible always speaks. Never, except in one
obscure passage, does the Bible seem to refer right and
wrong to the sovereignty of God, and declare it a matter of

Will : never does it imply that if He so chose, He could reverse evil and good. It says, " Is not my way equal ? are not your ways unequal ? " " Shall not the Judge of all the earth do right ? " was Abraham's exclamation in a kind of hideous doubt whether the Creator might not be on the eve of doing injustice. So the Bible *justifies* the ways of God to man. But it could not do so unless it admitted Eternal Laws, with which no will can interfere. Nay more, see what ensues from this mode of thought. If Right is right because God wills it, then if God chose, He could make injustice, and cruelty, and lying to be right. This is exactly what Balaam thought. If God could but be prevailed on to hate Israel, then for him to curse them would be right. And again : if power and sovereignty make right, then, supposing that the Ruler were a demon, devilish hatred would be as right as now it is wrong. There is great danger in some of our present modes of thinking. It is a common thought that Might makes Right, but for us there is no rest, no rock, no sure footing, so long as we feel right and wrong are mere matters of will and decree. There is no safety then, from these hankering feelings and wishes to alter God's decree. You are unsafe until you feel, " Heaven and earth may pass away, but God's word cannot pass away."

2. We notice, secondly, an attempt to blind himself. One of the strangest leaves in the book of the human heart is here turned. We observe here perfect veracity with utter want of truth. Balaam was veracious. He will not deceive Balak. Nothing was easier than to get the reward by muttering a spell, knowing all the while that it would not work. Many an European has sold incantations to rich savages for jewels and curiosities, thus enriching himself by deceit. Now Balaam was not super-

naturally withheld. That is a baseless assumption. Nothing withheld him but his consience. No bribe on earth could induce Balaam to say a falsehood—to pretend a curse which was powerless—to get gold, dearly as he loved it, by a pretence. " If Balak would give me his house full of silver and gold, I cannot go beyond the word of the Lord my God, to do less or more," was no mere fine saying, but the very truth. You might as soon have turned the sun from his course as induced Balaam to utter falsehood.

And yet, with all this, there was utter truthlessness of heart. Balaam will not utter what is not true ; but he will blind himself so that he may not see the truth, and so speak a lie, believing it to be the truth.

He will only speak the thing he feels ; but he is not careful to feel all that is true. He goes to another place, where the whole truth may not force itself upon his mind— to a hill where he shall not see the whole of Israel : from hill to hill for the chance of getting to a place where the truth may disappear. But there stands the stubborn fact— Israel is blessed ; and he will look at the fact in every way, to see if he cannot get it into a position where it shall be seen no longer. Ostrich like !

Such a character is not so uncommon as, perhaps, we think. There is many a lucrative business which involves misery and wrong to those who are employed in it. The man would be too benevolent to put the gold in his purse if he knew of the misery. But he takes care not to know. There is many a dishonourable thing done at an election, and the principal takes care not to inquire. Many an oppression is exercised on a tenantry, and the landlord receives his rent, and asks no questions. Or there is some situation which depends upon the holding of certain religious opinions, and the candidate has a suspicion that if he were to examine, he could not conscientiously profess these opinions, and perchance he takes care not to examine.

3. Failing in all these evil designs against Israel, Balaam tries his last expedient to ruin them, and that partially succeeds.

He recommends Balak to use the fascination of the daughters of Moab to entice the Israelites into idolatry. —(Numbers xxxi. 15, 16. Rev. ii. 14.) He has tried enchantments and sacrifices in vain to reverse God's Will. He has tried in vain to think that Will is reversed. It will not do. He feels at last that God has not beheld iniquity in Jacob, neither hath He seen perverseness in Israel. Now therefore, he tries to reverse the character of these favourites, and so to reverse God's Will. God will not curse the good; therefore Balaam tries to make them wicked ; he tries to make the good curse themselves, and so exasperate God.

A more diabolical wickedness we can scarcely conceive. Yet Balaam was an honourable man and a veracious man; nay, a man of delicate conscientiousness and unconquerable scruples—a man of lofty religious professions, highly respectable and respected. The Lord of heaven and earth has said there is such a thing as " straining out a gnat, and swallowing a camel."

There are men who would not play false, and yet would wrongly win. There are men who would not lie, and yet who would bribe a poor man to support a cause which he believes in his soul to be false. There are men who would resent at the sword's point the charge of dishonour, who would yet for selfish gratification entice the weak into sin, and damn body and soul in hell. There are men who would be shocked at being called traitors, who in time of war will yet make a fortune by selling arms to their country's foes. There are men respectable and respected, who give liberally and support religious societies, and go to church, and would not take God's name in vain, who have made wealth, in some trade of opium or spirits, out of the wreck of innumerable human lives. Balaam is one of the accursed spirits now, but he did no more than these are doing.

Now see what lay at the root of all this hollowness :— Selfishness.

From first to last one thing appears uppermost in this history—Balaam's self;—the honour of Balaam as a true prophet—therefore he will not lie ; the wealth of Balaam— therefore the Israelites must be sacrificed. Nay more, even in his sublimest visions his egotism breaks out. In the sight of God's Israel he cries, "Let *me* die the death of the righteous :" in anticipation of the glories of the Eternal Advent, "*I* shall behold Him, but not nigh." He sees the vision of a Kingdom, a Church, a chosen people, a triumph of righteousness. In such anticipations, the nobler prophets broke out into strains in which their own personality was forgotten. Moses, when he thought that God would destroy His people, prays in agony—" Yet now, if Thou wilt, forgive their sins ;—and if not, blot me, I pray Thee, out of Thy book." Paul speaks in impassioned words—" I have continual sorrow in my heart. For I could wish that myself were accursed from Christ for my brethren, my kinsmen according to the flesh, who are Israelites." But Balaam's chief feeling seems to be, " How will all this advance *me* ? " And the magnificence of the prophecy is thus marred by a chord of melancholy and diseased egotism. Not for one moment—even in those moments when uninspired men gladly forget themselves ; men who have devoted themselves to a monarchy or dreamed of a republic in sublime self-abnegation—can Balaam forget himself in God's cause.

Observe then : desire for personal salvation is not religion. It *may* go with it, but it is not religion. Anxiety for the state of one's own soul is not the healthiest or best symptom. Of course every one wishes, " Let me die the death of the righteous." But it is one thing to wish to be saved, another to wish God's right to triumph ;—one thing to wish to die safe, another to wish to live holily. Nay, not only is this desire for personal salvation not religion, but if soured, it passes into hatred of the good. Balaam's feeling became spite against the people who are to be blessed when he is not blessed. He indulges a wish that good may not prosper, because personal interests are mixed up with the failure of good.

We see anxiety about human opinion is uppermost. Throughout we find in Balaam's character semblances, not realities. He would not transgress a rule, but he would violate a principle. He would not say white was black, but he would sully it till it looked black.

Now consider the whole.

A bad man prophesies under the fear of God, restrained by conscience, full of poetry and sublime feelings, with a full clear view of death as dwarfing life, and the blessedness of righteousness as compared with wealth. And yet we find him striving to disobey God, hollow and unsound at heart ; using for the devil wisdom and gifts bestowed by God ; sacrificing all with a gambler's desperation, for name and wealth : tempting a nation to sin, and crime, and ruin ; separated in selfish isolation from all mankind ; superior to Balak, and yet feeling that Balak knew him to be a man that had his price ; with the bitter anguish of being despised by the men who were inferior to himself; forced to conceive of a grandeur in which he had no share, and a righteousness in which he had no part. Can you not conceive the end of one with a mind so torn and distracted?—the death in battle; the insane frenzy with which he would rush into the field, and finding all go against him, and that lost for which he had bartered heaven, after having died a thousand worse than deaths, find death at last upon the spears of the Israelites?

In application, we remark first, the danger of great powers. It is an awful thing, this conscious power to see more, to feel more, to know more than our fellows.

2. But let us mark well the difference between feeling and doing.

It is possible to have sublime feelings, great passions, even great sympathies with the race, and yet not to love man. To feel mightily is one thing, to live truly and charitably another. Sin may be felt at the core, and yet not be cast out. Brethren, beware. See how a man may be going on uttering fine words, orthodox truths, and yet be rotten at the heart.

VI.

THE TRANSITORINESS OF LIFE.

"So teach *us* to number our days, that we may apply *our* hearts unto wisdom."—Psalm xc. 12.

THIS is the key-note of the 90th Psalm. It numbers sadly the days and vicissitudes of human life ; but it does this, not for the sake of mere sentiment, but rather for practical purposes, that it may furnish a motive for a wiser life of the heart. We know nothing of the Psalm except that it was the composition of "Moses, the man of God." It was written evidently in the wilderness, after years of apparently fruitless wandering : its tone is that of deep sadness—retrospective ; its images are borrowed from the circumstances of the pilgrimage—the mountain-flood, the grass the night-watch of an army on the march.

See here again, what is meant by inspiration. Observe the peculiarly human character of this Psalm. Moses, "the man of God," is commissioned not to tell truths superhuman, but truths emphatically human. The utterances of this Psalm are true to nature. Moses felt as we feel, only God gave him a voice to interpret, and he felt more deeply than all, what all in their measure feel. His inspiration lay not in this, that he was gifted with legislative wisdom ; but rather in this, that his bosom vibrated truly and healthfully to every note of the still sad music of humanity. We will consider—

   I. The feelings suggested by a retrospect of the past.
   II. The right direction of those feelings.

   1. The analogies of nature which correspond with human life. All the images in this Psalm are suggested by the circumstances of their forty years' prilgrimage. Human life felt to be like a flood—the withering grass—a sleep broken —the pain—the start—death—the awakening—a nightwatch—a tale told, whose progress we watched with interest, but of which when done, the impression alone remains, the words are gone for ever. These are not artificial images, but natural. They are not similes forced by the writer into his service because of their prettiness, but similes which forced themselves on him by their truthfulness. Now this is God's arrangement. All things here are double. The world without corresponds with the world within. No man could look on a stream when alone by himself, and all noisy companionship overpowering good thoughts was away, without the thought that just so his own particular current of life will fall at last into the "unfathomable gulf where all is still."

No man can look upon a field of corn, in its yellow ripeness, which he has passed weeks before when it was green, or a convolvulus withering as soon as plucked, without experiencing a chastened feeling of the fleetingness of all earthly things.

No man ever went through a night-watch in the bivouac, when the distant hum of men and the random shot fired, told of possible death on the morrow; or watched in a sick room, when time was measured by the sufferer's breathing or the intolerable ticking of the clock, without a firmer grasp on the realities of Life and Time.

So God walks His appointed rounds through the year: and every season and every sound has a special voice for the varying phases of our manifold existence. Spring comes, when earth unbosoms her mighty heart to God, and anthems of gratitude seem to ascend from every created thing. It is something deeper than an arbitrary connection which compels us to liken this to the thought of human youth.

And then comes Summer, with its full stationariness, its noontide heat, its dust, and toil, an emblem of ripe manhood.—The interests of youth are gone by.—The interest of a near grave has not yet come.—Its duty is work. And afterwards Autumn, with its mournfulness, its pleasant melancholy, tells us of coming rest and quiet calm.

And now has come Winter again. This is the last Sunday in the year.

It is not a mere preacher's voice performing an allotted task. The call and correspondence are real. The young have felt the melancholy of the last two months. With a transient feeling—even amounting to a luxury—the prophetic soul within us anticipates with sentiment the real gloom of later life, and enables us to sympathize with what we have not yet experienced. The old have felt it as no mere romance—an awful fact—a correspondence between the world without and the world within. We have all felt it in the damp mist, in the slanting shadows, the dimmer skies, the pale, watery glow of the red setting sun, shorn of half its lustre. In the dripping of the woodland, in the limp leaves trodden by heaps into clay, in the depressing north wind, in the sepulchral cough of the aged man at the corner of the street under the inclement sky, God has said to us, as He said to Moses, " Pause, and number thy days, for they are numbered."

2. There is also a sense of loss. Every sentence tells us that this Psalm was written after a long period was past. It was retrospective, not prospective. Moses is looking back, and his feeling is *loss*. How much was lost? Into that flood of Time how much had fallen? Many a one consumed, like Korah, Dathan, and Abiram, by the wrath of God. Many a Hebrew warrior stricken in battle, and over him a sand-heap. And those who remembered these things were old men—" *consuming*," his strong expression, " their strength in labour and sorrow."

Such is life! At first, all seems given. We are acquiring associations—sensations—new startling feelings ; then comes the time when all give pleasure or pain by association—by touching some old chord, which vibrates again. And after that, all is loss—something gone, and more is going. Every day, every year—this year, like all others. Into that flood have fallen treasures that will not be recovered. Intimacies have been dissolved that will not be reunited. Affections cooled, we cannot say why. Many a ship foundered, and the brave hearts in her will be seen no more till the sea shall give up her dead. Many a British soldier fallen before Asiatic pestilence, or beneath the Kaffir assegai, above him the bush or jungle is waving green, but he himself is now where the rifle's ring is heard, and the sabre's glitter is seen, no more. Many a pew before me is full, which at the beginning of the year was filled by others. Many a hearth-stone is cold, and many a chair is empty that will not be filled again. We stand upon the shore of that illimitable sea which never restores what has once fallen into it ; we hear only the boom of the waves that throb over all—for ever.

3. There is, too, an apparent non-attainment.

A deeper feeling pervades this Psalm than that of mere transitoriness : it is that of the impotency of human effort. " We are consumed "—perish aimlessly like the grass. No man was more likely to feel this than Moses. After forty years, the slaves he had emancipated were in heart slaves still—idolators. He called them rebels, and shattered the stone tables of the Law, in sad and bitter disappointment. After forty years, the Promised Land was not reached. He himself never entered it.

No wonder if Life appeared to him like a stream, not merely transitory, but monotonous. Generation after generation, and no change ; much lost, apparently nothing was won. No prospect of better time had been. " The thing that hath been, it is that which shall be." Here too, is one of the great trials of all retrospect—the great trial of all earthly life.

The cycles of God's providences are so large that our narrow lives scarcely measure a visible portion of them. So large that we ask, What can we effect ? Yet there is an almost irrepressible wish in our hearts to see success attend our labours, to enter the Promised Land in our own life. It is a hard lesson : to toil in faith, and to die in the wilderness, not having attained the promises, but only seeing them afar off.

So in the past year, personally and publicly. Personally we dare not say that we are better than we were at the beginning. Can we say that we are purer ? more earnest ? Has the lesson of the Cross been cut sharply into our hearts ? Have we only learnt self-denial, to say nothing of self-sacrifice ?

And stagnation thus being apparently the case, or at most but very slow progress, the thought comes, Can such beings be destined for immortality?

On a larger scale, the young cries of Freedom which caused all generous hearts to throb with sympathy have been stifled; itself trodden down beneath the iron heel of despotism all over Europe and rendered frantic and ferocious. Can we wish for its success? Are the better times coming at all? So does the heart sicken over the Past. Every closing year seems to say, Shall we begin the old useless struggle over again? Shall we tell again the oft-told tale? Are not these hopes, so high, a mockery to a moth like man? Is all but a mere illusion, a mirage in the desert? Are the waters of life and home ever near, yet never reached, and the dry hot desert sand his only attainment?

Let us consider—

II. The right use of these sad suggestions. "So teach us to number our days."

"So," because the days may be numbered, as in this Psalm, and the heart *not* applied to wisdom. There are two ways in which days may be numbered to no purpose.

1. That of the Epicurean—"Let us eat and drink; for to-morrow we die." There is a strong tendency to reckless enjoyment when the time is felt to be short, and religion does not exist to restrain.

[For example. In times of plague.—Athens.—Milan.—London.—Danger only stimulates men to seize to-day the enjoyments which may not be theirs to-morrow. Again, at the close of the last century, when the prisons of Paris resounded with merriment, dance, and acting, a light and trivial people, atheists at heart, could extract from an hourly impending death no deeper lesson than this, "Let us eat and drink; for to-morrow we die."]

2. That of the sentimentalist.

It is no part of our Christian duty to think of decay in an abject spirit. That which the demoniac in the Gospels did, having his dwelling among the tombs, has sometimes been reckoned the perfection of Christian unworldliness. Men have looked on every joy as a temptation; on every earnest pursuit as a snare—the skull and the hour-glass their companions, curtaining life with melancholy, haunting it with visions and emblems of mortality. This is not Christianity.

Rather it is so to dwell on thoughts of death "that we may apply our hearts unto wisdom." If the history of these solemn truths does not stimulate us to duty and action, it were no duty to remind ourselves of them. Rather the reverse. Better shut out such gloomy and useless thoughts. But there is a way of dwelling amidst these facts which solemnizes life instead of paralyzing it. He is best prepared to meet change who sees it at a distance and contemplates it calmly. Affections are never deepened and refined until the possibility of loss is felt. Duty is done with all energy, then only, when we feel, "The night cometh, when no man can work," in all its force.

Two thoughts are presented to make this easier.

I. The Eternity of God. "Before the mountains were brought forth, even from everlasting to everlasting, thou art God." With God there is no Time—it is one Eternal Now. This is made conceivable to us by a recent writer, who has reminded us that there are spots in the universe which have not yet been reached by the beams of light which shone from this earth at its creation. If therefore, we were able on an angel's wings to reach that spot in a second or two of time, the sight of this globe would be just becoming visible as it was when chaos passed into beauty. A few myriads of miles nearer, we should be met by the picture of the world in the state of Deluge. And so in turn, would present themselves the spectacles of Patriarchal Life ; of Assyrian, Grecian, Persian, Roman civilization ; and, at a short distance from the earth, the scenes of yesterday. Thus a mere transposition in space would make the Past present. And thus, all that we need, is the annihilation of Space to annihilate Time. So that if we conceive a Being present everywhere in Space, to Him all past events would be present. At the remotest extremity of the angel's journey, he would see the world's creation. At this extremity, the events that pass before our eyes to-day. Omnipresence in Space is thus equivalent to ubiquity in Time. And to such a being, demonstrably, there would be no Time. All would be one vast Eternal Now.

Apply this to practical wisdom. And this comes in to correct our despondency. For with God, " a thousand years are as one day." In the mighty cycles in which God works, our years and ages are moments. It took fifteen hundred years to educate the Jewish nation. We wonder that Moses saw nothing in forty years. But the thought of the Eternity of God was his consolation. And so, shall we give up our hopes of heaven and progress, because it is so slow, when we remember that God has innumerable ages before Him ? Or our hopes for our personal improvement, when we recollect our immortality in Him who has been our refuge " from generation to generation ? "   Or for our schemes and plans which seem to fail, when we remember that they will grow after us, like the grass above our graves?

II. Next, consider the permanence of results. Read the conclusion of the Psalm, "Prosper Thou the work of our hands upon us, O prosper Thou our handiwork." It is a bright conclusion for a Psalm so dark and solemn. To correct the gloom that comes from brooding on decay, it is good to remember that there is a sense in which nothing perishes.

1. The permanence of our past seasons. Spring, summer, autumn, are gone, but the harvest is gathered in. Youth and manhood are passed, but their lessons have been learnt. The past is ours only when it is gone. We do not understand the meaning of our youth, our joys, our sorrows, till we look at them from a distance. We lose them to get them back again in a deeper way. The past is our true inheritance, which nothing can take from us. Its sacred lessons, its pure affections, are ours for ever. Nothing but the annihilation of our being could rob us of them.

2. The permanence of lost affections. Over the departed ones Moses mourned. But take his own illustration—"A tale that is told." The sound and words are gone, but the tale is indelibly impressed on the heart. So the lost are not really lost. Perhaps they are ours only truly when lost. Their patience, love, wisdom, are sacred now, and live in us. The Apostles and Prophets are more ours than they were the property of the generation who saw their daily life—"He being dead, yet speaketh."

3. The permanence of our own selves—"The beauty of the Lord our God be upon us." Very striking this. We survive. We are what the past has made us. The results of the Past are ourselves. The perishable emotions, and

the momentary acts of bygone years, are the scaffolding on which we build up the being that we are. As the tree is fertilized by its own broken branches and fallen leaves, and grows out by its own decay, so is the soul of man ripened out of broken hopes and blighted affections. The law of our Humanity is the common law of the universe,—Life out of death, Beauty out of decay. Not till those fierce young passions, over the decay of which the old man grieves, have been stilled into silence ; not until the eye has lost its fire, and the cheek its hot flush, can " the Beauty of the Lord our God be upon us "—the Beauty of a spirit subdued, chastened, and purified by loss.

4. Let us correct these sad thoughts by the thought of the permanence of work. " Prosper thou the *work* of our hands." Feelings pass, thoughts and imaginations pass : Dreams pass : Work remains. Through eternity, what you have done, that you are. They tell us that not a sound has ever ceased to vibrate through space ; that not a ripple has ever been lost upon the ocean. Much more is it true that, not a true thought, nor a pure resolve, nor a loving act, has ever gone forth in vain.

So then will we end our year.

Amidst the solemn lessons taught to the giddy traveller as he journeys on by a Nature hastening with gigantic foot-steps down to a winter grave, and by the solemn tolling of the bell of Time, which tells us that another, and another, and another, is gone before us, we will learn, not the lesson of the sensualist—enjoy while you can : not that of the feeble sentimentalist—mourn, for nothing lasts : but that of the Christian—work cheerfully.

" The beauty of the Lord our God be upon us."

" O prosper Thou our handiwork."

VII

VIEWS OF DEATH.

"Then said I in my heart, As it happeneth to the fool, so it happeneth even to me ; and why was I then more wise ? Then I said in my heart, that this also *is* vanity.—For *there is* no remembrance of the wise more than of the fool for ever : seeing that which now *is* in the days to come shall all be forgotten. And how dieth the wise *man ?* as the fool."—Eccles. ii. 15, 16.

THIS is the inspired record of a peculiar view of life. Paul, with his hopefulness of disposition, could not have written it, neither could John, with his loving, trustful spirit. We involuntarily ask who wrote this ? Was it written by a Voluptuary ?—a Sceptic ?—or a Philosopher? What sort of man was it ?

We detect the sated voluptuary in the expressions of the first eleven verses of this chapter. We see the sceptic in those of the 19th to the 22nd verses of the third chapter. And the philosopher who in avoidance of all extremes seeks the golden medium, is manifested in such a maxim as " Be not righteous overmuch ; neither make thyself overwise : why shouldest thou destroy thyself? Be not overmuch wicked, neither be thou foolish : why shouldest thou die before thy time ? "—Or was it written by a man deeply and permanently inspired ?

I believe it to have been written by none of these, or

rather by all four. It records different experiences of the same mind—different moods in which he viewed life in different ways. It is difficult to interpret, or to separate them ; for he says nothing by which they can be marked off and made distinct from each other. Nowhere does Solomon say, "I thought so then, but that was only a mood, a phase of feeling that I have since seen was false, and is now corrected by the experience and expressions of the present." Here is at first sight, nothing but inextricable confusion and false conclusions.

The clue to the whole is to be found in the interpreter's own heart. It is necessary to make these few preliminary remarks, as there is a tone of disappointment which runs through all this book, which is not the tone of the Bible in general. Two lines of thought are suggested by the text.

I. The mysterious aspect presented by death.

II. That state of heart in which it is mysterious no longer.

I. To Solomon, in his mood of darkness, "there is no remembrance of the wise more than of the fool for ever." But it is not only in moods of dark perplexity, it is *always* a startling thing to see the rapidity with which the wisest and the best are forgotten. We plough our lives in water, leaving no furrow ; two little waves break upon the shore, but no further vestige of our existence is left.

[An accident happens to one of England's greatest sons ; an announcement is made, which stagnates the blood in a country's veins for a moment, and then all returns to its former channel.—(Tennyson. " In Memoriam." " Let them rave," he sleeps well.)

Country church-yard—yew-tree—upheaving roots clasping round bones—a striking fact that vegetable life outlives and outlasts animal life.]

There is something exquisitely painful in the thought that we die out and are forgotten ; therefore it is, that in the higher walks of life people solace themselves with the hope of posthumous reputation ; they think, perhaps, that *then* only their true worth will be known. That posthumous reputation ! when the eye is for ever closed, and the heart for ever chilled here—what matters it to him, whether storms rage over his grave or men cherish his memory ? he sleeps well. The commentators on this book have disagreed among themselves about Solomon's character —some have even doubted whether he was finally saved or no. What matters it to him now what is said of him ? what does it signify to him what posterity thinks of him ? And so with us all : to the ear that is turned into dust the voice of praise or of censure is indifferent. One thing is certain. God says, " Time is short, eternity is long." The solemn tolling of the bell seems to cry, There is something to be done ; there is much to be done ;—do it ! and that quickly !

Then again there are some who say, " What use is there in doing anything in this world ? It scarcely seems worth while, in this brief span of life, to try to do anything." A man is placed in a high situation, receives an expensive education at school and college, and a still more expensive one of time and experience. And then, just when we think all this ripe wisdom, garnered up from so many fields, shall find its fullest use, we hear that all is over, he has passed from among us, and then the question, hideous in its suggestiveness, arises, " Why was he then more wise ? "

Asked from this world's stand-point—if there is no life beyond the grave, if there is no immortality, if all spiritual calculation is to end here, why then, the mighty work of God is all to end in nothingness : but if this is only a state of infancy, only the education for eternity, in which the soul is to gain its wisdom and experience for higher work, then to ask why such a mind is taken from us is just as absurd as to question why the tree of the forest has its first training in the nursery garden. This is but the nursery ground, from whence we are to be transplanted into the great forest of God's eternal universe. There is an absence of all distinction between the death of one man and another. The wise man dies as the fool with respect to circumstances.

In our short-sightedness we think there ought to be a certain correspondence between the man and the mode of the man's death. We fancy the warrior should die upon the battle-plain, the statesman at his post, the mean man should die in ignorance ; but it is not so ordered in God's world, for the wise man dies as the fool, the profligate man dies as the hero. Sometimes for the great and wise is reserved a contemptuous death, a mere accident ; *then*, he who is not satisfied unless the external reality corresponds with the inward hope, imagines that circumstances such as these cannot be ordained by Eternal Love, but rather by the spirit of a mocking demon.

There is always a disappointment of our expectations. No man ever lived whose acts were not smaller than himself. We often look forward to the hour of death in which a man shall give vent to his greater and nobler emotions. The hour comes, and the wise man dies as the fool. In the first place, in the case of holiness and humbleness, thoughts of deep despondency and dark doubt often gather round the heart of the Christian in his last hour, and the narrow-minded man interprets that into God's forgetfulness ; or else delirium shrouds all in silence ; or else there are only commonplace words, words tender, touching, and gentle, but in themselves nothing. Often there is nothing that marks the great man from the small man. *This* is the mystery of death.

II. It depends on causes within us and not without us. Three things are said by the man of pleasure :—1. That all things happen by chance. 2. That there is nothing new. 3. That all is vanity and nothing is stable.

There is a strange special penalty which God annexes to a life of pleasure : Everything appears to the worldly man as a tangled web—a maze to which there is no clue. Another man says, " There is nothing new under the sun." This is the state of the man who lives merely for excitement and pleasure—his heart becomes so jaded by excitement, that the world contains nothing for him which can awaken fresh or new emotions. Then again, a third says, " All is vanity." This is the state of him who is afloat on the vast ocean of excitement, and who feels that life is nothing but a fluctuating, changeful, heartless scene.

Some who read the Book of Ecclesiastes think that there is a sadness and uneasiness in its tone inconsistent with the idea of inspiration, that it is nothing but a mere kaleido-scope, with endlessly shifting moods. Therein lies the proof of its inspiration. Its value lies as much in the way of warning as of precept. Live for yourself here—live the mere life of pleasure, and then all is confusion and bewilderment of mind ; then the view which the mighty mind of Solomon took, inspired by God, will be yours : life will seem as nothing, and death a mere mockery. Be in harmony with the mind of Christ, have the idea He had, be one with Him, and you shall understand the machinery of this world. "The secret of the Lord is with them that fear Him." To the humble pious heart there is no mystery. The world is intelligible only to a mind in harmony with the Mind that made it. Else all is confusion, unless you are in possession of His idea, moved by His Spirit.

Hence it lies in a pure heart much more than in a clear intellect, to understand the mystery of life and death. Solomon's wisdom has left us only a confused idea.

Turn we now from the views of Solomon to the Life of the Son of Man. Men asked, "How knoweth this man letters, having never learned?" He gave a different explanation of His wisdom. "My judgment is just; because I seek not mine own will, but the will of the Father which hath sent me."

He gives directions to us how to gain the same discernment. "If any man will do His will, he shall know."

* * * * *

[One has just been taken from us to whom all eyes turned—Sir Robert Peel.]

VIII.

WAITING FOR THE SECOND ADVENT.

"And the Lord direct your hearts into the love of God, and into the patient waiting for Christ."—2 Thess. iii. 5.

THE two Epistles to the Thessalonians contain more expressly than any other, St. Paul's views respecting the Second Advent of Christ. The first Epistle was written to correct certain enthusiastic views respecting that Coming. But the Second Epistle tells us that the effort had failed. For in the meanwhile, another epistle had been forged in St. Paul's name, asserting that the day was near, and so opening the floodgates of fanaticism. To counteract this, he tells them not to be shaken in mind by any word or letter as from him, as that the Day of Christ was at hand. And, contrary to his usual practice, he writes the salutation at the close with his own hand, making it a test hereafter of the genuineness of his Epistles.

Let us try to paint a picture of the state of the Thessalonian Church. Such phenomena had appeared as might have been expected to arise from a belief that the end of the world was near. Men forsook their stated employments ; the poor would not work, but expected to be maintained by their richer brethren. Men, being idle, spent their time in useless discussions, neglected their own affairs, gossipped, and indulged a prying curiosity into the affairs of others. Hence arose the necessity for the admonition—" Study to be quiet, and to do your own business, and to work with your hands, as we commanded you;" and so the Apostle had said, "Now we command you, brethren, in the name of our Lord Jesus Christ, that ye withdraw yourselves from every brother that walketh disorderly, and not after the tradition which he received of us. For yourselves know how ye ought to follow us: for we behaved not ourselves disorderly among you; neither did we eat any man's bread for nought; but wrought with labour and travail night and day, that we might not be chargeable to any of you."

Moreover, two opposite lines of conduct were adopted by persons of different temperament. Some greedily received every wild tale and mysterious prediction of the Advent, and listened eagerly to every fanatic who could work upon the vulgar credulity. Others, perceiving that there was so much imposture, concluded that it was safest to believe nothing; and accordingly were sceptical of every claim to inspiration. In admonition of the first class, St. Paul says, " Prove all things; hold fast that which is good." In admonition of the second, " Quench not the Spirit. Despise not prophesyings."

The opposite tendencies of scepticism and credulity will be found very near together in all ages. Some men refusing to believe that God speaks in the signs of the times; others running after every book on prophecy, seeking after signs, believing in miracles and imposture, mesmerisms, electrobiologies, winking pictures—anything, provided it be marvellous—it is the same state of mind exactly !

To meet the evil of this feverish, disturbed state of the Thessalonian Church, St. Paul takes two grounds. He first points out the signs which will precede the second Advent : Self-idolatry, excluding the worship of God. Sinful humanity, "the man of sin," in the temple of God. And this self-worship deceiving by a show of godliness, and a power apparently miraculous (such as our present self-laudations, philanthropies, marvellous triumphs as with Divine power, over the material world). Besides this, punishment of falsehood on the rejection of the true. These signs worked then and now. St. Paul discerned the general law of Christ's kingdom and its development as applicable to all epochs down to the last. But next, St. Paul called the Church away from this feverishness to the real preparation for the Advent. The Church was on the tiptoe of expectation, and prepared in the way above described. St. Paul summons them to a real but not excited preparation. And this in two things :—1. The love of God. 2. Patience of the saints. We consider—

I. Preparation for the Redeemer's coming : the love of God.

1. The love of God is the love of goodness. The old Saxon word God is identical with Good. God the Good One —personified goodness. There is in that derivation not a mere play of words—there is a deep truth. None loves God but he who loves good. To love God is to love what God is. God is Pure, and he who loves purity can love God. God is True. God is Just ; and he who loves these things out of God may love them in God ; and God for them, because He is good, and true, and pure, and just.

No other love is real ; none else lasts. For example, love based on a belief of personal favours will not endure. You may be very happy, and believe that God has made you happy. While that happiness lasts you will love God. But a time comes when happiness goes. You will not be always young and prosperous. A time may come when misfortunes will accumulate on you as on Job. At last, Job had nothing left but life. The natural feeling would be, " Curse God and die." Job said, " Though He slay me, yet will I trust in Him." Plainly Job had some other reason for his love than personal favours. God, the all-pure, all-just, all-holy, adorable, *because* all-holy. Or again, you believe that Christ's sufferings have purchased heaven for you. Well, you are grateful. But suppose your evidence of personal salvation fades, what then?

Here however, let me make a remark. The love of goodness only becomes real by *doing* good. Without this it remains merely a sickly sentiment. It gets body and reality by acting. For example, we have been prating since the Great Duke's death, of Duty. Know we not that by merely *talking* of duty our profession of admiration for duty will become a cant? This is a truth a minister of Christ feels deeply. It is his business to be talking to others of self-sacrifice and devotedness. He of all men feels how little these words mean, unless they are acted out. For an indolent habit of admiring goodness is got easily, and is utterly without profit. Hence Christ says, " Not every man that saith unto me, Lord, Lord, shall enter into the kingdom of heaven ; but he that *doeth* the will of my Father which is in heaven ; " and hence, too, " If a man love me, he will keep my commandments, and I will love him." " If ye know these things, happy are ye if ye do them." " This is the love of God, that we keep His com- mandments." The love of goodness is real and healthy only when we *do* it.

2. The love of God is the love of man expanded and purified. It is a deep truth that we cannot begin with loving God, we must begin with loving man. It is an awful command, "Thou shalt love the Lord thy God with all thy heart and soul and mind." It is awful and impossible at first. Interrogate the child's conscience, he does not love God supremely; he loves his mother, and his sister, and his brother more. Now this is God's plan of nature. Our special human affections are given us to expand into a diviner Charity. We are learning "by a mortal yearning to ascend." Our affections wrap themselves round beings who are created in God's image; then they expand, widen in their range; become less absorbed, more calm, less passionate, more philanthropic. They become more pure, less selfish. Love was given, encouraged, sanctioned, chiefly for this end— . . . that self might be annulled. The testimony of St. John is decisive on this point. To him we appeal as to the Apostle who knew best what love is. His love to God was unearthly, pure, spiritual; his religion had melted into love. Let us listen to his account. "No man hath seen God at any time. If we love one another, God dwelleth in us, and His love is perfected in us." "He that loveth not his brother whom he hath seen, how can he love God whom he hath not seen?"

According to him, the thought of the invisible God is intolerable. It would be shorn of its dazzling splendour by being exhibited in our brethren. So we can gaze on the reflected sunlight on the moon. According to him, it is through the visible that we appreciate the invisible—through the love of our brother that we grow into the love of God.

An awful Day is coming to us all—the Day of Christ. A Day of triumph, but of judgment too. Terrible language describes it, " The sun shall be turned into darkness and the moon into blood." God shall be felt as He never has been yet. How shall we prepare for that august sight? Not by unnatural, forced efforts at loving Him whom no eye can see and live ; but by much persistence in the appointed path of our common affections, our daily intercourse, the talk man holds with man in the hourly walk of the world's intercourse. By being true to our attachments. Let not a humble Christian be over-anxious, if his spiritual affections are not as keen as he would wish. The love of God is the full-blown flower of which the love of man is the bud. To love man is to love God. To do good to man will be recognized hereafter as doing good to Christ. These are the Judge's words : " Verily, I say unto you, inasmuch as ye did it unto one of the least of these my brethren, ye did it unto Me."

3. Personal affections.

[Guard what is now said from any appearance of representing it as actually attained by the person who describes it. The love of God is a fearful and a lovely thing; but they who have reached it are the few.]

It is not merely love of goodness, but love of goodness concentrated on the Good One. Not merely the love of man, but the love of man expanded into the love of Him, of Whom all that we have seen of gentle and lovely, of true and tender, of honourable and bright in human character, are but the shadows and the broken imperfect lights.

It is here that the Jewish religion is the chief trainer of the world. Revelation began with the personality of God. All the Jew's discipline taught him this : that the law of

Right was the Will of a Lawgiver. Deliverance from Egyptian slavery, or Assyrian invasion, was always associated with the Name of a Deliverer. Moses and the prophets were His messengers and mediators. "Thus saith the Lord," is ever the preface of their message.

Consequently, only from Jews, and Christians trained through the Old Testament to know God, do we hear those impassioned expressions of personal love, which give us a sublime conception of the adoration of which human hearts are capable. Let us hear David—"Whom have I in heaven but Thee? and there is none upon earth that I desire in comparison of Thee." "My soul is athirst for God, yea, even for the living God." And that glorious outburst of St. Paul: "Let God be true, and every man a liar," which can be understood only by those who feel that the desertion of all, and the discovery of the falseness of all, would be as nothing compared with a single doubt of the faithfulness of God.

II. The other preparation is the patient waiting.

1. What is waited for?—an Advent of Christ. We must extend the ordinary meaning of this expression. There are many comings of Christ.

Christ came in the flesh as a Mediatorial Presence.

Christ came at the destruction of Jerusalem.

Christ came, a Spiritual Presence, when the Holy Ghost was given.

Christ comes now in every signal manifestation of redeeming power.

Any great Reformation of morals and religion is a Coming of Christ.

A great Revolution, like a thunderstorm, violently

sweeping the evil away, to make way for the good, is a Coming of Christ.

Christ will come at the end of the world, when the Spirit of all these comings will be concentrated.

Thus we may understand in what way Christ is ever coming and ever near. Why it was that St. James said, "Stablish your hearts : for the coming of the Lord draweth nigh ; " and " Behold, the Judge standeth before the door." And we shall also understand how it was that the early Church was not deceived in expecting Christ in their own day. He *did* come, though not in the way they expected.

2. What is meant by "waiting?"

Now it is remarkable that throughout the Apostle's writings, the Christian attitude of soul is represented as an attitude of expectation—as in this passage, "So that ye come behind in no gift ; waiting for the coming of our Lord Jesus Christ ; " and again, "We are saved by hope : but hope that is seen is not hope : for what a man seeth, why doth he yet hope for? But if we hope for that we see not, then do we with patience *wait* for it." Salvation in hope : that was their teaching. Not a perfection attained, but a perfection that is to be.

The Golden Age lies onwards. We are longing for, not the church of the Past, but the church of the Future. Ours is not an antiquated sentimental yearning for the imaginary perfection of ages gone by, not a conservative stagnation content with things as they are, but *Hope :*—for the Individual, and for the Society. By Him we have access by faith, and rejoice in hope of the glory that shall be revealed. A better, wiser, purer age than that of childhood. An age more enlightened and more holy than the world has yet seen. " Behold, the tabernacle of God is with men, and He will dwell with them, and they shall be His people, and God Himself shall be with them, and be their God." It is this spirit of expectation which is the preparation for the Advent. Every gift of noble origin is breathed upon by hope's perfect breath.

3. Let us note that it is *patient* waiting.

Every one who has ardently longed for any spiritual blessing knows the temptation to impatience in expecting it. Good men who, like Elijah, have sickened over the degeneracy and luxury of their times; fathers who have watched the obduracy and wild career of a child whom they have striven in vain to lead to God; such cry out from the deeps of the heart, " Where is the promise of His coming?"

Now the true preparation is, not having correct ideas of how and when He shall come but, being like Him. " It is not for you to know the times or the seasons which the Father hath put in His own power." " Every man that hath this hope in him purifieth himself, even as He is pure."

Application. " The Lord direct you " unto this.

Consider what the Thessalonians must have felt in their perplexity. Would that we had a Teacher such as St. Paul, ever at hand to tell us what is Truth—to distinguish between fanaticism and genuine enthusiasm — between wild false teaching and truth rejected by the many. " Here," might they have said, " were we bewildered. How shall we here-after avoid similar bewilderments without an infallible guide?" Instead of which St. Paul says, " The Lord direct your hearts into the love of God, and into the patient waiting for Christ."

God has so decreed, that except in childhood, our dependence must be on our own souls. " The way of truth is slow, hard, winding, often turning on itself." Good and evil grow up in the field of the world almost inseparably. The scanning of error is necessary to the comprehension and belief of truth. Therefore it must be done solitarily. Nay, such an infallible guide could not be given to us without danger. Such an one ever near would prove not a guide to us, but a hindrance to the use of our own eyes and souls. Reverence for such a guide would soon degenerate into slavishness, passiveness, and prostration of mind.

Hence, St. Paul throws us upon God.

IX

THE SINLESSNESS OF CHRIST.

"Whosoever committeth sin transgresseth also the law : for sin is the transgression of the law.—And ye know that he was manifested to take away our sins ; and in him is no sin."—1 John iii. 4, 5.

THE heresy with which the Apostle St. John had to contend in his day was an error of a kind and character which it is hard for us, with our practical, matter-of-fact modes of thinking, to comprehend. There were men so over-refined and fastidious, that they could not endure the thought of anything spiritual being connected with materialism. They could not believe in anything being pure that was also fleshly, for flesh and sinfulness were to them synonymous terms. They could not believe in the Divine Humanity, for humanity was to them the very opposite of that which was Divine : and accordingly, while admitting the Divinity of Jesus, they denied the reality of His materialism. They said of His earthly life exactly what the Roman Catholic says of the miracle he claims to be performed in the Supper of the Lord. The Roman Catholic maintains that it is simply an illusion of the senses ; there is the taste of the bread, the look of the bread, the smell of the bread, but it is all a deception : there is no bread really there, it is only the spiritual body of the Lord. That which the Romanist says now of the elements in the Lord's Supper, did these ancient heretics say respecting the Body and the Life of Jesus. There was, they said, the sound of the human voice, there was the passing from place to place, there were deeds done, there were sufferings undergone, but these were all an illusion and a phantasma—a thing that appeared, but did not really exist. The Everlasting Word of God was making Itself known to the minds of men through the senses by an illusion; for to say that the Word of God was made flesh, to maintain that He connected Himself with sinful, frail humanity—this was degradation to the Word—this was destruction to the purity of the Divine Essence.

You will observe that in all this there was an attempt to be eminently spiritual; and what seems exceedingly marvellous, is the fact withal that these men led a life of extreme licentiousness. Yet it is not marvellous, if we think accurately, for we find even now that over-refinement is but coarseness. And so, just in the same way, these ultra-spiritualists, though they would not believe that the Divine Essence could be mingled with human nature without degradation, yet they had no intention of elevating human nature by their own conduct. They thought they showed great respect for Jesus in all this; they denied the reality of His sufferings: they would not admit the conception that frail, undignified humanity was veritably His, but nevertheless they had no intention of living more spiritually themselves.

It was therefore that we find in another Epistle, St. John gives strict commands to his converts not to admit these heretics into their houses: and the reason that he gives is, that by so doing they would be partakers, not of their evil doctrines, but of their evil deeds. They were a licentious set of men, and it is necessary to keep this in view if we would understand the writings of St. John. It is for this reason therefore, that he says,—" That which was from the beginning, which we have heard, which we have seen with our eyes, which we have looked upon, and our hands have handled of the Word of Life, declare we unto you." It is for this reason that he, above all the Apostles, narrates with scrupulous accuracy all the particulars respecting the Redeemer's risen body—that He joined in the repast of the broiled fish and the honey-comb : and that he dwells with such minuteness on the fact that there came from the body of the Redeemer blood and water : " not water only, but water and blood ; " and it is for this reason that in speaking of Antichrist he says, " Every spirit that confesseth not that Jesus Christ is come in the flesh is not of God, and this is that Spirit of Antichrist whereof ye have heard that it should come."

So then we learn from this that the most spiritual of all the Apostles was the one who insisted most earnestly on the materialism of the Human Nature of our Lord. He who alone had penetrated into that Realm beyond, where the King was seen on His throne of Light, was the one who felt most strongly that in Humanity there was nothing degrading. In the natural propensities of human nature there is nothing to be ashamed of : there is nothing for a man to be ashamed of but Sin—there is nothing more noble than a perfect human nature.

My Brethren, though the error of the ancient times cannot be repeated in this age in the same form, though this strange belief commends itself not to our minds, yet there may be such an exclusive dwelling upon the Divinity of Jesus as absolutely to destroy His real Humanity; there may be such a morbid sensitiveness when we speak of Him as taking our nature, as will destroy the fact of His sufferings —yes, and destroy the reality of His Atonement also. There is a way of speaking of the sinlessness of Jesus that would absolutely make that scene on Calvary a mere pageant in which He was acting a part in a drama, during which He was not really suffering, and did not really crush the propensities of His human nature. It was for this reason we lately dwelt on the Redeemer's sufferings; now let us pass onward to the fact of the sinlessness of His nature.

The subject divides itself—first, into the sinlessness of His nature; and secondly, the power which He possessed from that sinlessness to take away the sins of the world.

With respect to the first branch, we have given us a definition of what sin is—"Sin is the transgression of the law." It is to be observed there is a difference between sin and transgression. Every sin is a transgression of the law, but every transgression of the law is not necessarily a sin. Whosoever committeth sin transgresseth also the law. Now mark the difference. It is possible for a man to transgress the law of God, not knowingly, and then in inspired language we are told that " sin is not imputed unto him." Yet for all that, the penalty will follow whenever a man transgresses, but the chastisement which belongs to sin, to known wilful transgression, will not follow.

Let us take a case in the Old Testament, which it may be as well to explain, because sometimes there is a difficulty felt in it. We read of the patriarchs and saints in the Old Testament as living in polygamy. There was no distinct law forbidding it, but there was a law written in the "fleshy tables of the heart," against which it is impossible to transgress without incurring a penalty. Accordingly, though we never find that the patriarchs are blamed for the moral fault, though you never find them spoken of as having broken the written law of God, yet you see they reaped the penalty that ever must be reaped—in the case of one, degradation ; in the case of the other, slavery. Jacob's many wives brought dissension and misery into his household, though he did it innocently and ignorantly, and he reaped the penalty—quarrels and wretchedness. In all this there is penalty, but there is not sin in all this, and therefore there was not excited that agony which comes from the pangs of conscience after wilful sin.

Every misery that falls on man has been the consequence of transgression, his own trespass or those of others. It may have been his parents, his grand-parents, or his far-back ancestors, who have given him the disadvantages under which he labours. How shall we explain the fact that misery falls alike on the good and on the evil ? Only by remembering whether it comes as the penalty of transgression ignorantly done : then it is but the gentle discipline of a Father's love, educating His child, it may be warning the child and giving him the knowledge of that Law of which he was hitherto ignorant. This wretchedness of the patriarchs, what was it but the corrective dispensation by which the world learnt that polygamy is against the Law of God ? So the child who cuts his hand with the sharp blade of the knife has learnt a lesson concerning his need of caution for the future, and if well and bravely borne, he is the better for it ; but if there has been added to that transgression the sin of disobedience to his parent's command, then there is something inflicted beyond the penalty ; there is all that anguish of conscience and remorse which comes as the consequence of sin. Now we have seen what transgression is, let us try to understand what sin is.

My Christian brethren, it is possible for us to mistake this subject by taking figurative expressions too literally. We speak of sin as if it were a thing, as if we were endowed with it, like memory, or judgment, or imagination, as a faculty which must be exercised. Now let us learn the truth of what sin is—it " is the transgression of the Law." There must be some voluntary act, transgressing some known law, or there is no sin. There were those in the days of St. John who held that sin was merely the infirmity of the flesh ; that if a man committed sin and he was to know that it was the working merely of his lower nature, not of his own mind—his faith would save him.

Another error was that of the Pharisees in the days of Jesus ; and their error was precisely opposite. " Yes," said the Pharisees, " sin is the transgression of the law. Holiness is conformity to the law, and the lives of the Pharisees being conformable to the ceremonial law, we stand before the world as, touching the righteousness which is in the law, blameless." The Redeemer comes, and He gives another exposition of sin. " Sin is the transgression of the law," but there is a law written for the heart, as well as for the outward man. There is a work to be done within as well as without. A murder may be committed, by indulging revenge and malice, though the hand has never been lifted to strike. It is not the outward act that constitutes alone the Morality of Christ, it is the feeling of the heart, the acts of the inner man.

But then, there is another error from which we have to guard ourselves. It is a sophistry in which some men indulge themselves. They say, " Well, if the thought is as bad as the act, why should we not therefore do the act? I am as guilty as if I had committed transgression; why should I debar myself from the enjoyment?" It is, I say, but sophistry, for no man that has any conscience can really so deceive himself. The Redeemer's doctrine was that many a man whose outward life was pure and spotless would have done the transgression if he had had the opportunity. It is one thing to say that he would have done it if he could, but it is quite another thing to say that a man who has indulged the thought, and has drawn back, is as guilty as if he had actually carried out the evil act. The difference lies in this—the one would have done it if he could, and the other could and would not.

We read in the Bible of two men who exemplify this. They both resolved to commit murder, and the opportunity was given to each. Saul threw his javelin with right good will at David's person; he did all that resolution could do, it was but what is called accident that left the javelin quivering in the wall. Opportunity was given also to David. He had resolved to slay Saul, but when the tempting opportunity came, when he was bending over Saul, full of the thought of destroying his enemy, at the very last moment he paused—his conscience smote him—he refused to strike. Which of these was the murderer? Saul was the murderer, he had slain in his heart. It was but an accident that prevented it. In the other case there had been the indulgence of a wrong thought, but it was subdued. He might say, he might as well have slain his foe, but would you say that he was in the same position as a murderer? No, Christian brethren, let there be no sophistry of this kind among us. It is but a subtle whisper from our great adversary that would beguile us. Generally there is first a rising of an inclination which is often no sin. This passes on to a guilty resolve—one step more, and the man has committed the sin.

Now let us turn to the character of our blessed Redeemer, and we shall find Him doubly free from all this—as free in desire as free in act. The proof of His perfect purity is to be found in the testimony of His enemies, of His friends, and of those indifferent to Him. We have first the evidence of His enemies. For three long years the Pharisees were watching their victim. There was the Pharisee mingling in every crowd, hiding behind every tree. They examined His disciples ; they cross-questioned all around Him ; they looked into His ministerial life, into His domestic privacy, into His hours of retirement. They came forward with the sole accusation that they could muster— that He had shown disrespect to the Roman governor. The Roman judge, who at least should know, had pro- nounced the accusation null and void. There was another spy. It was Judas. If there had been one act of sin, one failing in all the Redeemer's career that betrayed ambition, that betrayed any desire to aggrandize Himself,—in his hour of terrible remorse Judas would have remembered it for his own comfort ; but the bitterness of his feelings— that which made life insufferable—was that he had " betrayed innocent blood."

Pass we on to those who were indifferent. And first we have the opinion of Pilate himself. Contemporary historians tell us that Pilate was an austere and cruel man, a man of firm resolve, and one who shrank not from the destruction of human life ; but we see here that for once the cruel man became merciful : for once the man of resolve became timid. It was not merely that he thought Jesus was innocent ; the hard Roman mind would have cared little for the sacrifice of an obscure Jew.   The soul of Pilate was pervaded with the feeling that spotless innocence stood before him, and this feeling extended even to Pilate's wife ; for we find that she sent to him and said, " Have thou nothing to do with that just man."   It was not because he was going to pass an unjust sentence—he had often done so before—but she felt that here was an innocent one who must not be condemned.

Now let us consider the testimony of His friends.   They tell us that during their intercourse of three years His was a life unsullied by a single spot : and I pray you to remember that tells us something of the holiness of the thirty previous years ; for no man springs from sin into perfect righteousness at once.   If there has been any early wrong-doing—though a man may be changed—yet there is something left that tells of His early character—a want of refinement, of delicacy, of purity ; a tarnish has passed upon the brightness, and cannot be rubbed off.   If we turn to the testimony of John the Baptist, His contemporary, about the same age, one who knew Him not at first as the Messiah : yet when the Son of Man comes to him simply as a man, and asks him to baptize Him, John turns away in astonishment, shocked at the idea.   " I have need to be baptized of thee : and comest thou to me ? "   In other words, the purest, and the most austere man that could be found on earth was com- pelled to acknowledge that in Him who came for baptism there was neither stain nor spot that the water of Jordan was needed to wash away.   So we see there was no actual transgression in our blessed Lord.

Now let us see what the inward life was ; for it is very possible that there may be no outward transgression, and yet that the heart may not be pure. It is possible that outwardly all may seem right, through absence of temptation, and yet there may be the want of inward perfection. Of the perfection of Jesus we can have but one testimony; it cannot be that of the Apostles, for the lesser cannot judge the greater, and therefore we turn to Himself. He said, "Which of you can charge me with sin?" "I and my Father are one." Now we must remember that just in proportion as a man becomes more holy, does he feel and acknowledge the evil that is in him. Thus it was with the Apostle Paul; he declared, "I am the chief of sinners." But here is one who attained the highest point of human excellence, who was acknowledged even by His enemies to be blameless, who declares Himself to be sinless.

If then, the Son of Man were not the promised Redeemer —He, the humblest of mankind, might justly be accused of pride; the purest of mankind would be deemed to be unconscious of the evil that was in Him. He who looked so deeply into the hearts of others is ignorant of His own; the truest of mankind is guilty of the worst of falsehoods; the noblest of mankind guilty of the sin of sins—the belief that He had no sin. Let but the infidel grant us that human nature has never attained to what it attained in the character of Jesus, then we carry him still farther, that even He whom he acknowledges to be the purest of men declared Himself to be spotless, which, if it were false, would at once do away with all the purity which he grants was His. It was not only the outward acts, but the inner life of Jesus which was so pure. His mind regulates every other mind; it moves in perfect harmony with the mind of God. In all the just men that ever lived, you will find some peculiarity carried into excess. We note this in the zeal of St. John, in the courage

of St. Peter, in the truth-seeking of St. Thomas. It was not
so with Jesus : no one department of His human nature
ever superseded another : all was harmony there. The one
sound which has come down from God in perfect melody, is
His Life, the entire unbroken music of Humanity.

We pass on to our second subject—the power there is in
the manifested sinlessness of Jesus to take away the sins of
the world. There are two aspects in which we are to consider this: first in reference to man, and secondly in reference
to God. Our subject to-day will confine itself to the first ;
on the other, we simply say this : there is in the eternal
constitution of the heavenly government, that which makes
the life and death of Jesus the atonement for the world's
sins. Human nature which fell in Adam, rose again in
Christ ; in Him it became a different thing altogether in
God's sight—redeemed now, hereafter to be perfected.

But we leave this for the present, and consider how the
world was purified by the change of its own nature. " If I
be lifted up I will draw all men unto me." There are three
ways by which this may be done—by Faith, by Hope, and by
Love. It is done by Faith, for the most degrading thing in
the heart of man is the disbelief in the goodness of human
nature. We live in evil, and surrounded by evil, until we
have almost ceased to believe in greatness of mind or
character. The more a man increases in knowledge of the
world, the more does he suspect human nature ; a knowing
man, according to worldly phraseology, is one that will trust
no one. He knows that he himself has his price, and he
believes that he can buy any one else : and this may be
called the second fall of man—that moment when all our
boyish belief in goodness passes away ; when such degradation and anguish of soul comes on, that we cease to believe

in woman's purity or in man's integrity : when a man has fallen so low there is nothing in this world that can raise him, except faith in the perfect innocence of Jesus. Then it is that there bursts upon the world—that of which the world never dreamed—entire and perfect purity, spotless integrity —no mere dreaming of philosophers and sages—though the dream were a blessed thing to have; the tangible living Being before us, whom we can see, and touch, and hear, so that a man is able to come to his brother with trust in elevated Humanity, and to say, " This is He of whom the Prophets did write."

But secondly, trust in Divine Humanity elevates the soul by Hope. You must have observed the hopefulness of the character of Jesus—his hopefulness for human nature. If ever there were one who might have despaired, it was He. Full of love Himself, He was met with every sort of unkindness, every kind of derision. There was treachery in one of His disciples, dissension amongst them all. He was engaged in the hardest work that man ever tried. He was met by the hatred of the whole world, by torture and the Cross; and yet never did the hope of Human Nature forsake the Redeemer's soul. He would not break the bruised reed, nor quench the smoking flax. There was a spark mingling even in the lowest Humanity, which He would fain have fanned into a blaze. The lowest publican Jesus could call to Him, and touch his heart ; the lowest profligate that was ever trodden under foot by the world, was one for whom He could hope still. If He met with penitents, He would welcome them ;. if they were not penitents, but yet felt the pangs of detected guilt, still with hopefulness He pointed to forgiven Humanity :. this was His word, even to the woman brought to Him by her accusers, " Go, and sin no more ; " in His last moments on the cross, to one who was dying by His side, He promised a place in Paradise : and the last words that broke from the Redeemer's lips, — what were they but hope for our Humanity, while the curses were ringing in His ears ?—" Father, forgive them, for they know not what they do."

Now it is this hopefulness that raises hope in us. Christian brethren, we dare to hope for that nature which Jesus loved, we dare to forgive that nature which Jesus condescended to wear. This frail, evil, weak Humanity of ours, these hearts that yield to almost every gust of tempta-tion, the Son of Man hoped for them.

And thirdly, it is done also by Love ; hate narrows the heart, love expands the heart. To hate is to be miserable ; to love is to be happy. To love, is to have almost the power of throwing aside sin. See the power of love in the hearts of those around Him. He comes to a desponding man, nourishing dark thoughts of the world ; He speaks encou-ragingly, and the language of that man is, " Lord, I will follow thee whithersoever thou goest." He goes to a man who had loved money all his life. He treats him as a Man, and the man's heart is conquered : " Behold, Lord, the half of my goods I give to the poor." He comes to the coward, who had denied Him, and asks him simply, " Lovest thou Me ?" and the coward becomes a martyr, and dares to *ask* to be crucified. He comes to a sinful woman, who had spent large sums on the adornment of her person, and the ointment which was intended for herself was poured in love upon His feet, mingling with her tears. " She loved much," and much was forgiven.

And it was not during the Redeemer's life alone, that the power of His love extended. It was manifested also after

His death. There was the healing act done on the man who asked for alms. For this the Apostles were carried before the Sadducees, and the man on whom this miracle was done stood by them, full of strength and courage. The day before he had been a miserable, cringing suppliant, beseeching pity from the passers-by. But all the wailing tone is gone; the attitude of the suppliant has passed away, and the renovated cripple fronts the supreme judicature of Israel with a lion heart. Ask you what has inspired and dignified that man, and raised him higher in the scale of Humanity? It was the power of love. It is not so much the manifestation of this doctrine or that doctrine, that can separate the soul from sin. It is not the Law. It is not by pressing on the lower nature to restrain it, that this can be done, but it is by elevating it. He speaks not to the degraded of the sinfulness of sin, but He dwells upon the Love of the Father, upon His tender mercies; and if a man would separate himself from the bondage of guilt, there is no other way than this. My Christian brethren, forget that miserable past life of yours, and look up to the streams of mercy ever flowing from the right hand of God.

My brethren, it is on this principle that we desire to preach to the heathen. We would preach neither High Church nor Low Church doctrine. We desire to give Jesus Christ to the world; and in pleading for this society* I will not endeavour to excite your sympathies by drawing a picture of the heathen world suspended over unutterable misery, and dropping minute by minute into everlasting wretchedness. It is easy to do this; and then to go away calmly and quietly to our comfortable meals, and our hand-

* Church Missionary Society.

some habitations, satisfied with having demonstrated so tremendous a fact. But this we say, if we would separate the world from sin, and from the penalty of sin, and the inward misery of the heart attendant on sin in this world, and the world to come, it is written in Scripture, "There is none other name under heaven given among men, whereby we must be saved," than the name of Jesus.

X.

CHRIST'S WAY OF DEALING WITH SIN.

"And immediately when Jesus perceived in his spirit that they so reasoned within themselves, he said unto them, Why reason ye these things in your hearts?—Whether is it easier to say to the sick of the palsy, *Thy* sins be forgiven thee ; or to say, Arise, and take up thy bed, and walk?—But that ye may know that the Son of man hath power on earth to forgive sins (he saith to the sick of the palsy),—I say unto thee, Arise, and take up thy bed, and go thy way into thine house."— Mark ii. 8—11.

THIS anecdote is doubtless a familiar one to us all. The Son of God was teaching in a house full of listeners, round which crowds were pressing. The friends of a poor palsied man desired his aid. It was scarcely possible for one person to edge his way through the press, where all longed to hear, and none of the crowd were likely to give place ; but, for the cumbrous apparatus of a pallet borne by four, it was impossible. Therefore they ascended by the outside staircase, which, in Oriental countries leads to the flat roof, which they broke up, and let their friend down in the midst, before Jesus. No doubt this must have struck every one. But the impression produced on the spectators would probably have been very different from that produced on Christ. They that saw the bed descending from the roof over the heads of all, and who had before seen the fruitless efforts that had been made to get in, and now remembered

that he who had been farthest from Christ was unexpectedly
in a few minutes nearest to Him, could not have withheld
that applause which follows a successful piece of dexterity.
They would have admired the perseverance, or the ingenuity,
or the inventiveness.

On none of these qualities did Christ fix as an explanation
of the fact. He went deeper. He traced it to the deepest
source of power that exists in the mind of man. "When
Jesus saw their *faith*." For as love is deepest in the Being
of God, so faith is the mightiest principle in the soul of
man. Let us distinguish their several essences. Love is
the essence of the Deity—that which makes it Deity.
Faith is the essence of Humanity, which constitutes it what
it is. And, as here, it is the warring principle of this world
which wins in life's battle. No wonder that it is written in
Scripture—" This is the victory that overcometh the world,
even our faith." No wonder it is said, "All things are
possible to him that believeth." It is that which wrestles
with difficulty, removes mountains, tramples upon impossi-
bilities. It is this spirit which in the common affairs of
life, known as a "sanguine temperament," never says "impossible" and never believes in failure, leads the men of the
world to their most signal successes, making them believe a
thing possible because they hope it; and giving substantial
reality to that which before was a shadow and a dream.

It was this "substance of things hoped for" that gave
America to Columbus, when billows, miles deep, rose between
him and the land, and the men he commanded well-nigh rose
in rebellion against the obstinacy which believed in "things
not yet seen." It was this that crowned the Mahommedan
arms for seven centuries with victory : so long as they believed
themselves the champions of the One God with a mission

from Him, they were invincible. And it is this which so often obtains for some new system of medicine the honour of a cure, when the real cause of cure is only the patient's trust in the remedies.

So it is in religion. For Faith is not something heard of in theology alone, created by Christianity, but it is one of the commonest principles of life. He that believes a blessing is to be got, that " God is a rewarder of them that diligently seek Him," will venture much, and will likewise win much. For, as with this palsied man, faith is inventive, ever fertile in expedients—like our own English character, never knowing when it has been foiled ; and then nearest victory at the very moment when the last chance has seemed to fail. We divide our subject into—

I. The malady presented to Christ.
II. His treatment of it.

I. The malady, apparently, was nothing more than palsy. But not as such did Jesus treat it. The bystanders might have been surprised at the first accost of Jesus to the paralytic man. It was not, " Take up thy bed and walk ; " but " Thy sins be forgiven thee." As with their faith, so it was here. He went deeper than perseverance or ingenuity. He goes deeper than the outward evil ; down to *the* evil, the root of all evil, properly the only evil—Sin. He read in that sufferer's heart a deeper wish than appeared in the outward act, the consequences of a burden worse than palsy, the longing for a rest more profound than release from pain—the desire to be healed of guilt. It was in reply to this tacit application that the words " Thy sins be forgiven thee " were spoken.

Now, sin has a twofold set of consequences—1. The natural consequences. 2. The moral consequences.

1. By the natural, we mean those results which come inevitably in the train of wrong-doing, by what we call the laws of nature visiting themselves on the outward condition of a sinner, by which sin and suffering are linked together. As for example, when an intemperate man ruins his health, or an extravagant man leaves himself broken in fortune; or when tyrannical laws bring an uprising of a people against a tyrant :—these are respectively the natural penalties of wrong-doing.

Here apparently, palsy had been the natural result of sin ; for otherwise the address of Christ was out of place, and meaningless. And what we are concerned to remark is, that these natural consequences of sin are often invisible as well as inevitable. Probably not one of the four friends who bore him suspected such a connection. Possibly not even his physician. But there were two at least to whom the connection was certain—the conscience of the palsied man himself, whose awakened memory traced back the trembling of those limbs to the acts of a youth long past : and to the all-seeing eye of Him to whom Past, Present, and Future, are but one.

And such experience brethren, is true doubtless, much oftener than we imagine. The irritable temperament, the lost memory which men bewail, the over-sensitive brain, as if causeless—who can tell how they stand connected with sins done long ago? For nothing here stands alone and causeless. Every man, with his strength and his weaknesses, stunted in body or dwarfed in heart, palsied in nerve or deadened in sensibility, is the exact result and aggregate of all the past—all that has been done by himself, and all that has been done by his ancestors, remote or near. The Saviour saw in this palsied man the miserable wreck of an ill-spent life.

2. Now quite distinct from these are the moral consequences of guilt: by which I mean those which tell upon the character and inward being of the man who sins. In one sense, no doubt, it is a *natural* result, inasmuch as it is by a law, regular and unalterable, a man becomes by sin deteriorated in character, or miserable. Now these are twofold, negative and positive—the loss of some blessing : or the accruing of some evil to the heart. Loss—as when by sinning we lose the capacity for all higher enjoyments ; for none can sin without blunting his sensibilities. He has lost the zest of a pure life, the freshness and the flood of happiness which come to every soul when it is delicate, and pure, and natural. This is no light loss. If any one here congratulates himself that sin has brought to him no positive misery, my brother, I pray you to remember that God's worst curse was pronounced upon the serpent tempter. Apparently it was far less than that pronounced on the woman, but really it was far more terrible. Not pain, not shame—no, these are remedial, and may bring penitence at last,—but to sink the angel in the animal—the spirit in the flesh ; to be a reptile, and to eat the dust of degradation as if it were natural food. Eternity has no damnation deeper than that.

Then, again, a positive result—the dark and dreadful loneliness that comes from doing wrong—a conscious unrest which plunges into business, or pleasure, or society, not for the love of these things, but to hide itself from itself as Adam did in the trees of the garden, because it dare not hear the Voice of God, nor believe in His Presence. Do we not know something of a self-reproach and self-contempt, which alternating at times with pride, almost tear the soul asunder? And such was the state of this man. His pains were but the counterpart and reflection of a deeper sorrow. Pain had laid him on a bed, and said to him, "Lie there face to face with God—and think!" We pass on now to consider—

II. Christ's treatment of that malady.

By the declaration of God's forgiveness. Brethren, if the Gospel of our Master mean anything it means this—the blotting out of sin: "To declare His righteousness in the remission of sins that are past." It is the declaration of the highest name of God—Love. Let us understand what forgiveness is. The forgiveness of God acts upon the moral consequences of sin directly and immediately; on the natural, mediately and indirectly.

Upon the moral consequences directly. Remorse passes into penitence and love. There is no more loneliness, for God has taken up His abode there. No more self-contempt, for he whom God has forgiven learns to forgive himself. There is no more unrest, for "being justified by faith, we have peace with God." Then the fountains of the great deep are broken up, and unwonted happy tears can come— as with the woman in the gospels. I pray you to observe that this comes directly, with no interval—"Being justified by faith." For God's Love is not an offer but a gift ;—not clogged with conditions, but free as the air we breathe.

Upon the natural consequences, not directly, but indirectly and mediately. The forgiveness of Christ did not remove the palsy; that was the result of a separate, distinct act of Christ. It is quite conceivable that it might never have been removed at all—that he might have been forgiven, and the palsy suffered to remain. God might have dealt with him as He did in David's case :—on his repentance there came to him the declaration of God's pardon, his person was accepted, the moral consequences were removed, but the natural consequences remained. "The Lord hath put away thy sin, nevertheless the child which is born to thee shall die."

Consider too, that without a miracle, they *must* have remained in this man's case. It is so in every-day life. If the intemperate man repents he will receive forgiveness, but will that penitence give him back the steady hand of youth? Or if the suicide between the moment of draining the poisoned cup and that of death repent of his deed, will that arrest the operation of the poison? A strong constitution or the physician may possibly save life; but penitence has nothing to do with it. Say that the natural penal consequence of crime is the scaffold :—Did the pardon given to the dying thief unnail his hands? Did Christ's forgiveness interfere with the natural consequences of his guilt?

And thus, we are brought to a very solemn and awful consideration, awful because of its truth and simplicity. The consequences of past deeds remain. They have become part of the chain of the universe—effects which now are causes, and will work and interweave themselves with the history of the world for ever. You cannot undo your acts. If you have depraved another's will, and injured another's soul, it may be in the grace of God that hereafter you will be personally accepted and the consequences of your guilt inwardly done away, but your penitence cannot undo the evil you have done, and God's worst punishment may be that you may have to gaze half frantic on the ruin you have caused, on the evil you have done, which you might have left undone, but which being done, is now beyond your power for ever. This is the eternity of human acts. The forgiveness of God—the blood of Christ itself—does not undo the past.

And yet even here the grace of God's forgiveness is not in vain. It cannot undo the natural consequences of sin, but it may by His mercy, transform them into blessings. For example, suppose this man's palsy to have been left still with him, himself accepted, his soul at peace. Well, he is thenceforth a crippled man. But crippling, pain—are these necessarily evils? Do we not say continually that sorrow and pain are God's loving discipline given to His legitimate children, to be exempt from which were no blessing, proving them to be " bastards and not sons." And why should not that palsy be such to him, though it was the result of his own fault? Once, when it seemed in the light of a guilty conscience only the foretaste of coming doom—the outward a type of the inward, every pang sending him further from God, it was a curse. Now, when penitence and love had come, and that palsy was received with patience, meekness, why may it not be a blessing? What makes the outward events of life blessings or the reverse? Is it not all from ourselves? Did not dissolution become quite another thing by the Fall—changed into *death;* assuming thereby an entirely altered character : no longer felt as a natural blessed herald, becoming the messenger of God, summoning to higher life, but now obtaining that strange name—the " King of terrors ?" And in Christ, death becomes our minister again : " Ours," as St. Paul says, " with all other things." The Cross of Christ has restored to death something more blessed than its original peaceful-ness. A sleep now : not death at all. And will not a changed heart change all things around us, and make the worst consequence of our own misdoing minister to our eternal welfare? So that God's forgiveness, assured to us in the Cross of Christ, is a complete remedy for sin, acting on its natural consequences by transformation indirectly; on its moral results directly, by removing them.

Lastly, let us learn from this the true aim and meaning of Miracles. Let us attend to the account our Master gives us of the reason why he performed this miracle. Read verses 9, 10. To say, "Thy sins be forgiven thee," was easy, for no visible result could test the saying. To say, "Take up thy bed and walk," was not apparently so easy, for failure would cover with confusion. He said the last, leaving the inference—If I can do the most difficult, then of course, I can do the easier. Here we have the true character of a miracle: it is the outward manifestation of the power of God, in order that we may believe in the power of God in things that are invisible.

Now contrast this with the popular view. Miracles are commonly reckoned as proofs of Christ's mission, accrediting His other truths, and making them, which would be otherwise incredible, evidently from God. I hesitate not to say that nowhere in the New Testament are they spoken of in this way. When the Pharisees asked for evidences—and signs—His reply was, "There shall no sign be given you." So said St. Paul in his Epistle to the Corinthians—not signs, but "Christ crucified." He had no conception of our modern notion of miracles—things chiefly valuable because they can be collected into a portable volume of evidences to prove that God is Love: that we should love one another: that he is the Father of all men. These need no proofs, they are like the sun shining by his own light.

Christ's glorious miracles were not to prove these, but that through the seen the unseen might be known ; to show, as it were by specimens, the Living Power which works in ordinary as well as extraordinary cases. For instance here, to show that the One who is *seen* to say with power, " Take up thy bed and walk," arresting the natural consequences of sin, is. actually, though unseen, arresting its moral consequences. Or again, that He who bade the waves " Be still " in Galilee is holding now, at this moment, the winds in the hollow of His hand. That He who healed the sick and raised the dead, holds now and ever in His Hand the issues of life and death. For the Marvellous is to show the source of the Common. Miracles were no concession to that infidel spirit which taints our modern Christianity, and which cannot believe in God's presence, except it can see Him in the supernatural. Rather, they were to make us feel that all is marvellous, all wonderful, all pervaded with a Divine Presence, and that the simplest occurrences of life are miracles.

In conclusion. Let me address those who, like this sufferer, are in any degree conscious either of the natural or moral results of sin, working in them. It is apparently a proud and a vain thing for a minister of Christ, himself tainted with sin, feeling himself, perhaps more than any one else can feel, the misery of a palsied heart, for such an one to give advice to his brother men ; but it must be done, for he is but the mouthpiece of truths greater than himself, truths which are facts, whether he can feel them all or not.

Therefore, if there be one among us who in the central depths of his soul is conscious of a Voice pronouncing the past accursed, the present awful, and the future terrible—

I say to him, Lose no time in disputing, as these scribes did, some Church question, "whether the Son of man hath power on earth to forgive sins;" nor whether ecclesiastical etiquette permits you to approach God in this way or in that way—a question as impertinent as it would have been for the palsied man to debate whether social propriety permitted him to approach the Saviour as he did, instead of through the door.

My Christian brethren, if the crowd of difficulties which stand between your soul and God succeed in keeping you away, all is lost. Right into the Presence you must force your way, with no concealment, baring the soul with all its ailments, before Him, asking, not the arrest of the consequences of sin, but the "cleansing of the conscience from dead works to serve the living God;" so that if you must suffer you shall suffer as a forgiven man.

This is the time! Wait not for another opportunity nor for different means. For the saying of our Lord is ever fulfilled, "The Kingdom of Heaven suffereth violence, and the violent take it by force."

XI.

REGENERATION.

"Jesus answered, Verily, verily, I say unto thee, Except a man be born of water and *of* the Spirit, he cannot enter into the kingdom of God.—That which is born of the flesh is flesh ; and that which is born of the Spirit is spirit.—Marvel not that I said unto thee, Ye must be born again."—John iii. 5—7.

THE Church of England has apparently, selected this passage for the Gospel of Trinity Sunday, because the influences of the entire Godhead are named in different verses —the regenerating influence of the Spirit—the limitations of the Son of man, and the illimitable nature of the Father.

It is a threefold way in which God has revealed Himself to man—as Father, Son, and Holy Spirit. First, as a Father in opposition to that doctrine which taught that the whole universe is God, and every part of the universe is a portion of God. He is the Father who hath made this universe—God distinct from us : outside of us : the Creator distinguished from the creation.

Secondly, God has revealed Himself as a Son, as manifested in Humanity, chiefly in Christ. Throughout the ages past there has been a mediatorial Humanity. Man is in a way the reflection of God's nature—the father to the child. The prophets, the lawgivers, and especially Moses, are called mediators, through whom God's name was known. The mediatorial system culminated in Christ, attained the acme of perfection in one—the man Christ Jesus—the express image of His Father. The Son is the human side of the mind of God.

Thirdly, God has revealed himself as the Holy Spirit : not as a Father external to us, nor as reflected in Humanity still outside us, but as God within us mingling with our being. The body of man is His temple. " In Him we live and move, and have our being." This is the dispensation of the Spirit : He has told us that every holy aspiration, every thought and act, that has been on the side of right against wrong, is a part of His holy essence, of His spirit in us.

This is the threefold manifestation made of Himself to us by God. But this is not all, for this alone would not be the doctrine of the Trinity. It is quite conceivable that there might be one Living Force manifested in three different ways, without its being a Trinity. Let us try and understand this by an illustration.

Conceive a circular thin plate of metal : above it you would see it such ; at some yards distance as an oval ; sideways, edgeways, a line. This might be the account of God's different aspects : in one relationship to us seen as the Father, in another as the Son, in another as the Spirit ; but this is not the doctrine of the Trinity, it is a heresy, known in old times by the name of Sabellianism or modal Trinity, depending on our position in reference to Him.

Further. This is not merely the same *part* of His nature, seen in different aspects, but diverse parts of His complex being—persons :—three causes of this manifestation. Just as our reason, our memory, our imagination, are not the same, but really ourselves.

Let us take another illustration. A single white ray of light falling on a certain object appears red; on another, blue; on another, yellow. That is, the red alone in one case is thrown out, the blue or yellow in another. So the different parts of the one ray by turns become visible; each is a complete ray, yet the original white ray is but one.

So we believe that in that Unity of Essence there are three living Powers which we call Persons, distinct from each other. It is in virtue of His own incommunicable Essence that God is the Father. It is the human side of His nature by which He is revealed as the Son, so that it was not, so to speak, a matter of choice whether the Son or the Father should redeem the world. We believe that from all eternity there was that in the mind of God which I have called its human side, which made it possible for Him to be imaged in Humanity; and that again named the Spirit, by which He could mix and mingle Himself with us.

This is the doctrine of the Trinity, explained now, not to point the damnatory clause of the Athanasian creed, but only in order to seize joyfully the annual opportunity of professing a firm belief in the dogmatic truth of the Trinity.

We now pass on to notice more particularly the revelation to us of one mode in which that Blessed Trinity works. This will divide itself into two subjects. First, we shall endeavour to understand what is meant by the kingdom of God; and, secondly, we shall consider the entrance into that kingdom by regeneration.

Our blessed Lord says, "Except a man be born again, he cannot enter into the kingdom of God." Now that expression—the kingdom of God—is a Jewish one. Nicodemus was a Jew; and we must therefore, endeavour to comprehend how he would understand it.

By the kingdom of God, a Jew understood human society perfected. That domain on earth where God was visible and God ruled. The whole Jewish dispensation had trained Nicodemus to realize this. The Jewish kingdom was a theocracy, distinguished from an aristocracy and a democracy. There were two main things observable in this. First, it was a kingdom in which God's power was manifestly visible by miracles, marvels, the cloud and fire pillars, and by appearances direct from the King of Kings. The second matter of importance in this conception of the divine kingdom was that it was a society in which a Person ruled. God was the ruler of this society ; her laws all dated from God's will, and were right because the will of the Ruler was right. "Thus saith the Lord," was the preface to personal messages from their King.

Bear in mind then, that this was Nicodemus's conception of the kingdom, and we shall understand the conversation. He had seen in the works of Christ the assertion of a Living Will ruling over the laws of nature. He had seen wonders and signs. Therefore he said, "We know that Thou art a teacher come from God :" he saw that Christ in these two senses fulfilled the two requisites of a Divine mission. He had seen a society growing up in acknowledgment of the rule of a Person : but Christ told him that something more was needful than this : it was necessary that the subject should be prepared for the kingdom. It was not enough that God should draw nigh to man ; but that man must draw near to God. There must be an alteration in the man. " Except a man be born again he cannot enter the kingdom of God."

In other words, he distinguished between a kingdom that is visible and a kingdom that is invisible. He distinguished between that presence of God which man can see, and that which man can only feel. This will explain apparent contradictions in Christ's language.

To the Pharisee on one occasion, He said, " If I by the finger of God, cast out devils, no doubt the kingdom of God is come unto you." But again He said, " It is not lo here, nor lo there. For the kingdom of God is within you." There is a kingdom therefore, in which the Eternal Spirit moves, whereof the senses take cognizance. Nicodemus saw that kingdom when he gazed on the miracles and out-ward signs, and felt that they were evidences, and from these and from the gathering society around the Lord, drew the conclusion that no man could do these things except God were with him.

There was the outward manifestation. But there is another kingdom which is the peculiar domain of the Spirit, which " eye hath not seen, nor ear heard, nor hath it entered into the heart of man to conceive," into which flesh and blood cannot enter. Of this kingdom Jesus said to Peter, " Blessed art thou, Simon Barjona, for flesh and blood hath not revealed it." And of this St. Paul said, " Now this I say, brethren, that flesh and blood cannot inherit the kingdom of God."

Unless an inward change takes place, though surrounded by God's kingdom, we cannot enter into it. The eye, the ear, can take no cognizance of this; it must be revealed by the Spirit to the spirit.

Pass we on secondly, to consider the entrance into this kingdom by regeneration. As there is a twofold kingdom, so is there a twofold entrance.

1. By the baptism of water. 2. By the baptism of the Spirit. Now respecting the first of these, commentators

have been greatly at variance. A large number of Protestant commentators have endeavoured to explain this passage away, as if it did not apply to Baptism at all. But by all the laws of correct interpretation, we are compelled to admit that " born of water " has here a reference to baptism.

Into God's universe or kingdom we penetrate by a double nature—by our senses and by our spirit. To this double nature God has made a twofold revelation. God's witness to our senses is baptism; God's witness to our spirit is His Spirit. " He that believeth hath the witness in himself." Now let us observe the strength of that expression of Christ's, " Except a man be born of water and of the Spirit he cannot enter into the kingdom of God." A very strong expression, but not more so than the baptismal service of the Church of England. " Born of water " is equivalent to regeneration by baptism.

There are those who object to this formulary of our Church, because it seems to them to tell of a magical or miraculous power in the hands of the priest. In answer to them, we point to this passage of the inspired Word of God : let us try and understand in what sense it is true that a man is born of water. Now we hold baptism to be the sign, or proof, or evidence, of a spiritual fact. It is not the fact, but it substantiates the fact.

The spiritual fact is God's covenant. Let us take an illustration. The right of a man to his property is in right of his ancestor's will; it is in virtue of that will or intention, that the man inherits that property. But because that will is invisible, it is necessary that it should be made manifest in visible symbols ; and therefore there is a piece of parchment by which it is made tangible, and that, though only the manifestation of the will, is called "the will" itself. Nay, so strongly is this word with its associations rooted in our language, that it may never have occurred to us that it is but a figurative expression; and the law might, if it had been so chosen, have demanded another expression of the will.

There have been cases in which a high-minded heir-at-law has accepted the verbal testimony of another to the intentions of his ancestor, where there has been no outward manifestation whatever, and so has given away the property because the inward will of his ancestor was to him all in all.

Similarly, baptism is the revealed Will of God; that is, it is the instrument that declares God's Will. God's Will is a thing invisible; verbally, the will runs thus—"Fear not little flock, it is your Father's good pleasure to give you the kingdom."

And just as the instrument which declares a will is called by a figure of speech "the will" itself, although it is but the manifestation of it, so the ecclesiastical instrument which declares regeneration is called regeneration in the Bible and in our Church Service. Baptism is "regeneration" as a parchment is a "will;" and, therefore it is that we read in this passage, "born of water;" and, therefore it is that St. Peter says, "Baptism saves us;" and St. Paul says, "Buried with Christ in baptism."

Lastly, we pass on to consider the entrance into this kingdom by a spiritual change.

The ground on which Christ states it is our human nature. We have a twofold nature—the nature of the animal and the nature of God, and in the order of God's providence we begin with the animal. Howbeit says St. Paul, "that is not first which is spiritual, but that which is natural." Now the moment when these natures are exchanged is the moment of spiritual regeneration.

A man is to be born of water, but far rather of the Spirit. Of this expression there are several interpretations : first, the fanatical one—men of enthusiastic temperaments, chiefly men whose lives have been irregular, whose religion has come to them suddenly, interpreting all cases by their own experiences, have said that the exercise of God's spirit is ever sudden and supernatural, and it has seemed to them that to try and bring up a child for God in the way of education, is to bid defiance to that Spirit which is like the wind, blowing "where it listeth ; " and if a man cannot tell the day or hour when he was converted, to those persons he does not seem to be a Christian at all. He may be holy, humble, loving, but unless there is that visible manifestation of how and when he was changed, he must be still ranked as unregenerate.

Another class of persons, of cold, calm temperament, to whom fanaticism is a crime and enthusiasm a thing to be avoided, are perpetually rationalizing with Scripture, and explaining away in some low and commonplace way the highest manifestation of the spirit of God. Thus Paley tells us that this passage belongs to the Jews, who had forgotten the Messiah's kingdom ; but to speak of a spiritual, regenerative change, as necessary for a man brought up in the Church of England, is to open the door to all fanaticism.

There is a third class, who confound the regeneration of baptism with that of the Spirit, who identify in point of time, the being born of water and of the Spirit. And it seems to them that regeneration after that, is a word without meaning. Of this class there are two divisions : those who hold it openly in the Church of Rome, and those who do not go to the full extent of Romish doctrine on this subject. These will not say that a miracle has taken place, but they say that a seed of grace has thus been planted. Whichever of these views be taken, for all practical purposes the result must be the same. If this inward spiritual change has taken place at baptism, then to talk of regeneration *after* that must be an impertinence. But brethren, looking at this passage, we cannot be persuaded that it belongs to the Jew alone, nor can we believe that the strength of that expression is mere baptism by water. Here is recorded that which is true not for the Jew or heathen only, but for all the human race, without exception. "Except a man be born of water and of the Spirit, he cannot enter the kingdom of God."

In our life there is a time in which our spirit has gained the mastery over the flesh ; it is not important to know when, but whether it has taken place.

The first years of our existence are simply animal ; then the life of a young man is not that of mere instinct, it is a life of passion, with mighty indignations, strong aversions. And then passing on through life we sometimes see a person in whom these things are merged ; the instincts are there only for the support of existence ; the passions are so ruled that they have become gentleness, and meekness, and love. Between these two extremes there must have been a middle point, when the life of sense, appetite, and passion, which *had* ruled, ceased to rule, and was ruled over by the life of the spirit : that moment, whether it be long or short, whether it be done suddenly or gradually, whether it come like the rushing mighty wind, or as the slow, gentle zephyr of the spring—whenever that moment was, then was the moment of spiritual regeneration. There are cases in which this never takes place at all; there are grown men and old men merely children still—still having the animal appetites, and living in the base, and conscious, and vicious indulgence of those appetites which in the child were harmless. These are they who have not yet been born again. Born of water they may have been, born of God's eternal Spirit they have not been; before such men can enter into the eternal kingdom of their Father, that word is as true to them as to Nicodemus of old, " Marvel not that I said unto you, ye must be born again." Oh! it is an awful thing to see a spectacle such as that; an awful thing to see the blossom still upon the tree when the autumn is passed and the winter is at hand. An awful thing to see a man who ought to be clothed in Christ, still living the life of the flesh and of passion : the summer is past, the harvest is ended, and he is not saved.

Now let us briefly apply what has been said.

1. Do not attempt to date too accurately the transition moment.

* * * * *

2. Understand that the " flesh," or natural state, is wrong only when out of place. In its place it is imperfection, not evil. There is no harm in leaves or blossoms in spring,— but in autumn !—There is no harm in the appetites of child-hood, or the passions of youth, but great harm when these are still unsubdued in age. Observe therefore, the flesh is not to be exercised, but the spirit strengthened. This I say then, " Walk in the spirit, and ye shall not fulfil the lusts of the flesh."

3. Do not mistake the figurative for the literal.

Baptism is regeneration figuratively; " the like figure whereunto even baptism doth also now save us (not the putting away of the filth of the flesh, but the answer of a good conscience toward God,) by the resurrection of Jesus Christ.

*   *   *   *   *

The things to be anxious about are not baptism, not confirmation; but the spiritual facts for which baptism and confirmation stand.

XII.

AN ELECTION SERMON.

(A FRAGMENT.)

"And they appointed two, Joseph called Barsabas, who was sur-
named Justus, and Matthias.—And they prayed, and said, Thou, Lord,
which knowest the hearts of all *men*, shew whether of these two thou hast
chosen,—That he may take part of this ministry and apostleship, from
which Judas by transgression fell, that he might go to his own place.—
And they gave forth their lots ; and the lot fell upon Matthias ; and he
was numbered with the eleven apostles."—Acts i. 23—26.

THIS is the account of the earliest appointment of an
apostle or bishop over the Church of Christ.

It stands remarkably distinguished from the episcopal
elections of after ages. Every one acquainted with Church
history knows that the election of a bishop in the first
centuries, and indeed for many ages, was one of the bitterest
and fiercest questions which shook the Church of Christ.

    *   *   *   *   *

[Appointment by the people. — Presbyters. — Various
customs. Anecdote of Ambrose of Milan. Appointment
by the Emperor or Bishop of Rome. Quarrel of ages
between the Emperor and the Pope.]

Contradistinguished from this in spirit was the first
appointment which ended in the selection of Matthias.

Holy, calm, wise — presided over by an apostolic and Christian spirit.

It will be obvious at once why this subject has been selected. During the course of this week, England will be shaken to her centre with the selection of representatives who shall legislate for her hereafter, either in accordance with, or in defiance of, the principles of her constitution. In some places, as fiercely as the battle was formerly carried on between Guelph and Ghibelline, or between faction and faction in the choice of bishops, so fiercely will the contest rage in the choice of representatives.

Delicate and difficult as the introduction of such a subject from the pulpit must be, yet it seems to me the imperative duty of a minister of Christ—from which he cannot, except in cowardice, shrink—to endeavour to make clear the great Christian landmarks which belong to such an occurrence. But let me be understood. His duty is not to introduce politics in the common sense of the word, meaning thereby the views of some particular party. The pulpit is not to be degraded into the engine of a faction. Far, far above such questions, it ought to preserve the calm dignity of a voice which speaks for eternity, and not for time. If possible, not one word should drop by which a minister's own political leanings can be discovered.

Yet there must be broad principles of right and wrong in such a transaction as in any other. And, in discharge of my duty, I desire to place those before you. We shall consider—

    I. The object of the election spoken of in my text.

    II. The mode of the election.

    III. The spirit in which it was conducted.

I. The object of the election. To elect a bishop of the universal Church.

It might be that in process of time the apostle so chosen should be appointed to a particular city—as St. James was to Jerusalem. But it is plain his duty as an apostle was owed to the general assembly and Church of Christ, and not to that particular city; and if he had allowed local partialities or local interests to stand before the interests of the whole, he would have neglected the duty of his high office.

Also that if those who appointed him considered the interest of Jerusalem in the first instance, instead of his qualifications as a bishop of the Church universal, they would have failed in their duty.

In the third century, a bishop of Carthage, Cyprian, in a celebrated sentence has clearly and beautifully stated this principle—"*Episcopatus unus est, cujus,*" &c. The Episcopate, one and indivisible, held in its entirety by each bishop, every part standing for the whole. That is, if he were a bishop of Carthage or Antioch, he was to remember that it was not the interests of Carthage over which he had to watch, but those of the Church of Christ; Carthage being his special allotment out of the whole. And in a council he was to give his voice not for that which might be good for the men of Carthage, but for the Church of Christ.

The application is plain.

The nation is one—its life is a sacred life.—The nation is the Christian people, for whom Christ shed His blood.— Its life is unity.—Its death is division.—The curse of a Christian is sectarianism.—The curse of a nation is faction. —Each legislator legislates for the country, not for a county or town.—Each elector holds his franchise as a sacred trust, to be exercised not for his town, or for a faction of his town, not for himself, or his friends, but for the general weal of the people of England.

Let me expose a common fallacy.

We are not to be biassed by asking what charity does a candidate support, nor what view does he take of some local question, nor whether he subscribe to tractarian or to evangelical societies. We are, in our high responsibility, selecting, not a president for a religious society, nor a patron of a town, nor a subscriber to an hospital, but a legislator for England.

II. The mode of the election.

It was partly human, partly divine. The human element is plain enough in that it was popular. The choice lay not with the Apostles, but with the whole Church.—One hundred and twenty met in that upper chamber : all gave in their lots or votes. The Divine element lay in this that it was over-ruled by God.

Here is the main point observable. They at least took for granted that the popular element was quite separate from the Divine. The selected one might be the chosen of the people, yet not the chosen of God. Hence they prayed, " Thou Lord, which knowest the hearts of all men, show whether of these two thou hast chosen."

The common notion is, *vox populi vox Dei*. In other words, whatever the general voice wills is right. A law is right because it is a people's will. I do not say that we have got the full length of this idea in England. On the Continent it has long been prevalent. Possibly it is the expression of that Antichrist " who sheweth himself that he is God ; " self-will setting itself up paramount to the will of God.

The *vox populi* is sometimes *vox Dei*, sometimes not. The voice of the people was the voice of God when the children of Israel rescued Jonathan from his father's unjust sentence; and when the contest between Elijah and the prophets of Baal having been settled, they cried, " The Lord he is God."

Was the voice of the people the voice of God when, in Moses' absence, they required Aaron to make them a golden calf for a god?   Or when, led on by the demagogue Demetrius, they shouted, " Great is Diana of the Ephesians?" Or when, at the instigation of the priests, led blindfold by them they cried, " Crucify Him ? "

The politicians of this world eagerly debate the question, how best to secure a fair representation of the people's voice, whether by individuals or by interests fairly balanced?—a question doubtless, not to be put aside.   But the Christian sees a question deeper far than these—not how to obtain most fairly an expression of the people's will, but how that will shall truly represent the will of God.   There is no other question at last, than this.

And we shall attain this, not by nicely balancing interest against interest, much less by manœuvring, or by cunningly devised expedient, to defeat the cause which we believe the wrong one ; but by each doing all that in him lies to rouse himself and others to a high sense of responsibility.

It is a noble thought, that of every elector going to vote, as these men did, for the Church, for the People, for God, and for the Right, earnestly anxious that he and others should do *right*.

Else—to speak humanly—this was an appeal to chance and not to God ; and every election, by ballot or by suffrage, is else an appeal to chance.

All therefore, depends upon the *spirit* in which the election is conducted.

What constitutes the difference between an appeal to God and an appeal to chance?

III. The Spirit.

1. A *religious* spirit. "They prayed and said, Thou, Lord, which knowest the hearts of all men, show whether of these two Thou hast chosen." Now, we shall be met here at once, by an objection. This was a religious work—the selection of an apostle; but the choice of a representative is not a religious work, only a secular one.

Here we come therefore, to the very pith and marrow of the whole question. The distinction between religious and secular is true in a sense, but as we make it, it is false. It is not the occupation, but the spirit which makes the difference. The election of a bishop may be a most secular thing. The election of a representative may be a religious thing. St. Paul taught that nothing is profane. Sanctified by the Word of God and prayer, St. Peter learned that nothing is common or unclean.

*   *   *   *   *

[Many relics remain to us from our religious forefathers indicative of this truth. Grace before meals. *Dei gratia* on coins of the realm. "In the name of God," at the commencement of wills. Oaths in court of justice. Prayers in universities before election of scholars.—All proclaim that the simplest acts of our domestic and political life are sacred or profane according to the spirit in which they are performed; not in the question whether they are done for the State or the Church, but whether with God or without God.]

Observe—It is not the preluding such an election with public prayer that would make it a religious act. It is religious so far as each man discharges his part as a duty and solemn responsibility.

If looked on in this spirit by the higher classes, would the debauchery and the drunkenness which are fostered by rich men of all parties among the poor for their own purposes, be possible ? Would they, for the sake of one vote, or a hundred votes, brutalize their fellow-creatures ?

2. It is implied in this, that it must be done *conscientiously*.

Each Christian found himself in possession of a new right—that of giving a vote or casting a lot.

Like all rights, it was a duty. He had not a right to do what he liked. His right was only the duty of doing right. And if any one had swayed him to support the cause of Barnabas or that of Matthias on any motives except this one—" You ought "—he had so far injured his conscience.

The conscience of man is a holy, sacred thing. The worst of crimes is to injure a human conscience. Better kill the body. Remember how strongly St. Paul speaks, "When ye sin so against the brethren, and wound their weak conscience, ye sin against Christ." And that sin remember, consisted in leading them to do a thing which, though right in itself, they thought wrong.

Now there is an offence against the laws of the State which all men agree in treating with a smile.

My brethren, bribery is a *sin*—a sin against God. Not because a particular law has been made against it, but because it lowers the sense of personal responsibility, blunts the conscience, dethrones the God within the man's soul, and erects selfishness, and greed, and interest, in His stead.

And whether you do it directly or indirectly—directly by giving, indirectly by withdrawing, assistance, or patronage—you sin against Christ.

3. It was not done from personal interest.

There were two candidates, Barsabas and Matthias. Now if the supporters of these two had been influenced chiefly by such considerations as blood-relationship, or the chance of favour and promotion, manifestly a high function would have been degraded.

In secular matters however, we do not judge so. A man generally decides according to his professional or his personal interests. You know almost to a certainty beforehand which way a man will vote, if you know his profession. If a man be a farmer or a clergyman, or a merchant, you can pretty surely guess on which side he will range himself.

Partly no doubt, this is involuntary—the result of those prejudices which attach to us all from association. But it is party voluntary. We *know* that we are thinking not of the general good, but of our own interests. And thus a farmer would think himself justified in looking at a question simply as it affected his class, and a noble as it affected his caste, and a working-man as it bore upon the working-classes.

Brethren, we are Christians. Something of a principle higher than this ought to be ours. What is the law of the Cross of Christ? The sacrifice of the One for the whole, the cheerful surrender of the few for the many. Else, what do we more than others?

These are fine words—patriotism, public principle, purity.

Be sure these words are but sentimental expressions, except as they spring out of the Cross of Christ.

*   *   *   *   *

Application.—

I have endeavoured to keep entirely unseen my own political views. I may have failed, but not voluntarily.

Remember, in conclusion, the matter of paramount importance to be decided this week is, not whether a preponderance shall be ensured for one of the great parties which divide the country, or the other. That is important, but it is secondary. The important thing to be devoutly wished, is that each man shall give his vote as these men did—conscientiously, religiously, unselfishly, lovingly.

Better that he should support the wrong cause conscientiously than the right one insincerely. Better be a true man on the side of wrong than a false man on the side of right.

XIII.

ISAAC BLESSING HIS SONS.

"And it came to pass, that when Isaac was old, and his eyes were dim, so that he could not see, he called Esau his eldest son, and said unto him, My son : and he said unto him, Behold, *here am* I.—And he said, Behold now, I am old, I know not the day of my death :—Now therefore take, I pray thee, thy weapons, thy quiver and thy bow, and go out to the field, and take me *some* venison ;—And make me savoury meat, such as I love, and bring *it* to me, that I may eat ; that my soul may bless thee before I die."—Gen. xxvii. 1—4.

IN chapter xxv. we find Abraham preparing for death by a last will : making Isaac his heir, and providing for his other children by giving them gifts while he yet lived, and so sending them out into the world. In this chapter, the heir himself is preparing to die. The rapidity with which these chapters epitomize life, bringing its few salient points together, is valuable as illustrative of what human existence is. It is a series of circles intersecting each other, but going on in a line. A few facts comprise man's life. A birth—a marriage—another birth—a baptism—a will—and then a funeral : and the old circle begins again.

Isaac is about to declare his last will. It is a solemn act in whatever light we view it, if it were only for the thought that we are writing words which will not be read till we are gone. But it is solemn too, because it is one of those acts which tell of the immortal. First in the way of prophetic prescience. Is it not affecting to think of a human being, not sick, nor in pain, with his natural force unabated, calmly sitting down to make arrangements for what shall be when he is in his last long sleep? But the act of an immortal is visible also in that a dead man rules the world, as it were, long after his decease. Being dead, in a sense he yet speaketh. He is yet present with the living. His existence is protracted beyond its natural span. His will is law. This is a kind of evidence of his immortality : for the obedience of men to what he has willed is a sort of recognition of his present being.

Isaac was not left without warnings of his coming end. These warnings came in the shape of dimness of eyes and failing of sight. You can conceive a state in which man should have no warnings : and instead of gradual decay, should drop suddenly, without any intimation, into eternity. Such an arrangement might have been. But God has in mercy provided reminders. For we sleep in this life of ours a charmed sleep, which it is hard to break. And if the road were of unbroken smoothness, with no jolt or shock, or unevenness in the journey, we should move swiftly on, nothing breaking that dead slumber till we awake suddenly, like the rich man in the parable, lifting up our eyes in heaven or in hell. Therefore God has given these reminders. Some of them regular—such as failing of sight, falling out of hair, decay of strength, loss of memory—which are as stations in the journey, telling us how far we have travelled : others irregular—such as come in the form of sickness, bereavement, pain—like sudden shocks which jolt, arouse, and awaken. Then the man considers, and like Isaac, says, " Behold I am old, I know not the day of my death." We will consider—

I. Isaac's preparation for death.
II. The united treachery of Jacob and Rebekah.

I. Isaac's preparation for death.—First, he longed for the performance of Esau's filial kindness as for a last time. Esau was his favourite son : not on account of any similarity between them, but just because they were dissimilar. The repose, and contemplativeness, and inactivity of Isaac found a contrast in which it rested, in the energy and even the recklessness of his firstborn. It was natural to yearn for the feast of his son's affection for the last time. For there is something peculiarly impressive in whatever is done for the last time. Then the simplest acts contract a kind of sacredness. The last walk in the country we are leaving. The last time a dying man sees the sun set. The last words of those from whom we have parted, which we treasure up as more than accidental, almost prophetic. The winding up of a watch, as the last act at night. The signature of a will. In the life of Him in whom we find every feeling which belongs to unperverted Humanity, the same desire is found : a trait therefore, of the heart which is universal, natural, and right. "With desire I have desired to eat this passover with you before I suffer. *For* I say unto you, I will not drink henceforth of the fruit of the vine until that day when I drink it new with you in my Father's kingdom." It was the *Last* Supper.

2. By making his last testamentary dispositions. Apparently they were premature, but he did not defer them : partly because of the frailty of life, and the uncertainty whether there may be any to-morrow for that which is put off to-day : partly perhaps, because he desired to have all earthly thoughts done with and put away. Isaac lived

thirty or forty years after this : but he was a man set apart :
like one who in Roman Catholic language, had received
extreme unction, and had done with this world ; and when
he came to die, there would be no anxieties about the
disposition of property to harass him.　It is good to have
all such things done with before that hour comes : there is
something incongruous in the presence of a lawyer in the
death-room, agitating the last hours.　The first portion of
our lives is spent in learning the use of our senses and
faculties : ascertaining where we are and what.　The second
in using those powers, and acting in the given sphere : the
motto being, "Work, the night cometh."　A third portion
between active life and the grave, like the twilight between
day and night, not light enough for working, nor yet quite
dark, which nature seems to accord for unworldliness and
meditation.　It is striking doubtless, to see an old man, hale
and vigorous to the last, dying at his work like a warrior in
armour.　But natural feeling makes us wish perhaps, that an
interval might be given : a season for the statesman, such as
that which Samuel had, on laying aside the cares of office,
in the schools of the prophets ; such as Simeon had, and
Anna, for a life of devotion in the temple ; such as the
labourer has when, his long days' work done, he finds
an asylum in the almshouse ; such as our Church desires,
where she prays against sudden death : a season of interval
in which to watch, and meditate, and wait.

II. The united treachery of Jacob and Rebekah.—It
was treachery in both : in one sense it was the same
treachery.　Each deceived Isaac and overreached Esau.
But it would be a rough estimate to treat the two sins as
identical.　This is the coarse, common way of judging.

We label sins as by a catalogue. We judge of men by their acts ; but it is far truer to say that we can only judge the acts by the man. You must understand the man before you can appreciate his deed. The same deed done by two different persons ceases. to be the same. Abraham and Sarah both laughed when informed that they should have a son in their old age. But Sarah's was the laugh of scepticism : the other the result of that reaction in our nature by which the most solemn thoughts are balanced by a sense of strangeness or even ludicrousness. The Pharisees asked a sign in unbelief : many of the Old Testament saints did the same in faith. Fine discrimination is therefore necessary to understand the simplest deed. A very delicate analysis of character is necessary to comprehend such acts as these, and rightly to apportion their turpitude and their palliations.

In Rebekah's case the root of the treachery was ambition ; but here we find a trait of female character. It is a woman's ambition, not a man's. Rebekah desired nothing for herself, but everything for Jacob : for him spiritual blessing—at all events, temporal distinction. She did wrong, not for her own advantage, but for the sake of one she loved. Here is a touch of womanhood. The same is observable in the recklessness of personal consequences. So as only *he* might gain, she did not care. " Upon me be the curse, my son." And it is this which forces us, even while we must condemn, to compassionate. Throughout the whole of this revolting scene of deceit and fraud, we can never forget that Rebekah was a mother. And hence a certain interest and sympathy are sustained. Another feminine trait is seen in the conduct of Rebekah. It was devotion to a person rather than to a principle. A man's idolatry is for an idea, a woman's is for a person. A man suffers for a monarchy, a woman for a king. A man's martyrdom differs from a woman's. Nay even in their religion, personality marks the one, attachment to an idea or principle the other. Woman adores God in His personality, man adores Him in His attributes. At least that is on the whole the characteristic difference.

Now here you see the idolatry of the woman : sacrificing her husband, her elder son, high principle, her own soul, for an idolized person. Remark that this was properly speaking idolatry. For in nothing is a greater mistake made than in the conception attached to that word in reference to the affections. A mother's affection is called, by many religious people idolatry, because it is intense. Do not mistake. No one ever loved child, brother, sister, too much. It is not the intensity of affection, but its interference with truth and duty, that makes it idolatry. Rebekah loved her son more than truth, *i. e.* more than God. This was to idolize. And hence Christ says, " If any man love father or mother more than me, he is not worthy of me." You can only test that when a principle comes in the way. There are persons who would romantically admire this devotion of Rebekah, and call it beautiful. To sacrifice all, even principle, for another,—what higher proof of affection can there be ? O miserable sophistry ! The only true affection is that which is subordinate to a higher. It has been truly said, that in those who love little, love is a primary affection : a secondary one in those who love much. Be sure he cannot love another much who loves not honour more. For that higher affection sustains and elevates the lower human one, casting round it a glory which mere personal feeling could never give.

Compare for instance, Rebekah's love for Jacob with that of Abraham for his son Isaac. Abraham was ready to

sacrifice his son to duty. Rebekah sacrificed truth and
duty to her son. Which loved a son most?—which was the
nobler love? Even as a question of permanence, which
would last the longer? For consider what respect this
guilty son and guilty mother could retain for each other
after this:—would not love change into shame and lose
itself in recriminations? For affection will not long survive
respect, however it may protract its life by effort.

Observe again, monsters do not exist. When you hear
of great criminality, you think of natures originally mon-
strous, not like others. But none are liars for the sake of
lying. None are cruel for cruelty's sake. It is simply
want of principle that makes glaring sins. The best affections perverted—that is the history of great crimes. See
here : there is no touch of compunction from first to last.
The woman seems all unsexed. She has no thought of her
defrauded eldest son; none of her deceived husband.
There is an inflexible pursuit of her object, that is all. It
is wonderful how ambition and passion dazzle to all but the
end desired. It is wonderful how the true can become
false, and the tender-hearted hard and cruel for an end.
Nor is this lesson obsolete. Are there no women who
would do the same now? Are there none who would
sacrifice a son's principles or a daughter's happiness to a
diseased appetite for distinction? Are there none who
would conceal a son's extravagance, foster it, furnish it
means unknown, or in an underhand way, in what is called
the manœuvring of fashionable life; and do that for family
advancement from which the strong sense and principle of
a father would recoil and revolt? And all this, not because
they are monsters, but because their passion for distinction
is inflamed, and their affections unregulated.

Now look at Jacob's sin. He was not without ambition; but he had not that unscrupulous, inflexible will which generally accompanies ambition and makes it irresistible. A bad man naturally he was not: nor a false man: but simply a pliable and weak man. Hence he became the tool of another—the agent in a plan of villany which he had not the contrivance to originate. He was one of those who if they could, would have what they wish innocently. He would not play false, yet he would unjustly have. He was rather afraid of doing the deceit, than anxious that the deceit should not be done. Here was the guilt in its germ. He had indulged and pampered the fancy; and be sure he who wishes a temporal end for itself, does, or will soon, will the means. All temptations and all occasions of sin are power-less, except as far as they fall in with previous meditations upon the guilt. An act of sin is only a train long laid, fired by a spark at last. Jacob pondered over the desire of the blessing, dallied with it, and then fell. Now observe the rapidity and the extent of the inward deterioration. See how this plain, simple man, Jacob, becomes by degrees an accomplished deceiver; how he shrinks at nothing; how, at first unable to conceive the plan devised by another, he becomes at last inventive. At first the acted falsehood—a semblance; then the lie in so many words; then the impious use of the name, "The Lord thy God brought it me." How he was forced by fear and the necessities of begun guilt into enormity: deeper and deeper. Happy the man who cannot, even from the faint shadows of his own experience, comprehend the desperate agony of such a state: the horror mixed with hardening effrontery with which a man feels himself compelled to take step after step, and is aware at last that he is drifting, drifting, from the great shore of truth—like one carried out by the tide against his will, till he finds himself at last in a sea of falsehood, his whole life one great dream of false appearance.

Let us apply this briefly.

Doubtless perverted good is always different from original vice. In his darkest wanderings, one in whom the Spirit strives is essentially different from one who is utterly depraved. Sensibility to anguish makes the difference, if there were nothing else. Jacob lying in this way, plunging headlong, deeper and deeper, was yet a different man from one who is through and through hollow. Grant this,—and yet that fact of human pervertibility is an awful fact and mystery. Innocence may become depraved; delicate purity may pass into grossness. It is an appalling fact. Transparency of crystal clearness may end in craft, double-dealing, contrivance. Briefly, therefore,—

1. Learn to say " No."

2. Beware of those fancies, those day-dreams, which represent things as possible which should be for ever impossible. Beware of that affection which cares for your happiness more than for your honour.

Lastly, in the hour of strong temptations, throwing ourselves off self, distrusting ourselves; let us rest in Him who, having been tempted, knows what temptation is, who " will not suffer us to be tempted above that we are able, but will with the temptation also make a way to escape, that we may be able to bear it."

XIV.

SALVATION OUT OF THE VISIBLE CHURCH.

"Now there was at Joppa a certain disciple named Tabitha, which by interpretation is called Dorcas : this woman was full of good works and almsdeeds which she did," &c.—Acts ix. 36.

"There was a certain man in Cæsarea called Cornelius, a centurion of the band called the Italian band," &c.—Acts x. 1.

TWO events are connected with St. Peter's stay at Joppa : the miraculous restoration of Dorcas, and the vision which prepared for the reception of Cornelius into the Christian Church. The Apostle was at Lydda, when he was summoned by the news of the death of Dorcas to Joppa, about twelve miles distant. Now observe here the variety of the gifts which are bestowed upon the Christian Church. Four characters, exceedingly diverse, are brought before us in this ninth chapter : Paul, a man singularly gifted, morally and intellectually, with qualities more brilliant than almost ever fell to the lot of man ; Peter, full of love and daring, a champion of the truth ; Ananias, one of those disciples of the inward life whose vocation is sympathy, and who, by a single word, "Brother," restore light to those that sit in darkness and loneliness ; lastly, Dorcas, in a humbler, but not less true sphere of divine goodness, clothing the poor with her own hands, practically loving and benevolent.

We err in the comparative estimate we form of great and

small. Imagine a political economist computing the value
of such a life as this of Dorcas. He views men in masses :
considers the economic well-being of society on a large
scale : calculates what is productive of the greatest good for
the greatest number. To him the few coats and garments
made for a few poor people would be an item in the world's
well-being scarcely worthy of being taken into the reckoning.
Let the historian estimate her worth. The chart of time lies
unrolled before him. The fall of dynasties and the blending
together of races, the wars and revolutions of nations that
have successively passed across the world's stage—these are
the things that occupy him. What are acts like hers in the
midst of interests such as these and of contemplations so
large ? All this is beneath the dignity of history. Or again,
let us summon a man of larger contemplations still. To the
astronomer, lifting his clear eye to the order of the stars, this
planet itself is but a speck. To come down from the universe
to the thought of a tiny earth is a fell descent ; but to descend
to the thought of a humble female working at a few garments,
were a fall indeed.

Now rise to the Mind of which all other minds are but
emanations—and this conception of grand and insignificant
is not found in His nature. Human intellect, as it rises to
the great, neglects the small. The Eternal Mind condescends
to the small ; or rather, with It there is neither great nor
small. It has divided the rings of the earthworm with as
much microscopic care as the orbits in which the planets
move : It has painted the minutest feather on the wing of the
butterfly as carefully as It has hung the firmament with the
silver splendour of the stars. Great and small are words
which have only reference to us.

Further still—judging the matter by the heart, ascending

to the Heart of God, there is another aspect of the subject— great belongs only to what is moral—Infinitude and Eternity are true of feelings rather than of magnitude, or space, or time. The mightiest distance that mind can conceive, calculable only by the arrow flight of light, can yet be measured. The most vast of all the cycles that imagination ever wanted for the ages that are gone by, can yet be estimated by number. But tell us, if you can, the measure of a single feeling. Find for us, if you can, the computation by which we may estimate a single spiritual affection. They are absolutely incommensurable—these things together, Magnitude and Feeling. Let the act of Dorcas be tried thus. When the world has passed away, and the lust thereof, " he that doeth the will of God abideth for ever." The true Infinite, the real Eternal, is Love. When all that economist, historian, philosopher can calculate, is gone, the love of Dorcas will still be fresh, and living, in the eternity of the illimitable Mind.

Observe once more, the memorial which she left behind her. When Peter went into the upper chamber, he was surrounded by the poor widows, who showed him weeping the garments she had made. This was the best epitaph : the tears of the poor.

There is a strange jar upon the mind in the funeral, when the world is felt to be going on as usual. Traffic and pleasure do not alter when our friend lies in the upper chamber. The great, busy world rolls on, unheeding, and our egotism suggests the thought, So will it be when I am not. This world, whose very existence seems linked with mine, and to subsist only in mine, will not be altered by my dropping out of it. Perhaps, a few tears, and then all that follow me and love me now will dry them up again. I am but a bubble on the stream: here to-day, and then gone. This is painful to conceive. It is one of the pledges of our immortality that we long to be remembered after death—it is quite natural. Now let us inquire into its justice.

Dorcas died regretted: she was worth regretting, she was worth being restored ; she had not lived in vain, because she had not lived for herself. The end of life is not a thought, but an action—action for others. But you, why should you be regretted ? Have you discovered spiritual truth, like Paul ? Have you been brave and true in defending it, like Peter? or cheered desolate hearts by sympathy, like Ananias? or visited the widows and the fatherless in their affliction, like Dorcas ? If you have, your life will leave a trace behind which will not soon be effaced from earth. But if not, what is your worthless, self-absorbed existence good for, but to be swept away, and forgotten as soon as possible ? You will leave no record of yourself on earth, except a date of birth, and a date of death, with an awfully significant blank between.

The second event connected with St. Peter's stay at Joppa was the conversion of Cornelius.

A new doctrine was dawning on the Church. It was the universality of the love of God. The great controversy in the early history of Christianity was, not the atonement, not predestination, not even, except at first, the Resurrection, but the admissibility of the Gentiles to the Church of Christ. It was the controversy between Christianity, the universal religion, and Judaism, the limited one. Except we bear this in mind, the Acts of the Apostles and the Epistles will be alike unintelligible to us.

The germ of this truth had been planted by Stephen. St. Paul was now raised up as his successor, to develop it

still further. So that now a very important crisis had
arrived. For it has been well observed, that had St. Peter's
acceptance of this truth been delayed by leaving it to
gradual mental growth, the effects would have been incal-
culably disastrous to Christianity. A new Apostle had
arisen, and a new church was established at Antioch ; and
had St. Peter and the rest been left in their reluctance to this
truth, the younger Apostle would have been necessarily the
leader of a party to which the elder Apostles were opposed,
and the Church of Antioch would have been in opposition
to the Church at Jerusalem : a timely miracle, worthy of
God, prevented this catastrophe : at the very crisis of time
St. Peter's mind, too, was enlightened with the truth.

The vision was evidently in its form and in its direction
the result of previous natural circumstances. The death of
Stephen must have had its effect on the Apostle's mind.
That truth for which he died, the transient character of
Judaism, must have suggested strange new thoughts, to be
pondered on and doubted on ; add to this, the Apostle was
in a state of hunger. In ecstasy, or trance, or vision, things
meet for food presented themselves to his mental eye.
Evidently the *form* in which this took place was shaped
by his physical cravings, the direction depended partly
upon his previous thoughts concerning the opening question
of the Church. But the eternal Truth, the spiritual verity
conveyed by the vision, was clearly of a higher source. Here
are the limits of the natural and the supernatural closely
bordering on each other.

And this is only analogous to all our life. The human
touches on the Divine, earth borders upon heaven—the
limits are not definable. " I live," said St. Paul. Immediately after, he corrects himself : "yet not I, but Christ

liveth in me." Man's spirit prays : yet is it not " the Spirit making intercession for us with groanings which cannot be uttered ? " As if the mind of man were hardly to be distinguished from the mind of God. We are on the brink of the world unseen—on the very verge of the spirit-realm. Everywhere around us is God.

Now the contents of this vision were—a vessel let down from heaven, full of animals, domestic and wild, clean and unclean. This was let down from heaven, and taken up to heaven again. All had come from God, so that the truth conveyed was clear enough. These distinctions of clean and unclean were but conventional and artificial after all— temporal arrangements, not belonging to the unalterable. God had made all and given all. The analogy was not difficult to perceive. God is the Creator of mankind. He is the universal Father. All have come from Him. Sanctified by Him, there can be no man common or unclean.

Against even the first part of this St. Peter's mind revolted—" Not so, Lord." It is not a little remarkable that the two first to whom this expansive truth was revealed were bigoted men : St. Paul the Jewish, St. Peter the Christian bigot. For St. Peter was a Christian, yet a bigot still. Is this wonderful and rare ? or are we not all bigots in our way, the largest-minded of us all ? St. Peter was willing to admit a proselyte : the admission of an entire Gentile was a stumbling-block ; afterwards he could admit a Gentile, but hesitated to eat with him. There are some of us who can believe in the Christianity of those who are a little beyond our own Church pale ; some who even dimly suspect that God may love the Jew ; some, too, who will be ready, with qualifications, to acknowledge a benighted Roman Catholic for a brother ; but how many of us are there who would not be startled at being told to love a Unitarian? how many who would not shrink from the idea as over-bold, that he who is blind to the Redeemer's Deity, yet loving Him with all his heart, may perchance have that love accepted in place of adoration, and that it may be at our peril that we call him "common or unclean?" Oh! there was a largeness in the heart of Christ, of which we have only dreamed as yet—a something, too, in these words, "God hath showed me that I should not call any man common or unclean," which it will require, perhaps, ages to develop.

At the same, or nearly the same time when this was taking place at Joppa, a manifestation, somewhat similar, was going on at Cæsarea, a day's journey distant. Remark here the coincidence. There was an affinity, it seems, between the minds of these two men, Peter and Cornelius —a singular, mysterious sympathy. Nay, more than that, very shortly before, a similar phenomenon had been felt in the mind of St. Paul, more than a hundred miles off, in a valley near Damascus; concerning all which we can say little, except that it is very plain there is a great deal more going on upon earth than our ordinary life conceives of. In the scientific world, similar coincidences perpetually take place: discoveries, apparently unconnected, without any apparent link between the minds which make them, are announced from different parts of the world, almost simultaneously. No man perhaps, has been altogether unconscious of mental sympathies, coincidences of thought, which are utterly inexplicable. All that I deduce from this is the solemn awfulness of the universe in which we live. We are surrounded by Mystery. Mind is more real than matter. Our souls and God are real. Of the reality of nothing else are we sure: it floats before us, a fantastic shadow-world.

Mind acts on mind. The Eternal Spirit blends mind with mind, soul with soul, and is moving over us all with His mystic inspiration every hour.

In Cæsarea there was a cohort of soldiers, the body-guard of the governor who resided there. They were not, as was the case in other towns, provincial soldiers, but, being a guard of honour, were all Romans, called commonly the Italian Band. One of the centurions of this guard was Cornelius—"a devout man." A truth-loving, truth-seeking, truth-finding man; one of those who would be called in this day a restless, perhaps an unstable man; for he changed his religion twice. He had aspirations which did not leave him contented with Paganism. He found in Judaism a higher truth, and became a proselyte. In Judaism he was true to the light he had: he was devout, gave alms, and even influenced some of the soldiers of the guard, as it would appear (verse 7). The result was as might have been expected. "He that hath, to him shall be given." Give us such a man, and we will predict his history. He will be ever moving on; not merely changing, but moving on, from higher to higher, from light to light, from love to love, till he loses himself at last in the Fountain of Light and the Sea of Love. Heathenism, Judaism, Christianity. Not mere change, but true ever upwards progress. He could not rest in Judaism, nor anywhere else on earth.

To this man a voice said, "Thy prayers and thine alms are come up as a memorial before God." Prayers—that we can understand; but alms—are then works, after all, that by which men become meritorious in the sight of God? To answer this, observe—Alms may assume two forms. They may be complete or incomplete. Alms complete—works which may be enumerated, estimated—deeds done and put in as so much purchase—ten times ten thousand such will never purchase heaven. But the way in which a holy man does his alms is quite different from this. In their very performance done as pledges of something more ; done with a sense of incompleteness ; longing to be more nearly perfect —they become so many aspirations rising up to God ; sacrifices of thanksgiving, ever ascending like clouds of incense, that rise and rise in increasing volumes, still dissatisfied and still aspiring. Alms in this way become prayers —the highest prayers ; and all existence melts and resolves itself into a prayer. " Thy prayers and thine alms ; " or if you will, " Thy prayers and thy prayers," are come up to be remembered ; for what were his alms but devout aspirations of his heart to God ?

Thus, in the vision of the everlasting state which John saw in Patmos, the life of the redeemed presented itself as one eternal chant of grateful hallelujahs, hymned on harps whose celestial melodies float before the Throne for ever. A life of prayer is a life whose litanies are ever fresh acts of self-devoting love. There was no merit in those alms of Cornelius ; they were only poor imperfect aspirations, seeking the Ear of God, and heard and answered there.

All this brings us to a question which must not be avoided—the salvability of the heathen world. Let us pronounce upon this, if firmly, yet with all lowliness and modesty.

There are men of whose tenderness of heart we cannot doubt, who have come to the conclusion that without doubt the heathen shall perish everlastingly. A horrible conclusion : and if it were true, no smile should ever again pass across the face of him who believes it. No moment can, with any possible excuse, be given to any other enterprise than their evangelization, if it be true that eternity shall echo with the myriad groans and agonies of those who are dropping into it by thousands in an hour. Such men however, save their character for heart, at the expense of their consistency. They smile and enjoy the food and light just as gaily as others do. They are too affectionate for their creed; their system only binds their views; it cannot convert their hearts to its gloomy horror.

We lay down two principles:—No man is saved by merit, but only by faith. No man is saved, except in Christ. "There is none other name under heaven given among men whereby we must be saved."

But when we come to consider what is saving faith, we find it to be the broad principle of trust in God, above all misgivings, living for the invisible instead of the seen. In Hebrews xi. we are told that Noah was saved by faith. Faith in what? In the atonement? or even in Christ? Nay, but in the predicted destruction of the world by water; the truth he had, not the truth he had not. And the life he led in consequence, higher than that of the present-seeking world around him, was the life of faith, "by the which he condemned the world, and became heir of the righteousness which is by faith." Salvation therefore, is annexed to faith. Not necessarily faith in the Christian object, but in the truth, so far as it is given. Does God ask more?

Again: the Word revealed Itself to men before It was manifested in the flesh. Before this universe was called into being, when neither star nor planet was, the Father was not alone. From all eternity He contemplated Himself in Another—Himself in Himself; else God had not been Love. For another is required for love. To lose and find oneself again in another's being, that is love. Except this, we cannot conceive love possible to Him. But thus with the other, which was His very Self; in language theological, the Eternal Son in the bosom of the Father; God thrown into objectivity by Himself. There was a universe before created universe existed; there was Love when as yet there was none except Himself on whom that affection could be thrown; and the Expression of Himself to Himself, the everlasting Word, filled eternity with the anthem of the Divine Soliloquy. Now this Word expressed Itself to man before It mingled Itself with flesh. " Before Abraham was, I am." Read we not in the Old Testament of revelations made to men in visions, trances, day dreams, sometimes in voices, articulate or inarticulate, sometimes in suggestions scarcely distinguishable from their own thoughts?

Moreover, recollect that the Bible contains only a record of the Divine dealings with a single nation; His proceedings with the minds of other peoples are not recorded. That large other world—no less God's world than Israel was, though in their bigotry the Jews thought Jehovah was their own exclusive property—scarcely is—scarcely could be named on the page of Scripture except in its external relation to Israel. But at times, figures as it were, cross the rim of Judaism, when brought in contact with it, and passing for a moment as dim shadows, do yet tell us hints of a communication and a revelation going on unsuspected. We are told for example, of Job—no Jew, but an Arabian Emir, who beneath the tents of Uz contrived to solve the question to his heart which still perplexes us through life— the co-existence of Evil with Divine Benevolence; one who wrestled with God as Jacob did, and strove to know the shrouded Name, and hoped to find that it was Love. We find Naaman the Syrian, and Nebuchadnezzar the Baby-

Ionian, under the providential and loving discipline of God. Rahab the Gentile is saved by faith. The Syro-Phœnician woman by her sick daughter's bedside amidst the ravings of insanity, recognizes, without human assistance, the sublime and consoling truth of a universal Father's love in the midst of apparent partiality. The "Light which lighteth every man that cometh into the world" had not left them in darkness.

From all this we are constrained to the conviction that there is a Church on earth larger than the limits of the Church visible; larger than Jew, or Christian, or the Apostle Peter, dreamed; larger than our narrow hearts dare to hope even now. They whose soarings to the First Good, First Perfect, and First Fair, entranced us in our boyhood, and whose healthier aspirations are acknowledged yet as our instructors in the reverential qualities of our riper manhood —will our hearts *allow* us to believe that they have perished? Nay. "Many shall come from the east and west, and shall sit down with Abraham, and Isaac, and Jacob, in the kingdom of heaven." The North American Indian who worshipped the great Spirit, and was thereby sustained in a life more dignified than the more animalized men amongst his countrymen; the Hindoo who believed in the Rest of God, and in his imperfect way tried to "enter into rest," not forgetting benevolence and justice—these shall come, while "the children of the kingdom"—men who, with greater light, only did as much as they—"shall be cast out."

These, with an innumerable multitude whom no man can number, out of every kingdom, and tongue, and people, with Rahab and the Syro-Phœnician woman, have entered into that Church which has passed through the centuries, absorbing silently into itself all that the world ever had of great, and good, and noble. They were those who fought the battle of good against evil in their day, penetrated into the invisible from the thick shadows of darkness which environed them, and saw the open Vision which is manifested to all, in every nation, who fear God and work righteousness. To all, in other words, who live devoutly towards God, and by love towards man. And they shall hereafter " walk in white, for they are worthy." * * * It may be that I err in this. It may be that this is all too daring. Little is revealed upon the subject, and we must not dogmatize. I may have erred; and it may be all a presumptuous dream. But if it be, God will forgive the daring of a heart whose hope has given birth to the idea; whose faith in this matter simply receives its substance and reality from things hoped for, and whose confidence in all this dark, mysterious world can find no rock to rest upon amidst the roaring billows of uncertainty, except " the length, and the breadth, and the depth, and the height, of the Love which passeth knowledge," and which has filled the Universe with the fulness of His Christ.

XV.

THE WORD AND THE WORLD.

"And it came to pass, that, while Apollos was at Corinth, Paul having passed through the upper coasts, came to Ephesus: and finding certain disciples,—He said unto them, Have ye received the Holy Ghost since ye believed? And they said unto him, We have not so much as heard whether there be any Holy Ghost," &c.—Acts xix. 1, 2.

WE consider to-day the nineteenth chapter of the Acts of the Apostles, but first we must make some preliminary remarks.

The second missionary journey of St. Paul was done, and he had left Europe for Asia. The object of his travel was threefold. 1. To complete in the temple of Jerusalem the vow which he had begun at Corinth (xviii. 18, 21). 2. To visit Antioch, the mother church of Gentile Christianity, where his presence was much needed (xviii. 22). 3. To revisit the churches of Galatia, and strengthen those who had been tempted by false teaching in his absence (xviii. 23).

The two last of these objects were connected with one single point of interest. It was the Jewish controversy, which was then at its height. The council of Jerusalem had decided that a Gentile was not dependent for salvation on the Jewish law (xv. 23-29). But another question remained still open: Was a Christian who did not obey the law, on the same level as a Christian who did obey it?

Was it not a superior religious standing-ground, to add the Ritual life to the life of Faith ?

With this question the whole of the Epistle to the Galatians is occupied. That Epistle does not deal with the question, whether the ritual law is necessary for salvation ; but with this—whether a Gentile Christian became a higher man than before by a ceremonial life ; whether in St. Paul's words, " having begun in the spirit," he could be "made perfect through the flesh."

At Antioch that question assumed a practical form. The Jewish and Gentile Christians had lived in harmony, until certain zealous ritualists came from Jerusalem, where St. James presided. Then a severance took place. The Law-observing disciples admitted these new converts to be Christians, but would not admit their standing in the Church to be equal to their own. They denied their complete brotherhood. They refused to eat with them. A Christian, not observing the ceremonial law, was to a Christian who did observe it, very much what a proselyte of the gate was to an ancient Jew.

Two men of leading station yielded to this prejudice though it was destructive of the very essence of Christianity. These were St. Peter and Barnabas. The "dissimulation," as St. Paul calls it, of these two Apostles suggests two instructive lessons.

The yielding of Barnabas reminds us of the insecurity of mere feeling. Barnabas was a man of feeling and fine sensibilities. He could not bear to have his relative Mark severely judged (Acts xv. 36-39, and Col. iv. 10). It pained him to the heart to see that Paul, when he first essayed to join himself to his disciples, was misunderstood (Acts ix. 26, 27). He was a "Son of Consolation." He sold his property to distribute to the Christian poor (Acts iv. 36, 37).

He healed many a broken heart. But he wanted just that firmness which men of feeling so often want—the power of standing steadily by a principle.

The unsteadiness of St. Peter exhibits a different truth. It tells that a fall, however it may qualify a man for giving advice to others similarly tempted, does not qualify for future consistency, nor for the power of showing mercy in the highest way. No doubt St. Peter's fall, after his conversion, peculiarly fitted him for strengthening his brethren. But sin weakens the power of resistance. He who yields once will more easily yield the second time. He who shrunk from standing by his Master found it fearfully easy to shrink from abiding by a principle. Sin indulged breaks down the barriers between good and evil, and turns strength into weakness! And failure does not make men merciful to others. St. Peter is just as hard to the Gentile Christians, expelling them from Christian society for that which he knew to be indifferent, as if he had always been firm in his own integrity. He only can judge of error and show mercy, who has been "tempted, yet without sin." This nineteenth chapter is divisible into three chief subjects:—

I. The baptism of John's disciples.
II. The burning of the "Ephesian letters."
III. The tumult occasioned by the worshippers of Diana.

I. When St. Paul came to Ephesus, he found twelve disciples of John, bearing the name of Christians, but having a very imperfect form of Christianity. Now the baptism of John, which was all these men knew, means the doctrine of John—that cycle of teaching which is briefly symbolized by the chief ritual act of the system. The system of John was contained in a very narrow range of truth. It was such truth as we might have expected from a man who had been so disciplined. It was John's lot to be born into the world in a period of highly-advanced society; and in that hot-bed of life-fictions, Jerusalem, the ardent mind of the young man found nothing to satisfy the cravings of its desire. He wanted something deeper and truer than the existing systems could afford him. He went to the Sadducee and the Pharisee in vain. He found no life in the Jewish ritual—no assistance from the Rabbis. He went into the wilderness to commune with God, to try what was to be learned from Him by a soul in earnest, without church, ministers, or ordinances. The heavens spoke to him of purity, and the river by his side of God's eternity. Locusts and honey, his only food, taught him that man has a higher life to nourish than that which is sustained by epicurean luxuries. So disciplined John came back to his countrymen. As might be expected, no elaborate theology formed any part of his teaching. "We want a simpler, purer, austerer life. Let men be real. Fruits worthy of repentance—fruits, fruits, not profession. A new life. Repent." That was the burden of John's message.

A preparatory one evidently, one most incomplete in itself. It implied the need of something additional, as St. Paul told these converts. "John verily baptized with the baptism of repentance, saying unto the people that they should believe on Him who should come after him, that is, on Christ Jesus." And none felt more distinctly than John that his was merely an initial work. That was a touching acknowledgment of the subordinate part he had to perform in the construction of the World's new Life. "He must increase, but I must decrease." The work of John was simply the work of the axe. " The axe is laid to the root of the trees;" to destroy, not to build; to cut up by the roots ancient falsehoods; to tear away all that was unreal; to make a clearance that the light of day might come in. A great work, but still not the greatest.

And herein lay the difference between the two baptisms. John baptized with water, Christ with the Holy Ghost and fire. The one was simply the washing away of a false and evil past; the other was the gift of the power to lead a pure, true life.

This was all that these disciples knew; yet remark, they are reckoned as Christians. They are called " certain disciples "—that is, of Jesus. They knew little enough of Christianity; they had not so much as heard whether there be any Holy Ghost. The doctrine of the Trinity they knew not, nor that of Sanctification, nor probably that of the Atonement. And yet in the Word of God they are called disciples of Christ.

Let us learn from that a judgment of charity. Let not the religious man be too prone to talk with contempt of a legal spirit. Let him not sneer at " merely moral men." Morality is not religion, but it is the best soil on which religion grows. He who lives an honest, sincere, honourable life, and has strong perceptions of moral right and moral wrong, may not have reached the highest stages of spirituality; he may " know only the baptism of John;" he may aim as yet at nothing higher than doing his duty well, " accusing no man falsely, being content with his wages," giving one coat out of two to the poor; and yet that man, with scanty theology and small spiritual experience, may be a real " disciple" in the school of Christ, and one of the children of the Highest.

Nay, it is the want of this preparation which so often makes religion a sickly plant in the soul. Men begin with abundance of spiritual knowledge; they understand well the "scheme of salvation;" they talk of religious privilege, and have much religious liberty; they despise the formal spirit and the legal spirit. But if the foundation has not been laid deep in a perception of the eternal difference between right and wrong, the superstructure will be but flimsy. I believe it is a matter of no small importance that the baptism of John should precede the baptism of Christ; that is, that a strict life, scrupulous regularity, abhorrence of evil—perhaps even something too austere, the usual accompaniment of sincerity at the outset—should go before the peace which comes of faith in Christ. First the blade, *then* the ear, then the full corn in the ear. You cannot have the harvest first. There is an order in the development of the soul as there is in the development of the year of nature, and it is not safe to *force*. Nearly two thousand years were spent in the Divine government in teaching the Jews the meaning of holiness, the separation of right from wrong. And such must be the order of the education of children and of men. The baptism of Repentance before the baptism of the Spirit.

The result which followed this baptism was the gifts of tongues and prophecy. On a former occasion I endeavoured to explain what is meant by the gift of tongues. It appeared then that "tongues" were not so much the power of speaking various languages, as the power of speaking spiritual truths with supernatural and heavenly fervour. This passage favours that interpretation. The Apostle was there with twelve new converts. To what purpose was the supposed use of various languages among such a number, who already understood one another? It would seem more like the showing off of a new accomplishment than the humble character of Christian modesty permits. If this gift simply made them linguists, then the miracle was of a temporary and earthly character. But if it consisted in elevating their spiritual intuitions, and enabling them to speak, "not in the words which man's wisdom teacheth, but which the Holy Ghost teacheth, comparing spiritual things with spiritual," then you have a miracle,—celestial indeed, worthy of its Spirit-Author. If it were only a gift of languages, then the miracle has nothing to do with us; but if it were the elevating of the natural faculties by God's Spirit to a higher and diviner use, then we have a marvel and a truth which belongs to all ages. The Life is the light of men. Give life, and light follows. Expand the heart, and you enlarge the intellect. Touch the soul with love, and then you touch the lips with hallowed fire, and make even the stammering tongue speak the words of living eloquence.

This was the gift of tongues that followed the reception of the Divine spirit.

II. The second subject in the chapter is the burning of the "Ephesian letters."

Ephesus was the metropolis of Asia. Its most remarkable feature was the Temple of Diana—one of the wonders of the world. It contained a certain image, misshapen, of a human form, reported by tradition to have fallen from the skies; perhaps one of those meteoric stones, which, generated in the atmosphere, and falling to the ground, are reckoned by the vulgar to be thunderbolts from heaven.

This image represented Nature, the prolific nurse and source of all life, and the worship was a worship of Nature. Upon the base of the statue were certain mysterious sentences, and these, copied and written upon papers and amulets, were known far and wide by the name of "Ephesian letters." This was the heathen form of magical superstition. But it seems there was a Jewish practice of the occult art besides. They used certain incantations, herbs, and magical formulas, said by tradition to have been taught by Solomon, for the expulsion of diseases and the exorcism of evil spirits.

The state of Ephesus, like that of Corinth and Athens, was one of metropolitan civilization; and it is nothing strange that in such a stage of social existence, arts and beliefs like these should flourish. For there is always a craving in the soul of man for something supernatural, an irrepressible desire for communion with the unseen world. And where an over-refined civilization has choked up the natural and healthy outlets of this feeling, it will inevitably find an unnatural one. The restless spirit of those times, dissatisfied with their present existence, in spite of itself feeling the degradation of the life of epicurean indolence and selfishness, instinctively turned to the other world in quest of marvels. We do not wonder to find atheism and abject superstition co-tenants of the same town or the same mind. We do not marvel that in the very city where reasonable Christianity could scarcely find a footing, a mob could be found screaming for two hours, "Great is Diana of the Ephesians;" that when men had "not so much as heard whether there be any Holy Ghost," wise men and men in authority should be believers in "the image which fell down from Jupiter." Ephesus was exactly the place where Jewish charlatans and the vendors of "Ephesian letters" could reap a rich harvest from the credulity of sceptical voluptuaries.

It is difficult to know what to say about this Oriental magic. Shall we say that it was all imposture? or account for its success by the power of a highly-excited imagination? or believe that they were really making use of some unknown powers of nature, which they themselves in ignorance supposed to be supernatural? Little can now be decided. That the magicians themselves believed in their own art is plain, from the fact of the existence of these costly "Ephesian letters," and scientific "curious books," which had apparently reached the dignity of an elaborate system; and also from the fact that some of them, as the seven sons of Sceva, believed in Christianity as a higher kind of magic, and attempted to use its formula, as more efficacious than their own. "We adjure you by Jesus whom Paul preacheth." Had they been only impostors, they would have taken Paul for an impostor too.

Here was one of those early attempts, which in after ages became so successful, to amalgamate Christianity with the magical doctrines. Gnosticism was the result in the East, Romanism the result in the West.

But the spirit of Christianity brooks no amalgamation. The essence of magic consists in this : the belief that by some external act,—not connected with moral goodness, nor making a man wiser or better,—communication can be ensured with the Spiritual World; and the tutelage of God or some superior Spirit be commanded for a mortal. It matters not whether this be attempted by Ephesian letters, amulets, charms, curious books,—or by Sacraments, or by Church ordinances or Priestly powers,—whatever professes to bring God near to man, except by making man more like to God, is of the same spirit of Antichrist.

The spirit world of God has its laws, and they are unalterable. They are such as these: "Blessed are the pure in heart, for they shall see God." "Blessed are the merciful—the peacemakers—the meek—the poor in spirit." "If any man will do His will, he shall know." "If a man love Me he will keep my words: and My Father will love him, and We will come unto him, and make our abode with him." This is Christianity. There is no way of becoming a partaker of "the powers of the world to come," except by having the heart right with God. God's presence, God's protection, is the privilege of the humble, the holy, the loving. These are the laws of the kingdom of God's Spirit, and no magic can reverse them. The contest was brought to an issue by the signal failure of these magicians to work a miracle—the man possessed leaped upon the exorcisers, and they fled wounded, upon which there was great consternation in Ephesus. The possessors of curious books came, confessed their guilt, and burnt them with their own hands in the Apostle's presence.

You will observe in all this the terrible supremacy of conscience. There was struck a chord deep in the moral nature of these men, and it vibrated in torture. They could not bear their own secret, and they had no remedy but immediate confession. It is this arraigning accuser within the bosom, that compels the peculator, after years of concealed theft, to send back the stolen money to his employer, with the acknowledgment that he has suffered years of misery. It was this that made Judas dash down his gold in the Temple, and go and hang himself. It is this that again and again has forced the murderer from his unsuspected security in social life, to deliver himself up to justice, and to choose a true death rather than the dreadful secret of a false life. Observe how mightily our moral nature works —for health and peace, if there be no obstruction; but for disease and torture, if it be perverted. But, anyhow it works, and with living, indestructible force, as the juices of vigorous life, if obstructed, create and feed gigantic disease.

Consider in the next place, the test of sincerity furnished by this act of burning the Ephesian letters. First of all it was a costly sacrifice. They were valued at fifty thousand pieces of silver. In those days, copies were not multiplied by printing; and the possessor of a secret would take care not to multiply it. Rarity created costliness. The possession of one such book was the possession of a fortune. Then again, there was the sacrifice of livelihood. By these books they got their living. And a man who had lived to thirty or forty years of age in this mode of life was not young enough to begin the world again with a new profession. It was to throw themselves almost into beggary. Moreover, it was the destruction of much knowledge that was really valuable. As in the pursuit of alchemy real chemical secrets were discovered, so it cannot be doubted that these curious manuscripts contained many valuable natural facts. To burn them was to waste all these—to give the lore accumulated for years to the winds.

Once more, it was an outrage to feeling. Costly manuscripts, written with curious art, many of them probably the heirlooms of a family, many which were associated with a vast variety of passages in life, old feelings, old teachers, and companions, these were to be committed mercilessly to the flames. Remember too, how many other ways there were of disposing of them. Might they not be sold, and the proceeds " given to the poor ? " Might they not at least be made over to some relative who, not feeling anything wrong in the use or possession of them, would not have his conscience aggrieved ? Or might they not be retained, the use of them being given up, as curious records of the past, as the treasure stores of so much that was beautiful and wise ?

And then Conscience arose with her stern, clear voice. They are the records of an ignorant and guilty past. There must be no false tenderness ; the sacrifice must be real, or it is none. To the flames with them, till their ashes are strewed upon the winds, and the smoke will rise up to heaven a sweet savour before God.

Whoever has made such a sacrifice as this—and every real Christian in the congregation in some shape or other has—will remember the strange medley of feeling which accompanied the sacrifice. We should err if we expected such a deed to be done with feelings entirely single. There is a mixture in all such sacrifices. Partly fear constrained the act, produced by the judgment on the other exorcists ; partly genuine remorse ; partly there was a lingering regret as leaf after leaf perished in the flames ; partly a feeling of relief, and partly a heavy sense of loss in remembering that the work of years was obliterated, and that the past had to be lived afresh as a time wasted ; partly shame, and partly a wild tumult of joy, at the burst of new hope, and the prospect of a nobler life. We cannot, and dare not, too closely scan such things. The sacrifice was made, and He who knows the mixture of the earthly and the spiritual in His creatures' hearts doubtless accepted the sacrifice.

There is no Christian life that has not in it sacrifice, and that alone is the sacrifice which is made in the spirit of the conflagration of the "Ephesian letters," without reserve, without hesitation, without insincere tenderness. If the slaveholder, convinced of the iniquity of the traffic in man, sells the slaves on his estate to the neighbouring planter, the mark of sincerity is wanting; or if the trader in opium or in spirits quits his nefarious commerce, but first secures the value of all that remains in his warehouse or in his ships, again there is a something which betokens the want of a heart true and honest; or if the possessor of a library becomes convinced that certain volumes are unfit for his shelves, immoral, polluting the mind of him that reads them, and yet cannot sacrifice the brilliant binding and the costly edition without an equivalent, what shall we say of these men's sincerity?

Two things marked these Ephesians' earnestness—the voluntariness of their confession, and the unreserved destruction of these records and means of evil. And I say to you, if there be a man here before me with a sin upon his heart, let him remember Conscience *will* arise to do her dreadful work at last. It may be when it is too late. Acknowledgment at once, this is all that remains for him to relieve his heart of its intolerable load. If he has wronged a man, let him acknowledge it, and ask forgiveness; if he has defrauded him of his due, or kept from him his rights, let him repair, restore, make up; or, if the guilt be one with which man intermeddleth not, and of which God alone takes cognizance, on his bended knees this night, and before the sun of to-morrow dawn, let him pour out the secret of his heart, or else, it may be that in this world, and in the world to come, Peace is exiled from his heart for ever.

III. We shall consider thirdly, the sedition respecting Diana's worship. First under this head let us notice the speech of Demetrius—in which observe :

1. The cause of the slow death which error and false-hood die : shot through and through they still linger on. Existing abuses in Church and State are upheld because they are intertwined with private interests. The general good is impeded by private cupidity. The welfare of a nation, the establishment of a grand principle, is clamoured against because destructive of the monopoly of a few par-ticular trades. The salvation of the world must be arrested that Demetrius may continue to sell shrines of Diana. This is the reason why it takes centuries to overthrow an evil, after it has been proved an evil.

2. The mixture of religious and selfish feelings. Not only " our craft," but also the worship of the great goddess Diana. Demetrius was, or thought himself sincere ; a man really zealous for the interests of religion. And so it is with many a patriotic and religious cry. " My country " —" my church "—" my religion "—it supports *me.* " By this craft we have our wealth."

3. Numbers are no test of truth. What Demetrius said, and the town-clerk corroborated, was a fact—that the whole world worshipped the great goddess Diana. Antiquity, universality, popularity, were all on her side ; on the other, there were only Paul, Gaius, Aristarchus. If numbers tested truth, Apollos in the last chapter need not have become the brilliant outcast from the schools of Alexandria, nor St. Paul stand in Ephesus in danger of his life.

He who seeks Truth must be content with a lonely, little-trodden path. If he cannot worship her till she has been canonized by the shouts of the multitude, he must take his place with the members of that wretched crowd who shouted for two long hours, " Great is Diana of the Ephesians," till truth, reason, and calmness, were all drowned in noise.

Let us notice the judicious speech of the town-clerk, or chamberlain more properly, in which observe—

1. The impression made by the Apostle on the wiser and calmer part of the community. The Asiarchs, or magistrates, were his friends. The town-clerk exculpated him, as Gallio had done at Corinth. Herein we see the power of consistency.

2. The admitted moral blamelessness of the Christians. Paul had not " blasphemed" the goddess. As at Athens he had not begun by attacking errors, or prejudices, or even superstitions. He preached Truth, and its effect began to be felt already, in the decline of the trade which flourished by the sale of silver models of the wondrous Temple—a statistical fact, evidencing the amount of success. Overcome evil by good, error by truth. Christianity—opposed by the force of governments, counterfeited by charlatanism, sneered at by philosophers, cried down by frantic mobs, coldly looked at from a distance by the philosophical, pursued with unrelenting hatred by Judaism, met by unions and combinations of trades, having arrayed against it every bad passion of humanity—went swiftly on, conquering and to conquer.

The continental philosophers tell us that Christianity is effete. Let this narrative determine. Is *that* the history of a Principle which has in it the seeds of death ? Comes *that* from the invention of a transient thought of man's, or from the Spirit of the Everlasting ages ?

XVI.

SOLOMON'S RESTORATION.

"Did not Solomon king of Israel sin by these things? yet among many nations was there no king like him, who was beloved of his God."
—Nehem. xiii. 26.

THERE is one study, my Christian brethren, which never can lose its interest for us so long as we are men:—and that is the investigation of human character. The deep interest of Biography consists in this—that it is in some measure the description to us of our own inner history. You cannot unveil the secrets of another heart without at the same time finding something to correspond with, and perchance explain, the mysteries of your own. Heart answers here to heart. Between the wisest and the worst there are ten thousand points of marvellous resemblance; and so the trials, the frailties, the bitterness of any human soul, faithfully traced out, ever shadow out to us a portraiture of our own experience. Give but the inner heart history of the most elevated spirit that ever conquered in life's struggle, and place it before the most despicable that ever failed, and you exhibit to him so much of the picture of his own very self, that you perforce command his deepest attention. Only let the inarticulate life of the peasant find for itself a distinct voice, and a true biographer; let the inward struggles which have agitated that rough frame be given faithfully to the world, and there is not a monarch, whose soul will not be thrilled with those inner details of an existence with which outwardly he has not a single thought in common.

It is for this reason that Solomon's life is full of painful interest. Far removed as he is, in some respects, above our sympathies, in others he peculiarly commands them. He was a monarch, and none of us know the sensations which belong to Rule. He was proclaimed by God to be among the wisest of mankind, and few of us can even conceive the atmosphere in which such a gifted spirit moves, original, inquiring, comprehending, one to whom Nature has made her secret open. He lived in the infancy of the world's society, and we live in its refined and civilized manhood.

And yet, brethren, when we have turned away wearied from all those subjects in which the mind of Solomon expatiated, and try to look inwards at the *man*, straightway we find ourselves at home. Just as in our own trifling, petty history, so we find in him, Life with the same unabated, mysterious interest ; the dust and the confusion of a battle, sublime longings, and low weaknesses, perplexity, struggle ; and then the grave closing over all this, and leaving us to marvel in obscurity and silence over the strange destinies of man. Humbling, brethren, is all this, at the same time that it is most instructive. God's strange dealings with the human heart, when shall they cease their interest for us? When shall it be that life, with all its mysteries, will tire us to look upon ? When shall it be that the fate of man shall cease to wake up emotion in man's bosom ?

Now, we are to bear in mind that the career of Solomon is a problem which has perplexed many, and is by no means an easy one to solve. He belongs to the peculiar class of those who begin well, and then have the brightness of their lives obscured at last. His morning sun rose beautifully; it sank in the evening, clouded, and dark with earthy exhalations—too dark to prophesy with certainty how it should rise on the morrow.

Solomon's life was not what religious existence ought to be. The Life of God in the soul of man ought to be a thing of perpetual development; it ought to be more bright, and its pulsations more vigorous every year. Such certainly, at least to all appearance, Solomon's was not. It was excellence, at all events, marred with inconsistency. It was original uprightness disgraced by a fall, and that fall so prolonged and signal that it has always been a disputed question among commentators, whether he ever rose from it again at all. But the passage which I have selected for the text, in connection with one or two others, seems to decide this question. "Did not Solomon king of Israel sin by these things?" that is, marriage with foreign wives? "Yet among many nations was there no king like him who was beloved of his God." Now, there can be no doubt of the view given us in this verse. Six hundred years after Solomon had been sleeping in earthly dust, when all contemporaries were dead, and all personal feelings had passed away, when history could pronounce her calm verdict upon his existence as a whole, Nehemiah, in this passage, gave a summary of his character. He speaks to us of Solomon as a saint—a saint in whom saintliness had been wonderfully defaced—imperfect, tempted, fallen; but still ranked among those whom God's love had pre-eminently distinguished.

Now let us compare with this the prophecy which had been uttered by Nathan before Solomon was born. Thus he spoke in God's name to David of the son who was to succeed him on the throne :—" I will be his father, and he shall be my son. If he commit iniquity, I will chasten him with the rod of men,"—*i. e.* the rod as a human being uses it, for correction, not everlasting destruction—" and with the stripes of the children of men. But my mercy shall not depart away from him, as I took it from Saul." In this we have a distinct covenant, made prophetically. God foretold Solomon's terrible apostasy; and with it He foretold Solomon's restoration. And there is one point especially remarkable. He parallels Solomon's career with Saul's. Saul began well, and Saul ended ill. Just so it was with Solomon. Here was the parallel. But, farther than this, God distinctly warned, the parallel did not go. Saul's deterioration from good was permanent. Solomon's deterioration, dark as it was, had some point of essential difference. It was not for ever. Saul's life darkened from morning brightness into the gloom of everlasting night. Solomon's life darkened too, but the curtain of clouds was rolled aside at last, and before the night set in, the sun shone out, in serene, calm brilliancy.

We take up, therefore, for our consideration to-day the life of Solomon in these two particulars.

I. The wanderings of an erring spirit. "Did not Solomon king of Israel sin by these things?"

II. The guidance of that spirit, amidst all its wanderings, by God's love. "There was no king like unto him who was beloved of his God."

"Did not Solomon king of Israel sin by these things?" This is the first point for us to dwell on—the wanderings of a frail and erring human spirit from the right way. That which lay at the bottom of all Solomon's transgressions was his intimate partnership with foreigners. "Did not Solomon sin by these things?" that is, if we look to the context, marriage with foreign wives. The history of the text is this—Nehemiah discovered that the nobles of Judah, during the captivity, when law and religious customs had been relaxed, had married wives of Ashdod, of Ammon, and of Moab; and then, in his passionate expostulation with them, he reminds them that it was this very transgression which led to the fall of the monarch who had been most distinguished for God's favour. In the whole Jewish system, no principle was more distinct than this—the separation of God's people from partnership with the world. Exclusiveness was the principle on which Judaism was built. The Israelites were not to mix with the nations: they were not to marry with them: they were not to join with them in religious fellowship or commercial partnership. Everything was to be distinct—as distinct as God's service and the world's. And it was this principle which Solomon transgressed. He married a princess of Egypt. He connected himself with wives from idolatrous countries—Moabites, Ammonites, Edomites, Sidonians, Hittites. And then Nehemiah's argument, built on the eternal truth that friendship with the world is enmity with God, is this,—" Did not Solomon sin by these things?"

That Jewish law, my brethren, shadowed out an everlasting truth. God's people are an exclusive nation; God's Church is for ever separated from the world. This is her charter, "Come out from among them, and be ye separate, saith the Lord, and touch not the unclean thing; and I will receive you, and will be a Father unto you, and ye shall be my sons and daughters, saith the Lord Almighty." God's people may break that charter, but they do it at their own peril. And we may be very sure of this, when a religious person begins to feel an inclination for intimate communion with the world, and begins to break down that barrier which is the line of safety, the first step is made of a series of long, dark wanderings from God. We are to be separate, brethren, from the world. Mistake not the meaning of that word. The world changes its complexion in every age. Solomon's world was the nations of idolatry lying round Israel. *Our* world is not that. The world is that collection of men in every age who live only according to the maxims of their time. The world may be a profligate world, or it may be a moral world. All that is a matter of accident. Our world is a moral world. The sons of our world are not idolators, they are not profligate, they are, it may be, among the most fascinating of mankind. Their society is more pleasing, more lively, more diversified in information than religious society. No marvel if a young and ardent heart feels the spell of the fascination. No wonder if it feels a relief in turning away from the dulness and the monotony of home life to the sparkling brilliancy of the world's society. No marvel if Solomon felt the superior charms of the accomplished Egyptian and the wealthy Tyrian. His Jewish countrymen and countrywomen were but homely in comparison. What wonder if the young monarch felt it a relaxation to emancipate himself from the thraldom of a society which had little to interest his grasping and restless mind, and to throw himself upon a companionship which had more of refinement, and more of cultivation, and more of that enlargement of mind which his own gifted character was so fitted to enjoy?

It is no marvel, brethren. It is all most natural, all most intelligible—a temptation which we feel ourselves every day. The brilliant, dazzling, accomplished world—

what Christian with a mind polished like Solomon's does not own its charms? And yet now, pause. Is it in wise Egypt that our highest blessedness lies? Is it in busy, restless Sidon? Is it in luxurious Moab? No, my Christian brethren. The Christian must leave the world alone. His blessedness lies in quiet work with the Israel of God. His home is in that deep, unruffled tranquillity which belongs to those who are trying to know Christ. And when a Christian will not learn this; when he will not understand that in calmness, and home, and work, and love his soul must find its peace: when he will try keener and more exciting pleasures ; when he says, I must taste what life is while I am young, its feverishness, its strange, delirious, maddening intoxication, he has just taken Solomon's first step, and he must take the whole of Solomon's after and most bitter experience along with it.

The second step of Solomon's wandering was the unrestrained pursuit of pleasure. And a man like Solomon cannot do anything by halves. What he did, he did thoroughly. No man ever more heartily and systematically gave himself up to the pursuit. If he once made up his mind that pleasure was his aim, then for pleasure he lived. There are some men who are *prudent* in their epicureanism. They put gaiety aside when they begin to get palled with it, and then return to it moderately again. Men like Solomon cannot do that. No earnest man can. No ! if blessedness lies in pleasure, he will drink the cup to the dregs. Listen to what he says,—" I sought in mine heart to give myself unto wine, yet acquainting mine heart with wisdom ; and to lay hold on folly, till I might see what was that good for the sons of men, which they should do under the heaven all the days of their life." That was a pursuit of pleasure which was at least decided and systematic—manly. Observe, brethren, we have none of the cool, cautious sipping of enjoyment there. We have none of the feeble, languid attempts to enjoy the world which makes men venture ankle-deep into dissipation, and only long for courage to go a little further. It is the earnestness of an impassioned man, a man who has quitted God, and thrown himself, heart and soul, upon everything that he tries, and says he will try it fairly and to the full.

"Let us see what the world is worth." Perhaps some minds amongst us now are not altogether strangers to a feeling such as this. There is many a soul, formed for higher and better things, that has, at one time or another, lost its hold on God, and felt the impulse of its own desires urging it on for ever, dissatisfied, restless, panting for a celestial fruit which seems forbidden, and half expecting to find that fruit in life's excitement. These are the wanderings of an erring spirit.

But, my brethren, let us mark the wanderings of an immortal soul infinite in its vastness. There is a moral to be learnt from the wildest worldliness. When we look on the madness of life, and are marvelling at the terrible career of dissipation, let there be no contempt felt. It is an immortal spirit marring itself. It is an infinite soul, which nothing short of the Infinite can satisfy, plunging down to ruin and disappointment. Men of pleasure! whose hearts are as capable of an eternal blessedness as a Christian's, that is the terrible meaning and moral of your dissipation. God in Christ is your only Eden, and out of Christ you can have nothing but the restlessness of Cain ; you are blindly pursuing your destiny. That unquenched impetuosity within you might have led you up to God. You have chosen instead that your heart shall try to satisfy itself upon husks.

There was another form of Solomon's worldliness. It was not worldliness in pleasure, but worldliness in occupation. He had entered deeply into commercial speculations. He had alternate fears and hopes about the return of his merchant ships on their perilous three-years' voyage to India and to Spain. He had his mind occupied with plans for building. The architecture of the Temple, his own palace, the forts and towns of his now magnificent empire, all this filled for a time his soul. He had begun a system of national debt and ruinous taxation. He had become a slaveholder and a despot, who was compelled to keep his people down by armed force. Much of this was not wrong ; but all of it was dangerous. It is a strange thing how business dulls the sharpness of the spiritual affections. It is strange how the harass of perpetual occupation shuts God out. It is strange how much mingling with the world, politics, and those things which belong to advancing civilization, things which are very often in the way of our duty, deaden the delicate sense of right and wrong. Let Christians be on their guard by double prayerfulness when duty makes them men of business or calls them to posts of worldly activity. Solomon did things of questionable morality which he never would have done if he had not had the ambition to distinguish himself among the princes of this world. Business and worldliness dried up the springs of his spirituality. It was the climax of Solomon's transgression that he suffered the establishment of idolatry in his dominions.

There are writers who have said that in this matter Solomon was in advance of his age—enlightened beyond the narrowness of Judaism, and that this permission of

idolatry was the earliest exhibition of that spirit which
in modern times we call religious toleration. But my
brethren, Solomon went far beyond toleration. It is written,
when Solomon was old his wives turned away his heart after
other gods; for he went after Ashtoreth the goddess of
the Zidonians, and after Milcom the abomination of the
Ammonites. The truth seems to be, Solomon was getting
indifferent about religion. He had got into light and
worldly society, and the libertinism of his associations was
beginning to make its impression upon him. He was beginning to ask, Is not one religion as good as another, so
long as each man believes his own in earnest? He began to
feel there is a great deal to be said for these different religions. After all there is nothing certain; and why forbid
men the quiet enjoyment of their own opinion? And so
he became what men call liberal, and he took idolatry under
his patronage. There are few signs in a soul's state more
alarming than that of religious indifference, that is, the
spirit of thinking all religions equally true,—the real meaning
of which is, that all religions are equally false.

II. We are to consider, in the last place, God's loving
guidance of Solomon in the midst of all his apostasy. My
Christian brethren, in the darkest, wildest wanderings, a
man to whom God has shown his love in Christ is conscious
still of the better way. In the very gloom of his remorse,
there is an instinctive turning back to God. It is enumerated among the gifts that God bestowed on Solomon, that
He granted to him "largeness of heart." Now that largeness of heart which we call thoughtfulness and sensibility,
generosity, high feeling, marks out, for the man who has it,
a peculiar life. Life becomes an intense thing: if there be
guilt, then his life will be desolating remorse; if love, then

the very ecstasy of blessedness. But a cool, common-place life he cannot have. According to Scripture phraseology, Solomon had a great heart; and therefore it was that for such an one the discipline which was to lead him back to God must needs be terrible. " If he commit iniquity, I will chasten him with the rod of men." That was God's covenant, and with tremendous fidelity was it kept.

You look to the life of Solomon, and there are no outward reverses there to speak of. His reign was a type of the reign of the power of peace. No war, no national disaster, interrupted the even flow of the current of his days. No loss of a child, like David's, pouring cold desolation into his soul—no pestilences nor famines. Prosperity and riches, and the internal development of the nation's life, that was the reign of Solomon. And yet brethren, with all this, was Solomon happy? Has God no arrows winged in heaven for the heart, except those which come in the shape of outward calamity? Is there no way that God has of making the heart gray and old before its time, without sending bereavement, or loss, or sickness? Has the Eternal Justice no mode of withering and drying up the inner springs of happiness, while all is green, and wild, and fresh, out-wardly? We look to the history of Solomon for the answer.

The first way in which his aberration from God treasured up for him chastisement, was by that weariness of existence which breathes through the whole book of Ecclesiastes. That book bears internal evidence of having been written after repentance and victory. It is the experience of a career of pleasure; and the tone which vibrates through the whole is disgust with the world, and mankind, and life, and self. I hold that book to be inspired. God put it into the heart of Solomon to make that experience public. But my brethren, by " inspired," I do not mean that all the feelings to which that book gives utterance are right or holy feelings. Saint John could not have written that book. Saint John, who had lived in the atmosphere of love, looking on this world as God looks on it—calmly, with the deep peace of heaven in his soul, at peace with himself, and at peace with man—could never have penned the book of Ecclesiastes. To have written the book of Ecclesiastes a man must have been qualified in a peculiar way. He must have been a man of intense feeling—large in heart, as the Bible calls it. He must have been a man who had drunk deep of unlawful pleasure. He must have been a man in the upper ranks of society, with plenty of leisure and plenty of time to brood on self. Therefore, in saying it is an inspired book, I mean the inspired account of the workings of a guilty, erring, and yet, at last, conquering spirit. It is not written as a wise and calm Christian would write, but as a heart would write which was fevered with disappointment, jaded with passionate attempts in the pursuit of blessedness, and forced to God as the last resource.

My younger brethren, that saddest book in all the Bible stands before you as the beacon and the warning from a God who loves you, and would spare you bitterness if He could. Follow inclination now, put no restraint on feeling,— say that there is time enough to be religious by-and-by— forget that now is the time to take Christ's yoke upon you, and learn gradually and peacefully that serene control of heart which must be learnt at last by a painful wrench— forget all that, and say that you trust in God's love and mercy to bring all right, and then that book of Ecclesiastes is your history. The penalty that you pay for a youth of pleasure is, if you have anything good in you, an old age of weariness and remorseful dissatisfaction.

Another part of Solomon's chastisement was doubt. Once more turn to the book of Ecclesiastes. "All things come alike to all : there is one event to the righteous, and to the wicked ; to the good and to the clean, and to the unclean ; to him that sacrificeth, and to him that sacrificeth not." In this, brethren, you will observe the querulous complaint of a man who has ceased to feel that God is the Ruler of this world. A blind chance, or a dark destiny, seems to rule all earthly things. And that is the penalty of leaving God's narrow path for sin's wider and more flowery one. You lose your way ; you get perplexed ; doubt takes possession of your soul. And my Christian brethren, if I speak to any such, you know that there is no suffering more severe than doubt. There is a loss of aim, and you know not what you have to live for. Life has lost its meaning and its infinite significance. There is a hollowness at the heart of your existence. There is a feeling of weakness, and a discontented loss of self-respect. God has hidden his face from you because you have been trying to do without Him or to serve Him with a divided heart.

But now lastly, we have to remark, that the Love of God brought Solomon through all this to spiritual manhood. "Let us hear the conclusion of the whole matter: Fear God, and keep His commandments: for this is the whole duty of man." In this brethren, we have the evidence of his victory. Doubt, and imprisonment, and worldliness have passed away, and clear activity, belief, freedom, have taken their place. It was a terrible discipline, but God had made that discipline successful. Solomon struggled manfully to the end. The details of his life were dark, but the life itself was earnest; and after many a fall, repentance, with unconquerable purpose, began afresh. And so he struggled on, often baffled, often down, but never finally subdued; and still with tears and indomitable trust, returning to the conflict again. And so, when we come to the end of his last earthly work, we find the sour smoke, which had so long been smouldering in his heart and choking his existence, changed into bright, clear flame. He has found the secret out at last, and it has filled his whole soul with blessedness. God is man's happiness. " Fear God, and keep his commandments : for this is the whole duty of man."

And now brethren, let us come to the meaning and the personal application of all this. There is a way—let us not shrink from saying it—there is a way in which sin may be made to minister to holiness. "To whomsoever much is forgiven the same loveth much." There was an everlasting truth in what our Messiah said to the moral Pharisees : " The publicans and the harlots go into the kingdom of God before you." Now these are Christ's words ; and we will not fear to boldly state the same truth, though it be liable to much misinterpretation. Past sin brethren, may be made the stepping-stone to heaven. Let a man abuse that if he will by saying, " Then it is best to sin." A man may make the doctrine absurd, even shocking, by that inference, but it is true for all that. "All things work together for good to them that love God." All things, even sin. God can take even your sin, and make it work to your soul's sanctification. He can let you down into such an abyss of self-loathing and disgust, such life-weariness, and doubt, and misery and disappointment, that if he ever raises you again by the invigorating experience of the Love of Christ, you will rise stronger from your very fall, and in a manner secured against apostasy again. Solomon, King of Israel, sinned, and, by the strange power of the cross of Christ, that sin gave him deeper knowledge of himself, deeper insight into the mystery of human life, more marvellous power of touching the souls of his brother men, than if he had not sinned. But forget not this, if ever a great sinner becomes a great saint, it will be through agonies which none but those who have sinned know.

Brethren, I speak to those among you who know something about what the world is worth, who have tasted its fruits, and found them like the Dead Sea apples—hollowness and ashes. By those foretastes of coming misery which God has already given you, those lonely feelings of utter wretchedness and disappointment when you have returned home palled and satiated from the gaudy entertainment, and the truth has pressed itself icy cold upon your heart, "Vanity of vanities"—is this worth living for? By all that, be warned. Be true to your convictions. Be honest with yourselves. Be manly in working out your doubts, as Solomon was. Greatness, Goodness, Blessedness, lie not in the life that you are leading now. They lie in quite a different path: they lie in a life hid with Christ in God. Before God is compelled to write that upon your heart in disgust and disappointment, learn "what is that good for the sons of men which they should do" all the days of their life under the heaven. Learn from the very greatness of your souls, which have a capacity for infinite agony, that you are in this world for a grander destiny than that of frittering away life in uselessness.

Lastly, let us learn from this subject the covenant love of God. There is such a thing as love which rebellion cannot weary, which ingratitude cannot cool. It is the Love of God to those whom he has redeemed in Christ. " Did not Solomon, King of Israel, sin? and yet there was no king like him who was beloved of his God." Let that, my Christian brethren, be to us a truth not to teach carelessness, but thankfulness. Oh! trembling believer in Christ, are you looking into the dark future and fearing, not knowing what God will be to you at the last? Remember, Christ " having loved his own who are in the world loved them to the end." Your salvation is in the hands of Christ; the everlasting arms are beneath you. The rock on which your salvation is built is love, and the gates of hell shall not prevail against you.

XVII.

JOSEPH'S FORGIVENESS OF HIS BRETHREN.

"And when Joseph's brethren saw that their father was dead, they said, Joseph will peradventure hate us, and will certainly requite us all the evil which we did unto him.—And they sent a messenger unto Joseph, saying, Thy father did command before he died, saying,—So shall ye say unto Joseph, Forgive, I pray thee now, the trespass of thy brethren, and their sin; for they did unto thee evil: and now, we pray thee, forgive the trespass of the servants of the God of thy father. And Joseph wept when they spake unto him.—And his brethren also went and fell down before his face; and they said, Behold, we *be* thy servants. —And Joseph said unto them, Fear not: for *am* I in the place of God? —But as for you, ye thought evil against me; *but* God meant it unto good, to bring to pass, as *it is* this day, to save much people alive.— Now therefore fear ye not: I will nourish you, and your little ones. And he comforted them, and spake kindly unto them."—Genesis l. 15—21.

CHRISTIANITY is a revelation of the Love of God: a demand of our love by God based thereon. Christianity is a revelation of Divine forgiveness—a requirement thereupon that we should forgive each other.

"A new commandment I give unto you, That ye love one another; as I have loved you, that ye also love one another" (John xiii. 34). "Ye call me Master and Lord: and ye say well, for so I am. If I, then, your Lord and Master, have washed your feet; ye also ought to wash one another's feet. For I have given you an example, that ye should do as I have done to you" (John xiii. 13--15). "Forgive us our debts, as we forgive our debtors" (Matt. vi. 12). "Beloved, if God so loved us, we ought also to love one another" (1 John iv. 11). "Forbearing one another, and forgiving one another, even as God for Christ's sake hath forgiven you" (Ephes. iv. 32).

Now these duties of love, forgiveness, service, are called "new commandments." But we should greatly mistake if we suppose that they are new in this sense, that they were created by the Gospel, and did not exist before. The Gospel did not *make* God love us : it only revealed His love. The Gospel did not make it our duty to forgive and love : it only revealed the eternal order of things, to transgress which is our misery. These belong to the eternal order and idea of our Humanity. We are not planted by Christ in a new arbitrary state of human relationships, but redeemed into the state to which we were created.

So St. John says, "I write no new commandment unto you, but an old commandment which ye had from the beginning. The old commandment is the word which ye have heard from the beginning. Again, a new commandment I write unto you, which thing is true in him and in you ; because the darkness is past, and the true light now shineth"—old, because of the eternal order of Love ; new, because shown in the light of the Love of Christ. Christianity is the True Life—the Right Humanity.

Now the proof of this is, that ages before Christ appeared, they who gave themselves up to God to be led, instead of to their own hearts, did actually reduce to practice, and manifested in their lives, those very principles which, as principles, were only revealed by Christ.

Here for instance, three thousand years before Christ,

Joseph, a Hebrew slave, taught by life's vicissitudes, educated by God, acts out practical Christianity : one of its deepest and most difficult lessons.   There is nothing in the New Testament more childlike than this forgiveness of his brethren.   Some perhaps may be shocked at dwelling on this thought : it seems to them to derogate from Christ. This is as if they thought that they honoured Christ by believing that until He came no truth was known—that He created truth.   These persons tremble at every instance of a noble or pure life which can be shown in persons not enlightened by Christianity.   But in truth, this is a corroboration of Christianity.   Christianity is a full revelation of the truth of Life, into which every one who had been here had, in his measure, struck his roots before.   It is simply the Truth, " the same yesterday, to-day, and for ever."   And all instances of such a life only corroborate the truth of the Revelation.

We divide our subject into two parts :—

I. The petition of the brethren.
II. Joseph's forgiveness.

1. The petition was suggested by their own anticipations of vengeance.   Now whence came these anticipations ?   I reply, from their own hearts.   Under similar circumstances they would have acted so, and they took for granted that Joseph would.   We suspect according to our nature ; we look on others as we feel.   Suspicion proves character : so does Faith.   We believe and suspect as we are.   But unless there had been safety for them in Joseph's heart, a guarantee in the nobleness of Joseph's nature, their abject humiliation would have saved them nothing.   Little they knew the

power of hate, the sweetness of revenge, if they fancied that a grudge treasured up so many years would be foregone on the very verge of accomplishment for the sake of any satisfaction, prayer, apology.

Now the error of Joseph's brethren is our error towards God. Like them, we impute to God our own vindictive feelings : and, like them, we pray a prayer which is in itself an insult or absurd. We think that sin is an injury, a personal affront, instead of a contradiction of our own nature, a departure from the Divine harmony, a disfigurement of what is good. Consequently we expect that God resents it. Our vindictive feelings we impute to God : we would revenge, therefore we think He would. And then in this spirit, " Forgive us," means, " Forego thy vengeance. Do not retaliate. I have injured Thee ; but lo ! I apologize, I lie in the dust. Bear no malice, indulge no rancour, O God !" This is the heathen prayer which we often offer up to God. And just as it must have been unavailing in Joseph's case except there were safety in Joseph's character, so must it be useless in ours unless in God's nature there be a guarantee which we think our prayers create. Think you that God, if revengeful, can be bought off by prayer, by rolling in the dust, by unmanly cries, by coaxing, or flattery ? God's forgiveness is the regeneration of our nature. God cannot avert the consequences of our sin.

We must get rid of these heathen ideas of God. God's forgiveness is properly our regeneration. You cannot by prayer buy off God's vindictiveness : for God is not vindictiveness, but Love. You cannot by prayer avert the consequences of sin : for the consequences are boundless, inseparable from the act. Nor is there in time or eternity anything that can sever the connection. If you think that you can sin, and then by cries avert the consequences of sin, you insult God's character. You can only redeem the past by alteration of the present. By faith in God's love, by communion with His Spirit, you may redeem yourself; but you cannot win the love of God by entreaty, unless that love be yours already : yours, that is, when you claim it.

2. Next, observe the petition was caused by their father's insisting on their asking pardon.

He recognized the duty of apology. For Jacob knew that Joseph bore no malice. Not to change Joseph, but to fulfil their obligations, he gave the charge that required satisfaction. We know how false conceptions are of satisfaction : in the language of the old duel, to give satisfaction meant to give one who had been injured by you an opportunity of taking your life. In the language of semi-heathen Christianity, to satisfy God, means to give God an equivalent in blood for an insult offered. No wonder that with such conceptions the duty of apology is hard—almost impossible. We cannot say, " I have erred," because it gives a triumph. Now the true view of Satisfaction is this—to satisfy, not revenge, but the Law of Right. The Sacrifice of Christ satisfied God, because it exhibited that which alone can satisfy Him, the entire surrender of Humanity. The satisfaction of an apology is doing the right—satisfying—doing all that can be done.

It may be our lot to be in Jacob's circumstances : we may be arbiters in a dispute, or seconds in a quarrel. And remember, to satisfy in this sense is not to get for your friend all his vindictiveness requires, or to make him give as little as the other demands, but to see that he does all that should of right be done.

His honour ! Yes; but you cannot satisfy his honour

by glutting his revenge : only by making him do right. And if he has erred or injured, in no possible way can you repair his honour or heal his shame, except by demanding that he shall make full acknowledgment. " I have erred :" it *is* very hard to say, but because it is hard, it is therefore manly. You are too proud to apologize, because it will give your adversary an advantage ? But remember the advantage is already given to him by the wrong that you have done, and every hour that you delay acknowledgment you retain your inferiority : you diminish the difference and your inferiority so soon as you dare to say, " I did wrong ; forgive me."

3. Plea—as servant of the same God (v. 17). Forgiveness is not merely a moral, but a religious duty. Now remember this was an argument which was only available in behalf of Jews. It could not have been pleaded for an Egyptian. Joseph might have been asked to forgive on grounds of humanity : but not by the sanctions of religion, if an Egyptian had offended him. For an Egyptian did not serve the God of his fathers.

How shall we apply that ? According to the spirit in which we do, we may petrify it into a maxim narrower than Judaism, or enlarge it into Christianity. If by " servants of the God of our fathers," we mean our own sect, party, church, and that we must forgive *them*, narrow indeed is the principle we have learnt from this passage. But Judaism was to preserve truth—Christianity to expand it. Christianity says, just as Judaism did, " Forgive the servants of the God." Its pleas are, " Forgive : for he is thy fellow-servant. Seventy times seven times forgive thy *brother*." But it expands that word " brother " beyond what the Law ever dreamed of—God is the Father of Man. If there be a soul for which Christ did not die, then that man you are not, on Judaistic principles, bound to forgive. If there be one whom the love of God does not embrace in the Gospel family, then for that one *this* plea is unavailing. But if God be the Father of the Race, and if Christ died for all; if the word "neighbour" means even an alien and a heretic; then this plea, narrowed by the law to his nation, expands for us to all. Because the servant of our Maker and the child of our Father, therefore he must be forgiven, let him be whosoever he may.

II. Let us consider in the second place Joseph's forgiveness.

1. Joseph's forgiveness was shown by his renunciation of the office of avenger—"Am I in the place of God?" Now this we may make to convey a Christian or a heathen sense, as we read it. It might read—we often do read it— we often say it thus : " I will not avenge, because God will. If God did not, I would. But certain that He will do it, I can wait, and I will wait, long years. I will watch the reverses of fortune ; I will mark the progress of disease ; I will observe the error, failing, grief, loss ; and I will exult and say, ' I knew it, but my hand was not on him ; God has revenged me better than I could myself.' " This is the cold-blooded, fearful feeling that is sometimes concealed under Christian forgiveness. Do not try to escape the charge. That feeling your heart and mine have felt, when we thought we were forgiving, and were praised for it. That was *not* Joseph's meaning. Read it thus : "If God does not, dare I avenge ? 'Am I in the place of God?' Dare I—

> " ' Snatch from His hand the balance and the rod,
> Rejudge His justice, be the God of God?' "

So speaks St. Paul, "Vengeance is mine." Therefore wait, sit still, and see God's wrath? No! "Therefore, if thine enemy hunger, feed him ; if he thirst, give him drink." This is the Christian revenge.

I say not that there is no such thing as the duty of redressing wrongs, especially those of others. There is a keen sense of wrong, a mighty demand of the heart for justice, which cannot be put aside. And he who cannot feel indignation against wrong cannot, in a manly way, forgive injury. But I say, the only revenge which is essentially Christian is that of retaliating by forgiveness. And he who has ever tasted that Godlike feeling of forbearance when insulted ; of speaking well of one who has slandered him (pleasure all the more exquisite if the slanderer does not know it) ; of doing service in requital of an injury : he, and only he, can know how it is possible for our frail Humanity, by abnegating the place of God the avenger, to occupy the place of God the absolver.

2. Joseph forgave, or facilitated forgiveness, by observing the good results of what had seemed so cruel (v. 20). Good out of evil—that is the strange history of this world, whenever we learn God's character. No thanks to you. Your sin dishonoured you, though it will honour God. By our intentions, and not by the results, are our actions judged. Remember this tenaciously : forgiveness becomes less difficult, your worst enemy becomes your best friend, if you transmute his evil by good. No one can really permanently injure us but ourselves. No one can dishonour us : Joseph was immured in a dungeon. They spat on Christ. Did that sully the purity of the one, or lower the Divine dignity of the other ?

3. He forgot the injury. He spake kindly to them,

comforted them, and bade them fear not. An English proverb has joined forgiving and forgetting. No forgiveness is complete which does not join forgetfulness. You forgive only so far as you forget. But here we must explain: else we get into the common habit of using words without meaning. To forget, literally, is not a matter of volition. You can by will remember, you cannot by an act of will forget—you cannot give yourself a bad memory if you have a good one. In that sense, to forget is a foolish way of talking. And indeed, to forget in the sense of oblivion would not be truly forgiving: for if we forgive only while we do not recollect, who shall ensure that with recollection hate shall not return?

More than that. In the parable of the forgiven debtor, you remember his sin in this sense was not forgotten. Fresh sin waked up all the past. He was forgiven: then he was reminded of the past debt, and cast into prison. Not for his new offence, but for his old debt, was he delivered to the tormentors—it was not forgotten. But the true Christian forgiveness, as here in Joseph's example, is unconditional. Observe: he did not hold his brethren in suspense; he did not put them on their good behaviour; he did not say, "I hold this threat over you, if you do it again." That is forgiving and not forgetting. But that was a frank, full, free remission—consoling them—trying to make them forget —neither by look nor word showing memory, unless the fault had been repeated. It was unconditional, with no reserve behind. That was forgiving and forgetting.

To conclude. Forgiveness is the work of a long life to learn. This was at the close of Joseph's life. He would not have forgiven them in youth—not when the smart was fresh—ere he saw the good resulting from his suffering.

But years, experience, trial, had softened Joseph's soul. A dungeon and a government had taught him much ; also his father's recent death. Do not think that any formula will teach this. No mere maxims got by heart about forgiveness of injuries—no texts perpetually on the tongue will do this —God alone can teach it :—By experience ; by a sense of human frailty ; by a perception of " the soul of goodness in things evil;" by a cheerful trust in human nature ; by a strong sense of God's Love ; by long and disciplined realization of the atoning Love of Christ—only thus can we get that free, manly, large, princely spirit which the best and purest of all the patriarchs, Joseph, exhibited in his matured manhood.

XVIII.

A THANKSGIVING DAY.

"Afterwards Jesus findeth him in the temple, and said unto him, Behold, thou art made whole: sin no more, lest a worse thing come unto thee. — The man departed, and told the Jews that it was Jesus which had made him whole."—John v. 14, 15.

THE man to whom these words were spoken, had been lying only a few days before, a helpless, hopeless sufferer among the porches of Bethesda, together with a number of others affected in a similar manner. By a singular, unexpected, and miraculous event, he was rescued from his calamity, while the remainder were left to the mercies of public charity, or to avail themselves of the mysterious spring of Bethesda.

It was a time of festival in Jerusalem, the streets were probably echoing with the voice of mirth and festivity, with the sounds of them that kept holiday: but it was to this congregation of the sick and the miserable that the Redeemer bent his steps; it was what might have been expected from the Son of Man—"The whole need not a physician, but they that are sick." It was the office of the Man of Sorrows to soothe the wretched; and of all the crowded scenes that day enacting in the Holy City, the "great multitude of impotent folk, of blind, halt, withered," found that their abode was the most congenial atmosphere to the soul of the Redeemer.

And in all this we have but a miniature representation of the world as it is now. Jerusalem contained within its walls, within its proud battlements, and amidst its stately temples, as much wretchedness and as much misery, separated only by a thin partition from its abodes of luxury and state, as our own metropolis does now. It is a miniature representation of the world in this, so full of outward show and of inward wretchedness. It is a representation of the world we live in, inasmuch as it is a place where selfishness prevails ; for there was affixed a certain condition to the healing of the spring, that the man should be the first ; if he were not the first, no miracle took place, and there was one more friendless wretch.

This man had no one to give him the little assistance required. For thirty-eight years he had been lingering here, and there appeared to have been no visitor who would supply what was wanting of the ties of blood or relationship. It is I say, but a representation of what this world is, when the love of God has not touched the heart of man. It is a representation of the world too, in this, that with suffering there is frequently appointed the remedy. The remedy is often found side by side with the pain it may relieve, if we could but make use of it. It is so in both bodily and spiritual maladies—there is a remedial system, a pool of Bethesda, everywhere springing up by the side of sin and suffering.

It is a representation of the world also, that the presence of the Son of Man should be felt rather in scenes of sorrow than of joy. It is not in the day of high health and strength, when our intellect is powerful, our memory vigorous, when we

feel strong in our integrity and our courage, but when our
weakened powers have made us feel that we are " a worm
and no man ;" when our failing faculties convince us that,
except for our connection with immortality, our minds would
be as nothing ; when we feel temptation getting too strong
for us, and that we are on the brink of falling—then it is
that we are taught there is a strength not our own, beyond
anything that we possess of our own. It is then that the
presence of the Son of Man is felt ; then is the day of our
merciful and mysterious deliverance.

And there is another resemblance to be noted. The
Saviour of the world went into the Bethesda porches, and
out of the great number of sufferers he selected one—not
because of his superior righteousness, not for any merit on
his part, but for reasons hidden within His own Almighty
Mind. So it is in the world—one is taken, another is left ;
one nation is sterile, another is fertile ; one is full of diseases
from which another is exempted ; one man is surrounded
with luxuries and comforts, another with every suffering
which flesh is heir to. So much for the miniature of the
world exhibited by the Pool of Bethesda.

Now in connection with this subject there are two
branches in which we will arrange our observations.

I. The cause of this man's disease.
II. The history of his gratitude.

I. Concerning the cause of his disease, we are not left
in any doubt, the Redeemer's own lips have told us what it
was—" Sin no more, lest a worse thing come unto thee."
So we see there was a strange connection between this
bodily malady and moral evil, a connection that would

have startled all around if it had been seen. No doubt the men of science, versed in the healing art, would have found some cause for his malady connected with the constitution of his bodily frame; but the Redeemer went beyond all this. Thirty-eight years before, there had been some sin committed, possibly a small sin, in our eyes at least, of which the result had been thirty-eight years of suffering; and so the truth we gather from this is, there is a connection between physical and moral evil; a connection, my Christian brethren, more deep than any of us have been accustomed to believe in.

But most assuredly, many of the most painful forms of disease that come upon the body depend upon the nervous constitution; and the nervous system is connected inseparably with the moral state more than men suppose. Often where we have been disposed to refer the whole to external causes, there has been something of moral disorder in the character which makes that constitution exquisitely susceptible of suffering, and incapable of enjoyment. Every physician will tell us that indulged passions will lead to a disturbed state of body; that want of self-control in various ways will end in that wretched state when the light that falls on the eye inflicts torture, the sounds that are heard in the ear are all discord, and all this beautiful creation, so formed for delight, only ministers to the sufferings of the diseased and disorganised frame. Thus we see that external suffering is often connected with moral evil, but we must carefully guard and modify this statement, for this is not universally the case; and it is clear this was the Saviour's opinion, for when the disciples came to Him on another occasion asking whether the blind man or his parents did sin, He answered that neither had sinned, plainly showing that there was sometimes physical suffering for which there was no moral cause. In that case it was not for his own sin, or even that of others —it baffled all the investigations of man to explain it.

Now, we must remember this when we see cases of bodily suffering : we must consider that there is a great difference between the two senses in which the word punishment is used. It may be a penalty, it may be a chastisement—one meaning of punishment is, that the law exacts a penalty if it is broken—notice having been given that a certain amount of suffering would follow a certain course of action. All the laws of God, in the physical world, in the moral world, or in the political world, if broken, commonly entail a penalty. Revolutions beset a nation, shaking its very foundations, owing to some defects in the justice or wisdom of its government, and we cannot say that all this comes from the dust, or springs out of the ground. There are causes in the history of past events that will account for it. The philosophical historian of future years will show the results of some political mistake, continued perhaps for centuries, by the rulers of this nation. So in the moral and in the physical world there are laws, as it were, that execute themselves. If a man eat a deleterious herb, whether he does it willingly or unconsciously, the penalty will fall on his body. If a man touch the lightning-conductor, not knowing that the air is charged with electricity, no holiness on his part will prevent the deadly stroke. But there is another kind of law, written in the hearts of men, and given to the conscience, when the penalty is awarded as the result of moral transgression, and then it becomes a chastisement, and the language of Scripture then becomes the language of our hearts. It is the rod of God that hath done all this.

There is another thing that we must bear in mind, that there are certain evils which fall upon man, over which he can have no control. They come as the result of circumstances over which he has no power whatever. So, we read in the second book of Kings, the child of the Shunammite went out amongst the reapers ; he was suddenly seized with a deadly pain in his head, was taken to his mother, sate upon her lap, and died at noon. A sunstroke had struck that child ; but to say that from any fault of his he was selected as the object of suffering, when the rest of the reapers were spared, would be as unjust as to say that those upon whom the Tower of Siloam fell were sinners above all the Galileans.

Moreover, to understand this we must recollect that the laws of God and the penalties of God are not miracles. If the penalty comes as the consequence appointed by God Himself, to follow certain sins, it is a natural punishment, but if it comes with no connection, it is then an arbitrary punishment. So, if a man educates a child ill, and he turns out a bad man, there is the natural connection between the penalty and the guilt. But if a man, pursuing his journey, is struck with lightning, there is no penalty there. Now, in the Old Testament we find a natural punishment falling on Eli. He allowed his children to grow up without correction, and the contempt and scorn of the whole nation fell upon that family, and the father actually died in consequence of the shock of his children's misconduct. But if the father had died in battle, or by an accident, then it would have been unjust to say that there was any connection between his misconduct and his sudden death ; it would have been an arbitrary connection.

The punishments of God are generally not arbitrary :

each law, as it were, inflicts its own penalty. It does not execute one that belongs to another. So, if the drunkard lead a life of intoxication, the consequence will be a trembling hand and a nerveless frame; but if he be drowned in the seas when sailing in the storm, he is punished for having broken a natural law, not a moral law of God. Let us then bear in mind that if the ship convey across the ocean the heavenly-minded missionary and the scoffing infidel, if the working of the vessel be attended to, and there is nothing unusual in the winds and the waves, they will convey the one to his destination as safely as the other.

Now, the application we would make of all this is, if a man perish when out on a Sabbath-day, we have no right to say that he dies because he has broken the Sabbath. If famine or pestilence visit the land, it may be explained by the infringement of some of God's natural laws; the earth may not be rightly cultivated, sanitary means have not been taken to stop the pestilence; but we have no right to say that they come in consequence of political relations which are not to our mind, or of regulations of policy of which we disapprove.

There is one thing more. It is perfectly possible that transgressions against the natural laws of God may, in the end, become trespasses against His moral law, and then the penalty becomes chastisement. The first man that drank the fermented juice of the grape was perfectly innocent, even if it caused intoxication; but when he found how it affected his brain, it became sin to him thenceforward. The first time that a man enters into society which he finds hurtful to his religious feelings, he may have done it innocently; but when he sees how it lowers the tone of his character, he must mingle amongst them no more. So want of cleanliness in some Alpine regions may result from ignorance of the laws of nature; but when, in more crowded populations, it is ascertained that it is productive of disease, and injurious to those around them, then the infraction of the natural law is stigmatized as a higher degree of turpitude. That which was a penalty becomes something more of chastisement from the wrath of God. So it is that science goes on enlightening men more and more as to the laws of God's physical world, and telling them what they must, and what they must not do, in order to lessen the amount of bodily suffering around us.

My Christian brethren, we have spoken of these things at some length, because all these considerations have been brought into our view by that pestilence,* from which we celebrate our deliverance this day; partly the result of causes over which man has no control, and partly the result of the disregard of natural laws; partly, also, from the presence of moral evil amongst us. That these three distinct classes of causes have been present may be proved by tracing its history. They who have made it their duty to trace out its progress tell us that its origin was in 1818, in Bengal, when it arose during the overflow of the river Ganges; and then, dividing into two streams of pestilence and death, it passed through the world; one going to the east, the other to the west. The eastern current passed on till it reached the shores of China; the western moved slowly on with gigantic tread, decimating nations as it went, cutting off nine thousand of the British army; and, passing through Persia and Arabia, it destroyed twelve thousand of the pilgrims to Mecca, till it paused mysteriously and strangely on the very verge of Europe—as if the voice of

* The cholera.

God himself had said, " There is danger near ; set thine house in order." By 1830 it had reached the metropolis of Russia. In 1831 it was doing its dreadful work in our own capital, while eighteen thousand fell in Paris alone ; and it then passed on, as a winged messenger, across the ocean to America.

There was then a strange disappearance of the pestilence for four or five years, till 1837, when it appeared first in the southern parts of Europe, and gradually rolled its relentless course onward to our shores. In all this you will perceive something over which we have no control. It has pursued its way not guided by moral evil or by physical causes, but by some cause, explain it as you will—as electricity, or any other conjecture—it is one that baffles every effort to stay its progress. It has taken the same road, too, that it took on its former visitation. The common food of man seems changed into something poisonous, the very air is charged with contagion ; everything proclaims it as a visitation from the Almighty. And in the very character of the disease there is something that marks it out from all other diseases : it has been truly said, that in its worst cases there is but one symptom, and that one is death. A man is full of health and strength, and in two hours he is gone. It is a disease which in its best form is terrific. That being who just now stood before you in perfect health, is in a moment a cold, livid, convulsed mass of humanity, fighting with the foe that threatens to overcome him.

But yet we find, in spite of all this, that in the progress of this strange disease, great mistakes have been made by man. From the circumstance of the poorer classes being the chief sufferers, they fancied that it was inflicted by the higher ; and in some places they rose against them, accusing them of poisoning the wells. And we find Christians so mistaken, as to look on all this suffering, not as the natural connection between sin and its penalty, but as having some arbitrary connection with the sin of others, from which they themselves and their own party are free.

But in the next place we find that it really has been caused in some degree by the transgression of the laws of nature ; for whatever may have been the secret origin of the disease, whatever may be the mystery of its onward course, still we know that there are certain conditions usually necessary to make it destructive. So we find that in India it was the natives who for the most part suffered, those whose constitutions had less stamina than our own. And here we see that debility produced by over-work, bad air, crowded dwellings, have been the predisposing causes ; and this tells us, if ever visitation could speak, that affliction cometh not out of the dust, neither does sorrow spring from the ground. It has no direct connection with moral character, except on peculiar points. Place a worldly man and a holy man in the same unfavourable circumstances for receiving the disorder, and you will not find the one has any charm to escape the fate of the other.

But we do find that this disease is increased and propagated by human selfishness. We read of the crowds at Bethesda, of whom it was said, there was no man to put them into the water : and so it is now. The poor, the helpless, the neglected, have been the chief sufferers. Out of 243 who in this place have suffered from that and similar causes, 163 were receiving parish relief. And in this there is something that tells us not merely of ignorance, but of selfishness; for when commissioners went through the length and breadth of the country to examine into the statistics of the disease, we were met by the startling fact that medical science, that careful nursing could do nothing while our crowded graveyards, our teeming and airless habitations, our worn-out and unhealthy population, received and propagated the miasma ; and every time that a man in the higher classes perished, it was as if the poor neglected man had spoken from the grave ; or, as if God himself had been heard to speak through him. He seems to say, " I can prove to you *now* my relationship. You can receive evil from me, if nothing else has ever passed between us ;—the same constitution, the same flesh and blood, the same frame were once ours ; and if I can do it in no other way, I can prove, by infecting you, that I am your brother still.

Once more : it has been produced in a degree by moral evil ; vice has been as often the predisposing cause, as any other external circumstance, in certain cases. I say in certain cases, not in all. A man might have been a blasphemer, or a slanderer, but neither of these sins would affect him ; but those sins which are connected with the flesh, sensuality, drunkenness, gradually pervade the human frame, and fit it for the reception of this disease.

II. But we will pass on to consider the history of this man's recovery, and of his gratitude. The first cause for gratitude was his selection. He alone was taken, and others were left. He had cause for gratitude, also, in that he had been taught the connection between moral evil and its penalty. He had been taught the certainty of God's laws, how they execute themselves, and, more blessed than all, he had been taught that there was a Personal Superintendence over all the children of men. The relief had come from the personal interposition of the Son of Man. He went and told the Jews that it was Jesus who had done this. And this explains to us the meaning and the necessity of a public acknowledgment of our gratitude. It is meant to show this nation that it is not by chance, nor by the operation of science, nor by the might of man that we have been rescued, but that our deliverance comes direct from God.

Let us observe the popular account (for John gives us the popular account) of the angel troubling the water. It matters not whether it is scientifically to be proved or not, the secret causes lie hid beyond our investigation; but this you can observe, that it was a religious act, that it was not done by chance, that there were living agents in the healing process. The man of science in the present day would tell you what were the ingredients in the spring—how it told on the cellular tissue, or on the nervous fabric; but whatever he may make of it scientifically, it is true morally and religiously; for what is every remedy but the angel, the messenger of God sent down from the Father of all mercy, the Fountain of all goodness? So when we celebrate a day of National Thanksgiving, it is but the nation's voice, arising in acknowledgment of a Parent's protection—that these things come not by chance, but that there is personal superintendence over this world, and this deliverance is the proof of a Father's love.

Once more: a day of thanksgiving is meant to be a warning and a reminder against future sins. "Sin no more, lest a worse thing come unto thee." And it has ever been so, that the result of panic has been reaction. After excitement comes apathy; after terror has been produced, by danger especially, comes indifference, and therefore comes the warning voice from the Redeemer—"Sin no more, lest a worse thing come unto thee."

But we may perhaps say, " *My* sin did not produce this disease. It was no doing—no fault of mine ; it came from causes beyond my control. The pestilence now has wreaked its vengeance ; I find I had nothing to do with it, and I may dismiss the subject from my mind." My brethren, let us look into this a little more deeply. It was not directly your sin that nailed your Redeemer to the cross, but the sin of the cruel Pharisees, of the relentless multitude ; yet it is said " the Lord hath laid on Him the iniquity of us all." It arises all from this circumstance, brethren—there are two worlds, a world of evil, and a world of good. The Son of Man came as the perfect and entire representation of the kingdom of holiness. He came in collision with the world of evil ; He died for sinners—for the sins of others—of all who partake of the nature of moral evil : and therefore by their sin they nailed the Redeemer to the cross. All those who opposed themselves to Jesus, would have opposed themselves to Moses, Zacharias, and Abel ; they allowed the deeds of their fathers, and were partakers of the blood of all the prophets that had been slain upon the earth.

The men who join in a crowd, aiding and abetting the death of any individual, by the law of every country are held guilty ; and now, though there may have been no distinct act of selfishness by which any man has perished at your hands ; though there have been no distinct want of care for the poor—still I may fearlessly ask you all, Christian brethren, does not your conscience tell you how little the welfare and the comfort of others has been in your thoughts ? As far as we have taken a part in the world's selfishness ; as far as we have lived for self and not for our neighbours ; as far as we have forgotten the poor sufferers lying in the porches of Bethesda—not directly, but indirectly, all that

has fallen upon this land may have been sent as a chastisement to us.

And there is this to be explained—"Sin no more;"
meaning apparently, that if a man did not sin, nothing more
would happen. Are we to understand then, that if a man
has been blameless, he will never suffer from sorrow or
sickness? or that if a man will avoid sin, he will never be
visited by death? To have said that, would have been to
contradict the history of the Redeemer's own life and death.
He died, though He sinned not. How then, brethren, can
we understand it? Why, we can understand it but in this
way, by recalling to our memory what has been already said
of the difference between the punishment and the penalty.
If a man live a humble and holy life in Christ Jesus, there
is no promise that if plague visits his land it shall not come
nigh him. Live in purity, live in unselfishness; there is no
promise that you shall not be cut down in a day; there is
nothing in religion that can shield you from what the world
calls trouble—from penalty; but there is this—that which
would have been chastisement is changed into penalty.

The Redeemer suffered death as a penalty; but by no
means as chastisement; on the contrary, it was the richest
blessing which a Father's love could bestow upon His
well-beloved Son, in whom He was well pleased. So it will
be with every one of us. He who lives to God, rests in his
Redeemer's love, and is trying to get rid of his old nature—
to him every sorrow, every bereavement, every pain, will
come charged with blessings, and death itself will be no
longer the king of terrors, but the messenger of grace, the
very angel of God descending on the troubled waters, and
calling him to his Father's home.

XIX.

CHRISTIAN FRIENDSHIP.

"Then they that feared the Lord spake often one to another : and the Lord hearkened, and heard it, and a book of remembrance was written before him for them that feared the Lord, and that thought upon his name."—Malachi iii. 16.

THE first division of our subject is suggested by the word "*then*." When? They did thus in the times of Malachi. It is only in reference to those times that we can extract the true lesson from the conduct of the holy men whose behaviour he praises. We will consider—

I. The times of Malachi.
II. The patience of the saints in evil times.

I. Not much is known of the Prophet Malachi, or his exact date. We are sure, however, that he was the last prophet of the old dispensation. He lived somewhere between the restoration from captivity and the coming of Christ.

Thus much we know of those times from history :—The Jews were restored. From chap. iii. v. 10, we learn that the Temple had been rebuilt. But Israel's grandeur was gone, although still enjoying outward prosperity. The nation had sunk into a state of political degradation, and had become successively subject to the Persians, Syrians, Romans. It is precisely that political state in which national virtues do not thrive, and national decay is sure. * * * *

Italy—Spain.

They had a glorious past. They had the enlightenment of a present high civilization. But with this there was a want of unity, manhood, and simple virtues. There was just sufficient gallingness in the yoke to produce faction and sullenness ; but not enough curtailment of all physical comforts to rouse the nation as one man to reconquer freedom. It was a state in which there was no visible Divine interference.

Compare this period of Israel's history with all which had preceded it. These 400 years belong to profane history. The writings of that period are not reckoned inspired, so widely do they differ from the Scripture tone. There were no prophets, no flood of light, "no open vision." The Word of God was precious as in that time between the death of Joshua and the calling of Samuel.* Except this solitary voice, prophecy had hushed her harp.

Now, what was given to Israel in that period ?

I reply, Retrospect, Pause, and Prospect.

Retrospect, in the sublime past which God had given her for her experience. " They have Moses and the prophets, let them hear them." On them they were to live—their nation's sacred history ; God's guidance and faithfulness ; the sure truth that obedience was best.

Prospect, in the expectation of better times.

Dim, vague hints of the Old Testament had pointed them to a coming revelation—a day in which God should be

---

* Four hundred and thirty-one years.

nearer to them, in which society should be more pure. An Advent, in short.

And between these two there was a *Pause.*

They were left by God to use the grace and knowledge already given by Him.

Now this is parallel to God's usual modes of dealing. For example, the Pause of 400 years in the land of Egypt, between the bright days when Abraham talked with God, and the deliverance by Moses.

The Pause in Canaan when the Israelitish common-wealth was left, like a building to settle down before being built higher, between the times of Joshua and of Samuel.

The Pause in the Captivity, and now again a Pause.

A Pause after each revelation until the next.

So, in the natural world. Just as in summer there is a gush of nature's forces and a shooting forth; and then the long autumn and winter, in which is no growth, but an opportunity, taught by past experience, for the husbandman to manure his ground, and sow his seed, and to wait for a new outpouring of life upon the world.

And just as in human life, between its marked lessons there is a pause, in which we live upon past experience—looking back and looking on. Experience and hope, that is human life: as in youth, expecting manhood, and then looking for future changes in our condition, character, so in all God's revelation system, there have been periods of "open vision," and periods of pause—waiting; when men are left to experience and hope.

It is in vain that we have studied God's Word if we do not perceive that our own day and circumstances are parallel with those of the Prophet Malachi. We live in the World's fourth great Pause.

Miracles have ceased. Prophecy is silent. The Son of God is ascended. Apostles are no longer here to apply infallible judgment to each new circumstance as it arises, as St. Paul did to the state of the Corinthian Church.

But we are left to the great Gospel principles which have been already given, and which are to be our food till the next flood of God's Spirit, the next Revelation—that which the Scripture calls "the Second Advent."

And the parallel holds in another respect. The Jews had but undefined hints of that which was to be. Yet they knew the general outlines and character of the coming time ; they knew that it would be a searching time, it was to be the "Refiner's" day; they knew that he should turn the hearts of the fathers to the children : and they knew that the messenger age must be preceded by a falling back on simpler life, and a return to first principles, as Malachi had predicted, and as John the Baptist called them to. They knew that it was an age in which the true sacrifice would be offered.

And so now—we know not yet what shall be ; "but we know that when He shall appear we shall be like Him, for we shall see Him as he is." "And every man that hath this hope in Him *purifieth* himself."

We know that it will be the union of the human race— they will be "*one fold.*"

This is the outline and character of the Revelation ; and we may work at least, *towards* it. "Ye are not in darkness, that that day should overtake you as a thief. Ye are all the children of the light, and the children of the day." "Wherefore comfort yourselves together, and edify one another, even as also ye do." To strive after personal purity and attempt at producing unity, that is our work.

We rest on that we have, and hope for that we see not. And only for the glimpse that hope gives us of that, is life worth having.

II. Let us consider the conduct of different classes in these evil times.

1. Some lived recklessly.

Foremost among these were the priests, as has been always found in evil times. The riot of a priest is worse than that of the laity. Mutual corruption. Against the priests Malachi's denunciations are chiefly directed.

He speaks of the profanation of the sacred places (chap. i. 6, 7). Of sacrifice degraded (verses 12, 13). Vice honoured (chap. ii. 17). In that they called good evil and evil good. By these men belief in God was considered ridiculous.

And then it was that one of those glorious promises was made, to be fulfilled in after times. Malachi foresaw that the Gentiles would take up the neglected service (chap. i. 10, 11), and the vision of an universal Kingdom of God became the comfort of the faithful few.

2. Others lived uselessly, because despondingly.

The languor and despair of their hearts is read in the words (chap. iii. 14, 15); and indeed it is not surprising: to what point could good men look with satisfaction? The nation was enslaved, and worse—they had become slaves in spirit. Their ancient purity was gone. The very priests had become atheists. Where was the promise of His coming? Such too, is the question of these latter times. And our reply is from past experience.

That dark day passed, and a glorious Revelation dawned

on the world. From what has been, we justly infer what will be. Promises fulfilled are a ground of hope for those yet unfulfilled. Where is the promise *now* of holier times? Yes, but remember the question seemed to be just as unanswerable then; it was just as unanswerable in the days of the Judges, and in the captivity in Egypt and in Babylon.

This "Scripture was written for our admonition, on whom the ends of the world are come." Then the consolation of St. Peter becomes intelligible, "We have a more sure word of prophecy; whereunto ye do well that ye take heed, as unto a light that shineth in a dark place, until the day dawn, and the day-star arise in your hearts."

3. But in these evil times there were a few who compared with one another their hopes, and sought strength in Christian communion and fellowship. Of them the text speaks.

This communion of saints is twofold: it includes church fellowship and personal friendships.

It is plain that from church fellowship they could gain little in those days. Unity there was not, but only disunion. Over that state Malachi lamented in that touching appeal— "Have we not all one father? hath not one God created us? why do we deal treacherously every man against his brother, by profaning the covenant of our fathers?"—Israel had forgotten that she was a family.

And it is true that in our day church fellowship is almost only a name. The Christianity of the nation does not bind us as individuals. Well,—does the Church? Are there many traces of a common feeling? When church privileges are insisted on to produce unity, do they not produce division? Are not these words of the Prophet true of us? Where are the traces of Christian brotherhood?

Here—in this town? here—in this congregation? at the Holy Supper which we join in to-day? Shall we meet to get *private* good, or to feel we are partakers of the same Body and the same Blood? Therefore to insist on church union as the remedy would be to miss the special meaning of this verse. The malady of our disunion has gone too deep to be cured by you or me.

We will consider it therefore, in reference to Christian friendship. We find that within the outward Jewish Church there was an inner circle, knit together by closer bonds than circumcision or the passover—by an union of religious sympathies. "Then they that feared the Lord spoke often one to another:" they "thought upon His name."

Let us consider the blessing of Christian friendship. In such times it discharges a double office.

1. For the interchange of Christian hope and Christian feeling. It is dreary to serve God alone; it is desolate to have no one in our own circle or family from whom we can receive sympathy in our hopes. Hopes *die.*

2. It is a mighty instrument in guarding against temptation. It is a safeguard, in the way of example, and also as a standard of opinion. We should become tainted by the world if it were not for Christian friends.

In conclusion, cultivate *familiar* intimacy only with those who love good and God.

Doubtless there are circumstances which determine intimacies, such as rank, station, similarity of tastes. But one thing must be paramount to and modify them all—Communion in God. Not in a sectarian spirit. We are not to form ourselves into a party with those who think as we do, and use the formulas that we do. But the spirit of the text requires us to feel strongly that there is a mighty gulf between those who love and those who do not love God. To the one class we owe civility, courtesy, kindness, even tenderness. It is only those who love the Lord who should find in our hearts a home.

XX.

RECONCILIATION BY CHRIST.

"And you, that were sometime alienated and enemies in your mind
by wicked works, yet now hath he reconciled."—Colossians, i. 21.

THERE are two, and only two kinds of goodness possible : the one is the goodness of those who have
never erred : the other is the goodness of those who having
erred, have been recovered from their error. The first is
the goodness of those who have never offended ; the second
is the goodness of those who, having offended, have been
reconciled. In the infinite possibilities of God's universe,
it may be that there are some who have attained the first
of these kinds of righteousness. It may be that amongst
the heavenly hierarchies there are those who have kept
their first estate, whose performances have been commen-
surate with their aspirations, who have never known the
wretchedness, and misery, and degradation of a Fall. But
whether it be so or not is a matter of no practical importance
to us. It may be a question speculatively interesting, but it
is practically useless, for it is plain that such righteousness
never can be ours. The only religion possible to man is the
religion of penitence. The righteousness of man cannot be
the integrity of the virgin citadel which has never admitted
the enemy ; it can never be more than the integrity of the
city which has been surprised and roused, and which, having

expelled the invader with blood in the streets, has suffered great inward loss.

Appointed to these two kinds of righteousness there are two kinds of happiness. To the first is attached the blessing of entire ignorance of the stain, pollution, and misery of guilt—a blessed happiness; but it may be that it is not the greatest. To the happiness resulting from the other is added a greater strength of emotion; it may not have the calmness and peace of the first, but, perhaps, in point of intensity and fulness it is superior. It may be that the highest happiness can only be purchased through suffering: and the language of the Bible almost seems to authorize us to say, that the happiness of penitence is deeper, and more blessed than the happiness of the righteousness that has never fallen, could be.

There are two kinds of friendship, that which has never had a shock, and that which after having been doubted is at last made sure. The happiness of this last is perhaps the greater. Such seems to be the truth implied in the parable of the Prodigal Son: in the robe, and the ring, and the fatted calf, and the music, and dancing, and the rapture of a father's embrace: and once more, in those words of our Redeemer, "There is more joy among the angels of heaven over one sinner that repenteth, than over ninety and nine just persons that need no repentance." All these seem to tell of the immeasurable blessedness of penitence. And this then, is our subject, the subject of Reconciliation.

But the text divides itself into two branches: in the first place, Estrangement; in the second place, Reconciliation.

Estrangement is thus described: "You that were sometime" (that is, once,) "alienated and enemies in your mind by wicked works:" in which there are three things. The first is the cause of the estrangement—wicked works; the second is the twofold order; and thirdly, the degree of that estrangement; first of all mere alienation, afterwards hostility, enmity.

And first of all, we consider the cause of the estrangement — " wicked works." Wicked works are voluntary deeds; they are not involuntary, but voluntary wrong. There is a vague way in which we sometimes speak of sin, in which it is possible for us to lose the idea of its guilt, and also to lose the idea of personal responsibility. We speak of sin sometimes as if it were a foreign disease introduced into the constitution; an imputed guilt arising from an action not our own, but of our ancestors. It is never so that the Bible speaks of sin. It speaks of it as wicked works, voluntary deeds, voluntary acts; that you, a responsible individual, have done acts which are wrong, of the mind, the hand, the tongue. The infant is by no means God's enemy; he may become God's enemy, but it can only be by voluntary action after conscience has been aroused. This our Master's words teach, when He tells us, "Suffer little children to come unto me, for of such is the kingdom of Heaven." And such again, is the mystery of Christian baptism. It tells us that the infant is not the child of the Devil, but the child of God, the member of Christ, the heir of immortality. Sin then, is a voluntary action. If you close your ear to the voice of God, if there be transgression of an inward law, if you sacrifice the heart and intellect to the senses, if you let ease or comfort be more dear to you than inward purity, if you leave duties undone, and give the body rule over the spirit,—then you sin; for these are voluntary acts, these are wicked works.

The result of this is twofold. The first step is simply

the step of alienation. There is a difference between alienation and hostility: in alienation we feel that God is our enemy; in hostility we look on ourselves as enemies to God. Alienation — "you that were sometime alienated" —was a more forcible expression in the Apostle's time than it can be to us now. In our modern political society, the alien is almost on a level with the citizen. The difference now is almost nothing; in those days it was very great. The alien from the Jewish commonwealth had no right to worship with the Jews, and he had no power to share in the religious advantages of the Jews. The strength of the feeling that was existing against the alien you will perceive in that proverbial expression quoted by the Redeemer, "It is not meet to take the children's bread, and cast it to the *dogs*." In the Roman commonwealth, the word had a meaning almost stronger than this. To be an alien from the Roman commonwealth was to be separated from the authority and protection of the Roman law, and to be subjected to a more severe and degrading kind of penalty than that to which the Roman citizen was subject. The lash that might scourge the back of the alien offender might not fall on the back of a Roman citizen; and this it was that caused the magistrates of Philippi to tremble before their prisoners when the Apostle Paul said, "They have beaten us openly, uncondemned, being Romans." The lash was the alien's portion.

On reference to the second chapter of the Ephesians we find a conception given of alienation in the twelfth verse, where the Apostle, speaking of the Ephesian converts, says, "That at that time ye were without Christ, being aliens from the commonwealth of Israel, and strangers from the covenants of promise, having no hope, and without

God in the world." This brethren, is alienation, exclusion,
—to have no place in this world, to be without lot or
portion in the universe, to feel God as your enemy, to be
estranged from Him, and banished from his presence:
for the law of God acts as its own executioner within our
bosoms, and there is no defying its sentence; from it there
can be no appeal.

My Christian brethren,—hell is not merely a thing
hereafter, hell is a thing here; hell is not a thing banished
to the far distance, it is ubiquitous as conscience. Wherever
there is a worm of undying remorse, the sense of having
done wrong, and a feeling of degradation, there is hell
begun. And now respecting this. These words, "banish-
ment from God," "alienation," though merely popular
phrases, are expressions of a deep truth,—it is true they are
but popular expressions, for God is not wrath. You are not
absolutely banished from God's Presence. The Immutable
changes not. He does not become angry or passionate
whenever one of the eight hundred million inhabitants of
this world commits a sin. And yet you will observe there
is no other way in which we can express the truth but in
these popular words. Take the illustration furnished to us
last Sunday: it may be that it is the cloud and the mist that
obscure the sun from us: the sun is not changed in consequence: it is a change in our atmosphere. But if the
philosopher says to you, the sun in its splendour remains the
same in the infinite space above, it is only an optical delusion which makes it appear lurid: to what purpose is that
difference to you? to you it is lurid, to you it is dark. If
you feel a darkness in your eye, coldness in your flesh, to
what purpose, so far as feeling is concerned, is it that philosophy tells you the sun remains unchanged? And if it be

that God in the heaven above remains Love still, and that Love warms not your heart:—and that God is Light, in whom is no darkness at all, yet He shines not in your heart : my Christian brethren, let metaphysics and philosophy say what they will, these popular expressions are the true ones after all ; to you God *is* angry, from God you *are* banished, God's countenance *is* alienated from you.

The second step of this estrangement reaches a higher degree still ; it is not merely that God is angry, but that we have become enemies to God. The illustration of the process of this we have seen in our common every-day life.

It is sometimes the case that strength of attachment settles down to mere indifference, even changes to hatred. The first quarrel between friends is a thing greatly to be dreaded ; it is often followed by the cessation of all correspondence, the interruption of that intercourse which has gone on so long. Well, a secret sense of self-blame and of wrong will intrude, and the only way in which we can escape it is by throwing the blame elsewhere. You see by degrees a cankered spot begins, and you look at it and touch it; and irritate it until the mortification becomes entire, and that which was at first alienation settles down into absolute animosity.

And such is it in the history of the alienation of the soul from God. The first step is to become indifferent, communion is interrupted, irregularity is begun, sin by degrees widens the breach, and then between the soul and God there is a great gulf fixed. Observe by what different ways different classes of character arrive at that. Weak characters have one way, and strong and bold characters have another. The weak mind throws the blame on circumstances ; unable itself to subdue its own passions, it imagines there is some law in the universe that so ordains it; insists that the blame is on circumstances and destiny, and says, " If I am thus it is not my fault; if I am not to gratify my passions, why were they given to me ? ' Why doth He find fault, for who hath resisted His will ? ' " And so these weak ones become by degrees fatalists; and it would seem by their language, as if they were rather the patient victims of a cruel fate, the blame belonging not to them, but to God.

The way in which stronger and more vicious characters arrive at this enmity is different. Humiliation degrades, and degradation produces anger; you have but to go into the narrow and crowded streets of the most degraded portions of our metropolis, and there you will see the outcast turning with a look of defiance and hatred on respectability, merely because it is respectable : and this, brethren, many of us have seen, some of us have felt, in our relation towards God. That terrible demon voice stirs up within us, " curse God and die." Haunted by furies we stand, as it were, at bay, and dare to bid defiance to our Maker. Nothing so proves the original majesty of man as this terrible fact, that the creature can bid defiance to the Creator, and that man has it in him to become the enemy of God.

We pass on in the next place, to consider the doctrine of reconciliation. We need scarcely define what is meant by reconciliation. To reconcile is to produce harmony where there was discord, unity where before there was variance. We accept the Apostle's definition of reconciliation. He says that " Christ hath made of twain one new man so making peace." Now the reconciliation produced by Christ's Atonement is fourfold :—

In the first place, Christ hath reconciled man to God.

In the second place, He hath reconciled man to man.

In the third place, He hath reconciled man to himself.

And in the fourth place, He hath reconciled man to duty.

In the first place, the Atonement of the Redeemer has reconciled man to God, and that by a twofold step: by exhibiting the character of God; and by that exhibition changing the character of man.

Brethren, the Sacrifice of Christ was the Voice of God proclaiming Love. In this passage the Apostle tells us that "Christ has reconciled us to God in the body of His flesh through death.". We will not attempt to define what that Sacrifice was—we will not philosophize upon it; for the more we philosophize the less we shall understand it. We are well content to take it as the highest exhibition and the noblest specimen of the law of our Humanity—that great law—that there is no true blessedness without suffering, that every blessing we have comes through vicarious suffering. All that we have and enjoy comes from others' suffering. The life we enjoy is the result of maternal agony; our very bread is only obtained after the toil and anguish of suffering myriads; there is not one atom of the knowledge we possess now which has not, in some century of the world or other, been wrung out of nature's secrets by the sweat of the brow or the sweat of the heart. The very peace which we are enjoying at this present day, how has that been purchased? By the blood of heroes whose bodies are now lying mouldering in the trenches of a thousand battle-fields.

This is the law of our Humanity, and to this our Redeemer became subject—the law of life, self-surrender, without which Reconciliation was impossible. And when the mind has comprehended this, that the Sacrifice of Christ was the manifestation of the Love of God, then comes the happy and blessed feeling of reconciliation. When a man has surrendered himself in humbleness and penitence to God, and the proud spirit of self-excuse has passed away : when the soul has opened itself to all His influences and known their power : when the saddest and bitterest part of suffering is felt no longer as the wrath of the Judge but as the discipline of a Father : when the Love of God has melted the soul, and fused it into charity : then the soul is reconciled to God, and God is reconciled to the soul : for it is a marvellous thing how the change of feelings within us changes God to us, or rather those circumstances and things by which God becomes visible to us. His universe, once so dark, becomes bright : life, once a mere dull, dreary thing "dry as summer dust," springs up once more into fresh luxuriance, and we feel it to be a divine and blessed thing.

We hear the voice of God as it was once heard in the garden of Eden whispering among the leaves : every sound, once so discordant, becomes music, the anthem of creation raised up as it were, with everlasting hallelujahs to the eternal throne. Then it is that a man first knows his immortality, and the soul knows what is meant by infinitude and eternity ; not that infinitude which can be measured by miles, nor that eternity which can be computed by hours ; but the eternity of emotion. Let a man breathe but one hour of the charity of God, and feel but one true emotion of the reconciled heart, and then he knows for ever what is meant by immortality, and he can understand the reality of his own.

The second consequence of the Redeemer's Atonement is the reconciliation of man to man. Of all the Apostles none have perceived so strongly as St. Paul that the death of Christ is the reconciliation of man to man. Take that one single expression in the Epistle to the Ephesians—" For he

is our peace who hath made both one." Observe, I pray
you, the imagery with which he continues, "and hath broken
down the middle wall of partition." The veil or partition
wall between the court of the Jew and Gentile was broken
asunder at the Crucifixion. St. Paul saw in the death of
Christ a spiritual resemblance to that physical phenomenon.
Christ was not only born of woman, but under the law ; and
He could not become as such, the Saviour of the world ; but
when death had taken place, and He was no longer the Jew,
but the Man, no longer bound by limitations of time, and
place, and country, then He became, as it were, a Spirit in
the universe, no longer narrowed to place and to century,
but universal, the Saviour of the Gentile as well as the
Messiah of the Jew.

Therefore it was that St. Paul called the flesh of Christ a
veil, and said the death of Christ was the taking down of
"the middle wall of partition" between Jew and Gentile :
and therefore it is by the Sacrifice of Christ, and by that
alone, man can be thus reconciled to man : and on no other
possible basis can there be a brotherhood of the human race.
You may try other ways ; the men of the world have tried,
and doubtless will go on trying, until they find that there is
no other way than this. They may try by the principle of
selfishness, the principle of moral rule, or the principle of
civil authority. Let the political economist come forward
with his principle of selfishness, and tell us that this is that
by which alone the wealth of nations can accrue. He may
get a nation in which there are a wealthy few and miserable
many, but not a brotherhood of Christians. Suppose you
say men should love one another. Will that *make* them love
one another ? You may come forward with the crushing rule
of political authority. Papal Rome has tried it and failed.

She bound up the masses of the human race as a gigantic iceberg; but she could give only a temporary principle of unity and cohesion.

Therefore we turn back once more to the Cross of Christ: through this alone we learn there is one God, one Father, one Baptism, one Elder Brother in whom all can be brothers. But there is a something besides, a deeper principle still. We are told in this passage we can be reconciled to man by the body of Christ through death. And now brethren, let us understand this. By the Cross of Christ the Apostle meant reconciled by the Spirit of the Cross. And what was that spirit? It was the spirit of giving, and of suffering, and of loving, because he had suffered. Say what we will, love is not gratitude for favours which have been received. Why is the child more beloved by the parent than the parent by the child? Why did the Redeemer love His disciples more than they loved their Master? Benefits will not bind the affection; you must not expect that they will. You must suffer if you would love; you must remember that " it is more blessed to give than to receive." The Apostle Paul felt this when he said reconciliation was produced through the body of the flesh of Christ by death.

Once more man becomes by the Redeemer's Atonement reconciled to himself.

That self-reconciliation is necessary, because we do not readily forgive ourselves. God may have forgiven us, but we cannot forgive ourselves. You may obtain a remission of the past, but you cannot forgive yourself and get back the feeling of self-respect, unity within, rest, by sitting still and believing that God has forgiven you, and that you have nothing left to look for? My brethren, there is a spirit of self-torture within us which is but a perversion of nobleness, a mistake of the true principle. When you have done wrong, you want to suffer. Love demands a sacrifice, and only by sacrifice can it reconcile itself to self. Then it is that the Sacrifice of Christ replies to this, answers it, satisfies it, and makes it plain. The Sacrifice of Christ was suffering in Love, it was surrender to the Will of God. The Apostle Paul felt this; when that Spirit was with him he was reconciled to himself. He says, "I am crucified with Christ, nevertheless I live, yet not I, but Christ liveth in me." If ever you devoted yourself to another's happiness or amelioration, so far and so long as you were doing that, you forgave yourself; you felt the spirit of inward self-reconciliation, and what we want is only to make that perpetual, to make that binding which we do by fits and starts, to feel ourselves a living sacrifice, to know that we are, in our highest and best state, victims, offered up in love on the great altar of the kingdom of Christ, offered by Him to God as the first-fruits of His Sacrifice; then we are reconciled to ourselves "by the body of His flesh through death."

And lastly, through the Atonement of the Redeemer, man becomes reconciled to duty. There is no discord more terrible than that between man and duty. There are few of us who fancy we have found our own places in this world; our lives, our partnerships, our professions, and our trades, are not those which we should have chosen for ourselves. There is an ambition within us which sometimes makes us fancy we are fit for higher things, that we are adapted for other and better things than those to which we are called. But we turn again to the Cross of Christ, and the mystery of Life becomes plain. The Life and Death of Christ are the reconciliation of man to the duties which he has to do. You cannot study His marvellous Life without perceiving that the whole of Its details are uncongenial, mean, trivial, wretched circumstances — from which the spirit of a man revolts.

To bear the sneer of the Sadducee and the curse of the Pharisee ; to be rejected by His family and friends ; to be harassed by the petty disputes and miserable quarrels of His followers about their own *personal* precedence ; to be treated by the government of His country as a charlatan and a demagogue ; to be surrounded by a crowd of men, coming and going without sympathy ; to retire and find His leisure intruded on and Himself pursued for ignoble ends— these were the circumstances of the Redeemer's existence here. Yet in these it was that the noblest Life the world has ever seen was lived. He retired into the wilderness, and one by one put down all those visions that would have seduced Him from the higher path of duty ; the vision of comfort which tempted Him to change the stones of this world into bread ; the vision of ambition which tempted Him to make the kingdoms of this world His own by seeking good through evil ; the vision which tempted Him to distrust God, and become important by pursuing some strange, unauthorized way of His own, instead of following the way of submission to the will of God.

He ascended into the Transfiguration Mount, and there His spirit converses with those of an elder dispensation, who had fought the fight before Him, Moses and Elias, and they spoke to Him of the triumph which He had to accomplish in death at Jerusalem. And He went down again with calm, serene, and transfigured faith, and there, at the very foot of the Mount, He found His disciples engaged in some miserable squabble with the scribes and the Pharisees about casting out a devil. And this Life of His is the only interpretation of this life of ours—the reconciliation of our hearts with what we have to do. It is not by change of circumstances, but by fitting our spirits to the circumstances in which God has placed us, that we can be reconciled to Life and Duty. If the duties before us be not noble, let us ennoble them by doing them in a noble spirit; we become reconciled to Life if we live in the spirit of Him who reconciled the Life of God with the lowly duties of servants.

And now one word in conclusion. The central doctrine of Christianity is the Atonement. Take that away, and you obliterate Christianity. If Christianity were merely the imitation of Christ, why then the imitation of any other good man, the Apostle Paul or John, might become a kind of Christianity. If Christianity were merely martyrdom for truth, then, with the exception of a certain amount of degree, I see no difference between the death of Socrates and the death of Jesus Christ. But Christianity is more than this. It is the At-one-ment of the Soul. It is a reconciliation which the Life and Death of Christ have wrought out for this world,—the reconciliation of man to God, the reconciliation of man to man, the reconciliation of man to self, and the reconciliation of man to duty.

XXI.

THE PRE-EMINENCE OF CHARITY.

"And above all things have fervent charity among yourselves: for charity shall cover the multitude of sins."—1 Peter iv. 8.

THE grace of charity is exalted as the highest attainment of the Christian life by St. Paul, St. Peter, and St. John. These three men were very different from each other. Each was the type of a distinct order of character. And it is a proof that the Gospel is from God, and that the sacred writings are inspired from a single Divine source, that personal peculiarities are not placed foremost in them, but the foremost place is given by each to a grace which certainly was not the characteristic quality of all the three.

It is said in these modern days that Christianity was a system elaborated by human intellect. Men, they say, philosophized, and thought it out. Christianity, it is maintained, like ethics, is the product of human reason. Now had this been true, we should have found the great teachers of Christianity each exalting that particular quality which was most remarkable in his own temperament. Just as the English honour truthfulness, and the French brilliancy, and the Hindoos subtlety, and the Italians finesse—and naturally, because these are predominant in themselves—we should have found the Apostles insisting most strongly on those graces which grew most naturally in the soil of their own hearts.

Indeed in a degree it is so. St. John's character was tender, emotional, and contemplative. Accordingly, his writings exhibit the *feeling* of religion, and the predominance of the inner life over the outer.

St. Paul was a man of keen intellect, and of soaring and aspiring thought which would endure no shackles on its freedom. And his writings are full of the two subjects we might have expected from this temperament. He speaks a great deal of intellectual gifts; very much of Christian liberty.

St. Peter was remarkable for personal courage. A soldier by nature: frank, free, generous, irascible. In his writings accordingly, we find a great deal said about martyrdom.

But each of these men, so different from each other, exalts Love above his own peculiar quality. It is very remarkable. Not merely does each call charity the highest, but each names it in immediate connection with his own characteristic virtue, and declares it to be more divine.

St. John, of course, calls love the heavenliest. That we expect from St. John's character. "God is Love. He that dwelleth in love dwelleth in God." "No man hath seen God at any time: if we love one another God dwelleth in us."

But St. Paul expressly names it in contrast with the two feelings for which he was personally most remarkable, and, noble as they are, prefers it before them. First, in contrast with intellectual gifts. Thus, "Covet earnestly the best gifts: and yet show I unto you a more excellent way: though I speak with the tongue of men and of angels, and have not charity, it is nothing." Gifts are nothing in comparison of charity. Again, "We know that we all have knowledge: knowledge puffeth up, but charity buildeth up." Knowledge is nothing in comparison.

Next, in comparison of that liberty which was so dear to him. Christian liberty permitted the converts the use of meats, and the disregard of days from which the strict law of Judaism had debarred them. Well, but there were cases in which the exercise of that liberty might hurt the scruples of some weak Christian brother, or lead him to imitate the example against his conscience. "If thy brother be grieved with thy meat, now walkest thou not *charitably*." Liberty said, You have a right to indulge ; but Charity said, Refrain.

So that, according to St. Paul, there is one thing, and one only, to which Christian liberty must be sacrificed. That one is Christian love.

Now let us see how St. Peter does honour to the same grace, at the expense of that which we should have expected him to reckon the essential grace of manhood. Just before the text, we find the command, "Be sober, and watch unto prayer." This is a sentence out of St. Peter's very heart. For in it we have prayer represented as the night-watch of a warrior, armed, who must not sleep his watch away. "Be sober, and watch"—the language of the soldier and the sentinel ; words which remind you of him who drew his sword to defend his Master, and who in penitence remembered his own disastrous sleep when he was surprised as a sentry at his post. But immediately after this,—"And, *above all things,* have fervent charity amongst yourselves." Sobriety, self-rule, manhood, courage, yes ; but the life of them all, says St. Peter, the very crown of manhood, without which sobriety is but prudent selfishness, and courage is but brute instinct—is Love.

Now I take that unanimity as a proof that the Gospel comes from one Living Source. How came St. Peter and

St. John, so different from each other, and St. Paul, who had had almost no communion with either of them, to agree, and agree so enthusiastically, in this doctrine—Love is over all and above all; above intellect, freedom, courage—unless there had streamed into the mind and heart of each one of them Light from One Source, even from Him the deepest principle of Whose Being, and the law of Whose life and death, were love?

We are to try, to-day, to understand this sentence of St. Peter. It tells us two things,—

I. What charity is.

II. What charity does.

I. It is not easy to find one word in any language which rightly and adequately represents what Christ and His Apostles meant by charity. All words are saturated with some imperfect meaning. Charity has become identified with almsgiving. Love is appropriated to one particular form of human affection, and that one with which self and passion mix inevitably. Philanthropy is a word too cold and negative.

Let us define Christian charity in two sentences :— 1. The desire to give. 2. The desire to bless.

1. The desire to give. Let each man go deep into his own heart. Let him ask what that mysterious longing means which we call love, whether to man or God, when he has stripped from it all that is outside and accidental; when he has taken from it all that is mixed with it and perverts it. Not in his worst moments—but in his best, what did that yearning mean? I say it meant the desire to give. Not to get something, but to give something. And the

mightier, the more irrepressible this yearning was, the more truly was his love love. To give—whether alms in the shape of money, bread, or a cup of cold water, or else self. But be sure, sacrifice, in some shape or other, is the impulse of love, and its restlessness is only satisfied and only gets relief in giving. For this, in truth, is God's own love, the will and the power to give. "It is more blessed to give than to receive." Therefore God is the only blessed One, because He alone gives and never receives. The universe, teeming with life, is but God's love expressing itself. He creates life by the giving of Himself. He has redeemed the world by the giving of His Son. "God so loved the world that He gave His only begotten Son." The death of Christ was sacrifice. The Life of God is one perpetual sacrifice, or giving of Himself and shedding forth of His Spirit. Else it would not be love.

And so, when the poor sinful woman gave her costly ointment with a large profuseness, Christ saw in it an evidence of love. "She loved much." For love gives.

2. The desire to bless.

All love is this in a degree. Even weak and spurious love desires happiness of some kind for the creature that it loves. Almsgiving is often nothing more than indolence. We give to the beggar in the street to save ourselves the trouble of finding out fitter objects. Still, indolent as it is, it is an indolent desire to prevent pain.

What we call philanthropy is often calm and cool—too calm and cool to waste upon it the name of charity. But it is a calm and cool desire that human happiness were possible. It is in its weak way a desire to bless. Now, the love whereof the Bible speaks, and of which we have but one perfect personification—viz., in the Life of Christ, is the desire for the best and true blessedness of the being loved. It wishes the well-being of the whole man—body, soul, and spirit; but chiefly spirit.

Therefore, He fed the poor with bread. Therefore, He took His disciples into the wilderness to rest when they were weary. Therefore "He gave Himself for us, that we, being dead unto sin, might live unto righteousness." For the Kingdom of God is not bread only and repose, which constitute physical happiness, but goodness, too; for that is blessedness.

And the highest love is, therefore, the desire to make men good and godlike; it may wish, as a subordinate attainment, to turn this earth into a paradise of comfort by mechanical inventions; but far above that, to transform it into a Kingdom of God, the domain of love, where men cease to quarrel and to envy, and to slander and to retaliate. "This, also, we wish," said St. Paul, "even your perfection."

Concerning this charity we remark two points: 1. It is characterized as fervent. 2. It is capable of being cultivated.

1. "Fervent." Literally intense, unremitting, unwearied. Now, there is a feeble sentiment which wishes well to all so long as it is not tempted to wish them ill, which does well to those who do well to them. But this being merely sentiment, will not last. Ruffle it, and it becomes vindictive. In contrast with that St. Peter calls Christ's spirit, which loves those who hate it, "fervent" charity, which does not tire, and cannot be worn out; which loves its enemies, and does good to them that hate it. For Christian love is not the dream of a philosopher, sitting in his study, and benevolently wishing the world were better than it is, congratulating himself, perhaps, all the time on the superiority shown by

himself over other less amiable natures. Injure one of these beaming sons of good humour, and he bears malice : deep, unrelenting, refusing to forgive. But give us the man who, instead of retiring to some small, select society, or rather association, where his own opinions shall be reflected, can mix with men where his sympathies are unmet, and his tastes are jarred, and his views traversed, at every turn, and still can be just, and gentle, and forbearing.

Give us the man who can be insulted and not retaliate ; meet rudeness and still be courteous ; the man who, like the Apostle Paul, buffeted and disliked, can yet be generous, and make allowances, and say, "I will very gladly spend and be spent for you, though the more abundantly I love you, the less I be loved." That is "fervent charity."

2. Again, it is capable of being cultivated.

We assume that, simply because it is enjoined. When an Apostle says, " *Have* fervent charity among yourselves," it is plain that it would be a cruel mockery to command men to attain it if they could do nothing towards the attainment. It would be the same insult as saying to the deformed, "be beautiful." For it is wanton cruelty to command where obedience is impossible.

How shall we cultivate this charity ?

Now I observe first, love cannot be produced by a direct action of the soul upon itself. You cannot love by a resolve to love. That is as impossible as it is to move a boat by pressing it from within. The force with which you press on is exactly equal to that with which you press back. The reaction is exactly equal to the action. You force back-wards exactly as much as you force on. There are religious persons who, when they feel their affections cooled, strive to warm them by self-reproach, or by unnatural effort, or by the excitement of what they call revivals—trying to work themselves into a state of warm affection. There are others who hope to make feeble love strong by using strong words. Now, for all this they pay a price. Effort of heart is followed by collapse. Excitement is followed by exhaustion. They will find that they have cooled exactly in that proportion in which they warmed, and at least as fast.

It is as impossible for a man to work himself into a state of genuine fervent love as it is for a man to inspire himself. Inspiration is a breath and a life coming from without. Love is a feeling roused not from ourselves, but from something outside ourselves. There are, however, two methods by which we may cultivate this charity.

1. By doing acts which love demands. It is God's merciful law that feelings are increased by acts done on principle. If a man has not the feeling in its warmth, let him not wait till the feeling comes. Let him act with such feeling as he has; with a cold heart if he has not got a warm one ; it will grow warmer while he acts. You may love a man merely because you have done him benefits, and so become interested in him, till interest passes into anxiety, and anxiety into affection. You may acquire courtesy of feeling at last, by cultivating courteous manner. The dignified politeness of the last century forced man into a kind of unselfishness in small things, which the abrupter manners of to-day will never teach. And say what men will of rude sincerity, those old men of urbane manners were kinder at heart with real good will, than we are with that rude bluffness which counts it a loss of independence to be courteous to any one. Gentleness of manner had some influence on gentleness of heart.

So in the same way, it is in things spiritual. If our

hearts are cold, and we find it hard to love God and be affectionate to man, we must begin with duty. Duty is not Christian liberty, but it is the first step towards liberty. We are free only when we love what we are to do, and those to whom we do it. Let a man begin in earnest with—I ought —he will end, by God's grace, if he persevere, with the free blessedness of—I will. Let him force himself to abound in small offices of kindliness, attention, affectionateness, and all those for God's sake. By-and-by he will feel them become the habit of his soul. By-and-by, walking in the conscientiousness of refusing to retaliate when he feels tempted, he will cease to wish it : doing good and heaping kindness on those who injure him, he will learn to love them. For he has spent a treasure there : "And where the treasure is there will the heart be also."

2. The second way of cultivating Christian love is by contemplating the love of God. You cannot move the boat from within ; but you may obtain a purchase from without. You cannot create love in the soul by force from within itself ; but you may move it from a point outside itself. God's Love is the point from which to move the soul. Love begets love. Love believed in, produces a return of love : we cannot love because we must. "Must" kills love ; but the law of our nature is that we love in reply to love. No one ever yet hated one whom he believed to love him truly. We may be provoked by the pertinacity of an affection which asks what we cannot give ; but we cannot hate the true love which does not ask but gives. Now this is the central truth of Christ's Gospel : "We love Him because He first loved us." "Beloved, if God so loved us, we ought also to love one another." "God is love."

It is the one, almost only struggle of religious life, to

believe this. In spite of all the seeming cruelties of this life; in spite of the clouded mystery in which God has shrouded Himself; in spite of pain, and the stern aspect of human life, and the gathering of thicker darkness and more solemn silence round the soul as life goes on, simply to believe that God is Love, and to hold fast to that, as a man holds on to a rock with a desperate grip when the salt surf and the driving waves sweep over him and take the breath away—I say that is the one fight of Christian life, compared with which all else is easy : when we believe that, human affections are easy. It is easy to be generous, and tolerant, and bene-volent, when we are sure of the Heart of God, and when the little love of this life, and its coldnesses, and its unreturned affections are more than made up to us by the certainty that our Father's Love is ours. But when we lose sight of that, though but for a moment, the heart sours, and men seem no longer worth the loving : and wrongs are magnified, and injuries cannot be forgiven, and life itself drags on, a mere death in life. A man may doubt anything and everything, and still be blessed, provided only he holds fast to that con-viction. Let all drift from him like seaweed on life's ocean. So long as he reposes on the assurance of the eternal faith-fulness of the Eternal Charity, his spirit at least cannot drift. There are moments, I humbly think, when we understand those triumphant words of St. Paul, "Let God be true, and every man a liar."

II. What charity does.

It covereth a multitude of sins.

Now the only question is, *whose* sins does charity cover? Is it that the sins of the charitable man are covered by his charity in God's sight? Or is it the sins of others over which charity throws a mantle so as not to see them?

Some wise and good men have said the first. Love obliterates sin in the sight of God; and assuredly it *might* be this that St. Peter meant. No doubt whole years of folly we outlive " in His unerring sight, who measures life by love." Recollect our Master's own words,—" Her sins, which are many, are forgiven her : *for* she loved much."

Nevertheless, that does not seem to be the meaning of this passage. A large number of deep thinkers have been convinced that St. Peter is here describing Christianity, and the description which he gives of it as most characteristic is, that it hides out of sight, and refuses to contemplate, a multitude of sins which malevolence would delight to see. It throws a veil over them and covers them. At all events, this is true of Christian charity : and we shall consider the passage in that sense to-day.

There are three ways, at least, in which Love covers sin.

1. In refusing to see small faults.

Every man has his faults, his failings, peculiarities, eccentricities. Every one of us finds himself crossed by such failings of others, from hour to hour. And if he were to resent them all, or even notice all, life would be intolerable. If for every outburst of hasty temper, and for every rudeness that wounds us in our daily path, we were to demand an apology, require an explanation, or resent it by retaliation, daily intercourse would be impossible. The very science of social life consists in that gliding tact which avoids contact with the sharp angularities of character, which does not argue about such things, does not seek to adjust or cure them all, but covers them, as if it did not see.

Exceedingly wise was that conduct of the Roman proconsul at Corinth which we read of in the Acts. The Jews, with Sosthenes at their head, had brought a charge of heresy against the Christians, and tried it at the Roman law. Gallio perceived that it was a vexatious one, and dismissed it; drove them from the judgment seat. Whereupon the Greeks, indignant at the paltry virulence of the accusation, took Sosthenes, in his way from the judgment seat, and beat him even in Gallio's presence. It is written "Gallio cared for none of these things." He took no notice. He would not see. It was doubtless illegal and tumultuous, a kind of contempt of court—a great offence in Roman law. But Gallio preferred permitting a wholesome outburst of healthy indignation, to carrying out the law in its letter. For he knew that in that popular riot human nature was throwing off an incubus. It was a kind of irregular justice, excusable because of its provocation. And so Gallio would not see. He *covered* the transgression in a wise and wilful blindness.

That which the Roman magistrate did from wise policy, the Christian spirit does in a diviner way. It throws over such things a cloak of love. It knows when it is wise not to see. That microscopic distinctness in which all faults appear to captious men, who are for ever blaming, dissecting, complaining, disappears in the large, calm gaze of Love. And oh ! it is this spirit which our Christian society lacks, and which we shall never get till we begin each one with his own heart. What we want is, in one word, that graceful tact and Christian art which can bear and forbear.

That was a rude, "unpardonable" insult offered by Peter to his Master when he denied Him. In His hour of trial, he refused to seem even to know Him. We should have said, I will never forget that. The Divine Charity covered all. Ask ye how? "Simon, son of Jonas, lovest thou me? Feed my sheep."

2. Love covers sin by making large allowances.

In all evil there is a "soul of goodness." Most evil is perverted good. For instance, extravagance is generosity carried to excess. Revenge is sometimes a sense of justice which has put no restraint upon itself. Woman's worst fault is perverted self-sacrifice. Incaution comes from innocence. Now there are some men who see all the evil, and never trace, never give themselves the trouble of suspecting the root of goodness out of which it sprung. There are others who love to go deep down, and see *why* a man came to do wrong, and whether there was not some excuse, or some redeeming cause : in order that they may be just. Just, as " God is just, *and* the justifier of him that believeth in Jesus."

Not as the passage is sometimes quoted—just, and *yet* the justifier ; as if there were some difficulty in reconciling God's justice and God's mercy : but just *and* the justifier, just and therefore the justifier. Merciful because just.

Now human life, as it presents itself to these two different eyes, the eye of one who sees only evil, and that of him who sees evil as perverted good, is two different things. Take an instance. Not many years ago, a gifted English writer presented us with a history of Ancient Christianity. To his eye the early Church presented one great idea, almost only one. He saw corruption written everywhere. In the history of the ascetics, of the nuns, of the hermits, of the early bishops, he saw nothing noble, nothing aspiring. Everywhere the one dark spectacle of the Man of Sin. In public and in private life, in theology and practice, within and without, everywhere pollution. Another historian, a foreigner, has written the history of the same times, with an intellect as piercing to discover the very first germ of error, but with a calm, large heart, which saw the good out of which the error sprung, and loved to dwell upon it, delighting to trace the lineaments of God, and discern His Spirit working where another could see only the spirit of the Devil. And you rise from the two books with different views of the world; from the one, considering the world as a devil's world, corrupting towards destruction; from the other, notwithstanding all, feeling triumphantly that it is God's world, and that His Spirit works gloriously below it all. You rise from the study with different feelings: from the one, inclined to despise your species; from the other, able joyfully to understand in part, why God so loved the world, and what there is in man to love, and what there is, even in the lost, to seek and save.

Now that is the "charity which covereth a multitude of sins."

It understands by sympathy. It is that glorious nature which has affinity with good under all forms, and loves to find it, to believe in it, and to see it. And therefore such men —God's rare and best ones—learn to make allowances; not from weak sentiment, which calls wrong right, but from that heavenly charity which sees right lying at the root of wrong. So the Apostle Paul learned to be candid even towards himself. "I obtained mercy, because I did it ignorantly, in unbelief." His very bigotry and persecuting spirit could be justified by God, and by men who see like God. It was wrong, very wrong; he did not palliate it; he felt that it had made him "the chief of sinners," but he discerned that his had been zeal directed wrongly,—not hate, but inverted love.

So too, over the dark grave of Saul the suicide, the love of friendship could shed one ray of hope. He who remembered of Saul, only his nobler nature and his earlier days, when his desolate character was less ambiguous,—the man after God's own heart—whose love refused to part with the conviction that that light which was from God was not quenched for ever, though it had set in clouds and thick darkness—dared to say, "Saul and Jonathan were lovely in their lives, and in their deaths they were not divided." Would you or I have dared to hope over a grave like Saul's? So too, over the grave of the prophet whose last act was disobedience, love still dared to hope, and the surviving prophet remembered only that he had shared the gift of prophecy with himself. "Alas, my *brother!*" A sinner, who had died in sin, but as our own Burial Service nobly dares to say, in the hope of intense charity, "To rest in Thee, as our hope is this our brother doth." And so, lastly, in the blackest guilt the earth has seen—in memory of which we, in our Christian charity, after eighteen hundred years, brand the descendant Jews with a curse, which is only slowly disappearing from our minds—there was one Eye which could discern a ground on which to make allowance, "Father, forgive them; for they know not what they do."

Let us dismiss from our minds one false suspicion. The man who can be most charitable is not the man who is himself most lax. Deep knowledge of human nature tells us it is exactly the reverse. He who shows the rough and thorny road to heaven, is he who treads the primrose path himself. Be sure that it is the severe and pitiless judge and censor of others' faults, on whom, at a venture, you may most safely fix the charge, "Thou art the man!" I know not why, but unrelenting severity proves guilt rather than innocence. How much purity was proved by David's sentence of an imaginary criminal to death? How much, by the desire of those Pharisees to stone the woman taken in adultery? Convicted by their own consciences, they went out one by one ; yet they had longed to stone her. No. Be sure you must be free from sin in proportion as you would judge with the allowance and the charity of Christ Jesus. "Tempted in all points, yet without sin." " *Wherefore* also, He is a merciful High Priest."

3. Lastly, charity can tolerate even intolerance.

Let no man think that he can be tolerant or charitable as a matter of self-indulgence. For real charity and real toleration he must pay a price. So long as they are merely negative—so long as they mean only the permission to every one to think his own thoughts and go his own way—the world will bear them. But so soon as charity becomes action, and toleration becomes earnest, basing themselves on a principle, even this—the conviction that at the root of many an error there lies a truth, and within much evil a central heart of goodness, and below unwise and even opposite forms, the same essential meaning—so soon Charity and Toleration exasperate the world secular, or so-called religious.

For instance, if with St. Paul, you affirm, " He that observeth the day, observeth it to the Lord ; and he that observeth not the day, to the Lord he observeth it not," tolerating both the observance and the non-observance, when you perceive the desire of doing God's will existing in both, you cannot avoid the charge of being careless about the question of the sanctities of a day of rest. Or if, with St. Paul, you say of some superstitious idolatry, that men ignorantly worship God in it, their worship being true, their form false—you cannot avoid the stigma of seeming for the time to be tending to that idolatry. Or if, with the Son of God, you recognize the enthusiasm of nature, which passion had led astray in devious paths, you cannot escape the

imputation of being "a friend of publicans and sinners."
This is the price which a man must pay for Charity.   His
Master could not escape the price, nor can he.

And then comes the last and most difficult lesson of
Love, to make allowances even for the uncharitable.   For
surely below all that uncharitableness which is so common,
there is often a germ of the Life of Love ; and beneath that
intolerance, which may often wound ourselves, a loving and
a candid eye may discern zeal for God.   Therefore St. Paul
saw even in the Jews, his bitterest foes, that "they had a
zeal for God, but not according to knowledge."   And therefore St. Stephen prayed, with his last breath, "Lord, lay not
this sin to their charge."   Earth has not a spectacle more
glorious or more fair to show than this—Love tolerating
intolerance ; Charity covering, as with a veil, even the sin
of the lack of charity.

XXII.

THE UNJUST STEWARD.

"And the lord commended the unjust steward, because he had done wisely: for the children of this world are in their generation wiser than the children of light.—And I say unto you, Make to yourselves friends of the mammon of unrighteousness ; that, when ye fail, they may receive you into everlasting habitations."—Luke xvi. 8, 9.

THERE is at first sight a difficulty in the interpretation of this parable ; apparently there is a commendation of evil by Christ. We see a bad man is held up for Christian imitation. Now let us read the parable.

"And He said also unto His disciples, There was a certain rich man, which had a steward ; and the same was accused unto him that he had wasted his goods.—And he called him, and said unto him, How is it that I hear this of thee ? give an account of thy stewardship ; for thou mayest be no longer steward.—Then the steward said within himself, What shall I do ? for my lord taketh away from me the stewardship : I cannot dig ; to beg I am ashamed.—I am resolved what to do, that, when I am put out of the stewardship, they may receive me into their houses.—So he called every one of his lord's debtors unto him and said unto the first, How much owest thou unto my lord ?—And he said, An hundred measures of oil. And he said unto him, Take thy bill, and sit down quickly, and write fifty.—Then said he to another, And how much owest thou? And he said, An hundred measures of wheat. And he said unto him, Take thy bill, and write fourscore.—And the lord commended the unjust steward, because he had done wisely: for the children of this world are in their generation wiser than the children of light."

The difficulty we have spoken of passes away when we have learnt to distinguish the essential aim of the parable from its ornament or drapery. There is in every parable the main scope, and the ornament or drapery. Sometimes, if we press too closely the drapery in which the aim and intention of a parable is clothed, we get quite the contrary of our Redeemer's meaning. For example, in the parable of the Unjust Judge there is the similarity, that both God and the unjust judge yield to importunate prayer; but there is this difference, that the judge does it from weariness, and God from love. The judge grants the widow's request, lest, he says, " by her continual coming she weary me ;"—and God answers the petitions of His people from Love : and encourages earnestness and sincerity in prayer because it brings man nearer to Him, elevating and ennobling him, while it makes him feel his entire dependence on God.

So here in this parable : it is the lord—it is not Christ, but the master—who commended the unjust steward. And he did so, not because he had acted honourably, faithfully, gratefully, but because he had acted *wisely*. He takes the single point of prudence, foresight, forecast.

Let us consider the possibility of detaching a single quality from a character, and viewing it separately.

So do we speak in every-day life. We quote a passage admiringly, from an infidel writer—for example, Gibbon ;

but thereby we do not approve his infidelity. We may admire the manly bearing of a prisoner in the dock or on the scaffold while we reprobate the crime which brought him there. We may speak enthusiastically of a great philosopher; we do not therefore say he is a great man, or a good man. Perhaps we are charmed by a tale of successful robbery; we wonder at its ingenuity, its contrivance, feel even a kind of respect for the man who could so contrive it: but no man who thus relates it is understood to recommend felony. We admire the dexterity of a juggler *as* dexterity.

So it was with this parable of Christ. He fastened on a single point, excluding all other considerations. The man had planned, he had seen difficulties, overcome them, marked out his path, held to it steadily, crowned himself with success. So far he is an example. The way in which he used his power of forecasting may have been bad; but forecast itself is good. Our subject to-day includes :—

I. The wisdom of this world.
II. The pattern of Christian consistency.

I. The wisdom of this world. There are three classes of men. Those who believe that one thing is needful, and choose the better part, who believe in and live for eternity;—these are not mentioned here: those who believe in the world, and live for it: and those who believe in eternity, and half live for the world.

Forethought for self made the steward ask himself, "What shall I do?" Here is the thoughtful, contriving, sagacious man of the world. In the affairs of this world, the man who does not provide for self, if he enter into competition with the world on the world's principles, soon finds himself thrust aside; he will be put out.   It becomes necessary to jostle and struggle in the great crowd if he would thrive.   With him it is not, first the kingdom of God ; but first, what he shall eat, and what he shall drink, and wherewithal shall he be clothed.

Note the kind of superiority in this character that is commended.   There are certain qualities which really do elevate a man in the scale of being.   He who pursues a plan steadily is higher than he who lives by the hour.   You cannot but respect such an one.   The value of self-command and self-denial is exemplified in the cases of the diplomatist who masters his features while listening ; the man of pleasure who is prudent in his pleasures ; the man of the world who keeps his temper and guards his lips.   How often, after speaking hastily the thought which was uppermost, and feeling the cheek burn, you have looked back in admiration on some one who held his tongue even though under great provocation to speak.

Look at some hard-headed, hard-hearted man, with a front of brass, carrying out his worldly schemes with a settled plan, and a perseverance which you perforce must admire. There may be nothing very exalted in his aim, but there is something very marvellous in the enduring, patient, steady pursuit of his object.

You see energies of the highest order are brought into play.   It is not a being of mean powers that the world has beguiled, but a mind far-reaching, vast ; throwing immortal powers on things of time ; on a scheme, perhaps, which breaks up like a cloud phantom, or melts like an ice-palace.

It is a marvellous spectacle—a man reaching forward to secure a habitation, a home, that will last.   A man counting

his freehold more his own than the pension for life : sagacious, meeting with entire success : the success which always
attends consistency in any pursuit. If a tradesman resolve
to save and be frugal, barring accidents, he will realize a
competency or a fortune. If you make it your business
to please, you will be welcome in society. So we find it in
this parable. This man, one of the world, contrived to
secure for himself a home. And the children of this world
are consistent, and force the world to yield them a home. It
is no use saying the people of the world are not happy.

I shall now endeavour to explain this parable. The term
" steward " is not to be taken exactly in its modern meaning.
The tenants paid their rents, not in money, but in kind, that
is in produce, and the rent was a certain proportion of the
crop, and would therefore vary according to the harvest.
Say, for illustration, the landlord—here called " the lord "—
received as rent the tenth part of the crop ; then, if the
produce of an olive yard was a thousand measures of oil,
" the lord " was entitled to a hundred measures. And
similarly in the case of an arable farm, a rent of a hundred
measures of wheat would represent a crop of a thousand
measures. According to the parable it appears that it
depended on the good faith of the tenant to state truly the
amount gathered in ; and against false returns the chief
check was provided in the steward. If he acquiesced in the
deception, there was generally no detection or check. We
read in this case he permitted the bill to be taken, and an
account given, in the one instance of eight hundred, in the
other, of five hundred instead of a thousand measures. Thus
he got gratitude from the tenants, who considered him a
benevolent man, and counted his expulsion an injustice.
We have here a specimen of the world's benevolence and

the world's gratitude. Let us do the world justice. Gratitude is given profusely. Help a man to build his fortune, and you will win gratitude.

The steward got commendation from his lord for his worldly wisdom. Such is the wisdom of this world—wise in its contriving selfishness ; wise in its masterly superiority ; wise in its adaptation of means to ends ; wise in its entire success.

But the success is only in their generation, and their wisdom is only for their generation. If this world be all, it is wise to contrive for it, and live for it. But if not, then consider,—the word is, " Thou fool, this night thy soul shall be required of thee ; then whose shall those things be that thou hast gotten ? "

II. In contrast with the wisdom of the children of this world, the Redeemer shows the inconsistencies of the children of light. " The children of this world are wiser in their generation than the children of light."

This is evidently not true of all. There have been men who have given their bodies to be burned for the truth's sake ; men who have freely sacrificed this present world for the next. To say that the wisest of the sons of this world is half as wise as they, were an insult to the sanctifying Spirit.

But " children of light " is a wide term. There is a difference between Life and Light. To have Light is to perceive truth and know duty. To have Life is to be able to live out truth and to perform duty. Many a man has clear light who has not taken hold of life. Many a man is the child of light who does not walk as the child of life.

So far as a man feels that eternity is long, time short, so far he is a child of light. So far as he believes the body nothing in comparison with the soul, the present in comparison with the future ; so far as he has felt the power of sin, and the sanctifying power of the death of Christ ; so far as he comprehends the character of God as exhibited in Jesus Christ,—he is a child of light.

Now the accusation is, that in his generation he does not walk so wisely as the child of the world does in his. The children of the world believe that this world is of vast importance. They are consistent with their belief, and live for it. Out of it they manage to extract happiness. In it they contrive to find a home.

To be a child of light implies duty as well as privilege. It is not enough to have the light, if we do not " walk in the light." " If we say we have fellowship with Him, and walk in darkness, we lie, and do not the truth."

And to hold high principles and live on low ones is Christian inconsistency. We are all more or less inconsistent. There is no man whose practice is not worse than his profession. No one who does not live below his own standard. But absolute inconsistency is, when a man's life taken as a whole, is in opposition to his acknowledged views and principles. If a man say that " it is more blessed to give than to receive," and is for ever receiving, scarcely ever giving, he is inconsistent. If he profess that to please God is the only thing worth living for, and his plans, and aims, and contrivances are all to please men, he is wise for the generation of the children of the world ; for the generation of the " children of light" he is not wise.

See then, the contrast.

The wisdom of the steward consisted in forecasting. He felt that his time was short, and he lost not a moment. Every time he crossed a field it was with the feeling, This is no longer mine. Every time he left his house he felt, I shall soon leave it to come back no more. Every time he went into a tenant's cottage he felt, the present is all that may be given me to make use of this opportunity. Therefore, he says with despatch, " Take thy bill, and write down."

Now the want of Christian wisdom consists in this, that our stewardship is drawing to a close, and no provision is made for an eternal future. We are all stewards. Every day, every age of life, every year, gives us superintendence over something which we have to use, and the use of which tells for good or evil on eternity.

Childhood and manhood pass. The day passes : and, as its close draws near, the Master's voice is heard—" Thou mayest be no longer steward." And what are all these outward symbols but types and reminders of the darker, longer night that is at hand ? One by one, we are turned out of all our homes. The summons comes. The man lies down on his bed for the last time ; and then comes that awful moment, the putting down the extinguisher on the light, and the grand rush of darkness on the spirit.

Let us now consider our Saviour's application of this parable.

" And I say unto you, Make to yourselves friends of the mammon of unrighteousness ; that, when ye fail, they may receive you into everlasting habitations.—He that is faithful in that which is least is faithful also in much : and he that is unjust in the least is unjust also in much.—If therefore ye have not been faithful in the unrighteous mammon, who will commit to your trust the true riches ?—And if ye have not been faithful in that which is another man's, who shall give you that which is your own ? "

There are two expressions to be explained.

1. "Mammon of unrighteousness."

Mammon is the name of a Syrian god, who presided over wealth. Mammon of unrighteousness means the god whom the unrighteous worship—wealth.

It is not necessarily gold. Any wealth; wealth being weal or well-being. Time, talents, opportunity, and authority, all are wealth. Here the steward had influence.

It is called the mammon of unrighteousness, because it is ordinarily used, not well, but ill. Power corrupts men. Riches harden more than misfortune.

2. "Make friends of." This is an ambiguous expression. Those who know it to be so scarcely are aware how widely it is misunderstood. To make friends of, has in English, two meanings. To make friends of a man, in our idiom, is to convert him into our ally. We meet with those who imagine that the command is to make riches our friends instead of our enemies.

But the other meaning is " of," *i. e.* out of, by the use of, to create friends,—in a word, to use these goods of Time in such a way as to secure Eternal well-being.

"Make to yourselves friends." I will explain "friends" as a home. There may seem to be great legality in this injunction.

Yet on this subject the words of Scripture are very strong. "Sell that thou hast, and give unto the poor, and thou shalt have treasure in heaven." "Provide yourselves bags that wax not old; a treasure in the heavens, that fadeth not away." "Lay up for yourselves treasure in heaven, where neither moth nor rust doth corrupt, and where thieves do not break through and steal." Do not be afraid of the expression.   Let it stand in all its bold truthfulness.   Goodness done in Christ secures blessedness.   A cup of cold water, given in the name of Christ, shall not lose its reward.

Merit in these things there is none.   Oh, the man who knows the torment of an evil heart !—and the man who is striving to use his powers wisely, is not the man to talk of merit in the sight of God.   There is no truth more dear to our hearts than this—not by merit, but by grace, does heaven become ours.

But let us put it in another way.   Wise acts, holy and unselfish deeds, secure friends.   Wherever the steward went he found a friend.   The acts of his beneficence were spread over the whole of his master's estate.   Go where he would, he would receive a welcome.   In this way our good actions become our friends.

And if it be no dream which holy men have entertained, that on this regenerated earth the risen spirits shall live again in glorified bodies, then it were a thing of sublime anticipation, to know that every spot hallowed by the recollection of a deed done for Christ, contains a recollection which would be a friend.   Just as the patriarchs erected an altar when they felt God to be near, till Palestine became dotted with these memorials, so would earth be marked by a good man's life with those holiest of all friends, the remembrance of ten thousand little nameless acts of piety and love.

Lastly, they are *everlasting* habitations.

If the children of the world be right, it is not all well with them ; but if the children of light be right, it is well everlastingly.

Nothing is eternal but that which is done for God and

others. That which is done for self dies. Perhaps it is not wrong : but it perishes. You say it is pleasure, well—enjoy it. But joyous recollection is no longer joy. That which ends in self is mortal; that alone which goes out of self into God lasts for ever.

XXIII.

THE ORPHANAGE OF MOSES.

(*A Sermon Preached on behalf of the Orphan Society.*)

"And when she had opened it, she saw the child: and, behold, the babe wept. And she had compassion on him, and said, This is one of the Hebrews' children.—Then said his sister to Pharaoh's daughter, Shall I go and call to thee a nurse of the Hebrew women, that she may nurse the child for thee?—And Pharaoh's daughter said to her, Go. And the maid went and called the child's mother.—And Pharaoh's daughter said unto her, Take this child away, and nurse it for me, and I will give thee thy wages. And the woman took the child, and nursed it."—Exodus, ii. 6—9.

THIS is the account given of the discovery of a foundling orphan. Moses was an orphan—ὀρφανὸς, bereaved; ordinarily it means one bereaved by death. But it matters not whether it is by death or otherwise; it is truly an orphan if it be in any manner deprived of a parent's care. Here the child Moses was not bereaved by death, but by political circumstances.

In the book from whence our text is taken, we are told that three laws were enacted against the liberties of Israel :—

1. To keep down the population, the political economy of those days devised, as a preventive check, the slaughter of the males.

2. To prevent their acquiring any political importance, the officers set over them were Egyptians. No Israelite was eligible to any office—not even as a taskmaster.

3. To prevent their acquiring knowledge, they were prohibited from the slightest leisure : their lives were made bitter with hard bondage, in brick and mortar.

No penal statutes were ever more complete than these. If any penal statutes could have prevented the growth of this injured nation, these must have succeeded. Numerically limited, rendered politically insignificant, and intellectually feeble, the slavery of Israel was complete.

But wherever governments enact penal laws which are against the Laws of God, those governments or nations are, by the sure and inevitable process of revolution, preparing for themselves destruction. As when you compress yielding water, it bursts at last.

Pharaoh's laws were against all the laws of Nature, or, more properly speaking, against the Laws of God : and Nature was slowly working against Pharaoh. He had made God his enemy.

Against these laws of Pharaoh a mother's heart revolted. She hid her child for three months. Disobedience to this Egyptian law, we read, was faith in God—so says the Epistle to the Hebrews. " By faith Moses, when he was born, was hid three months of his parents, because they saw he was a proper child ; and they were not afraid of the king's commandment."

At last concealment was no longer possible, and the mother placed her child in an ark among the reeds of the river Nile. And there a foundling orphan he lay, who was to be the future emancipator and lawgiver of Israel.

In order to understand these verses, I divide them into two branches :—

    I. The claims of the orphan.
    II. The orphan's education.

And first. By apparent accident, if there be such a thing in this world of God's, the daughter of Pharaoh came down to the river to wash, and, among the reeds, she saw the chest, in which lay the child.

Now the first claim put forward on her compassion was the claim of infancy.

The chest was opened. The princess " saw the child." That single sentence contains an argument. It was an appeal to the woman's heart. It mattered not that she was a princess, nor that she belonged to the proudest class of the most exclusive nation in the world. Rank, caste, nationality, all melted before the great fact of womanhood. She was a woman, and before her lay an outcast child.

Now, let us observe, that feeling which arose here was spontaneous. She did not feel compassion because it was her duty so to feel, but because it was her nature. The law of Egypt forbade her to feel so for a Hebrew child.

We commit a capital error when we make feeling a matter of command. To make feelings a subject of law destroys their beauty and spontaneity.

When we say ought—that a woman ought to feel so and so—we state a fact, not a command. We say that it is her nature, and that she is unnatural if she does not. There is something wrong—her nature is perverted. But no command can *make* her feel thus or thus. Law, applied to feeling, only makes hypocrites.

God has provided for Humanity by a plan more infallible than system, by implanting feeling in our natures. It was a heathen felt thus.

Do not fancy that Christianity created these feelings of tenderness and compassion by commanding them. Christianity declares them, commands them, and sanctions them, because they belong to man's unadulterated nature. Christianity acknowledges them, stamps them with the divine seal; but they existed before, and were found even among the Egyptians and Assyrians. What Christianity did for all these feelings was exactly what the creation of the sun, as given in the Mosaic account, did for the light then existing. There was light before, but the creation of the sun was the gathering all the scattered rays of light into one focus. Christian institutions, asylums, hospitals, are only the reduction into form of feelings that existed before.

So it is, that all that heathenism held of good and godlike, Christianity acknowledges and adopts—centralizes. It is human—Christian—ours.

2. Consider the degradation of this child's origin.

"This is one of the Hebrews' children." The exclusiveness of the Egyptian social system was as strong as that of the Hindoo. There was no intermixture between caste and caste—between priest and merchant. This child was, moreover, a Hebrew—a slave—an alien—reckoned an hereditary enemy, and to be crushed.

In these rigid feelings of caste distinction the princess was brought up. The voice of Society said, It is but a Hebrew. The mightier voice of nature—no, of God—spake within her, and said, It is a human being—bone of your bone, and sharing the same life.

That moment the princess of Egypt escaped from the

trammels of time-distinctions and temporary narrowness, and stood upon the rock of the Eternal. So long as the feeling lasted, she breathed the spirit of that Kingdom in which there is "neither Jew nor Gentile, barbarian, Scythian, bond, nor free." So long as the feeling lasted, she breathed the atmosphere of Him who "came not to be ministered unto but to minister."

She was animated by His spirit Who came to raise the abject, to break the bond of the oppressor. She felt as He felt, when she recognized that the very degradation of the child was a claim upon her royal compassion.

3. The last reason we find for this claim was its unprotected state :—it wept.

Those tears told of a conscious want—the felt want of a mother's arms. But they suggested to the Egyptian princess the remembrance of a danger of which the child was unconscious—helpless exposure to worse evils—famine ; the Nile flood ; the crocodile. And the want of which the exposed child was conscious was far less than the danger of which it was unconscious.

Such is the state of orphanage. Because it is unprotected, it is therefore exposed to terrible evils. There are worse evils than the Nile, the crocodile, or starvation.

Suppose the child had lived. Then, as a boy in the hands of a taskmaster or slave-driver, he would have become callous, hard, and vicious, with every feeling of tenderness dried up. Nothing can replace a parent's tenderness. It is not for physical support merely that parents are given us, but for the formation of the heart. He wept now; but the fountain of the orphan's tears would have been withered and dried up, and instead of the tender man which he afterwards became, he would have become a hard-hearted slave.

Let us suppose again the case of a girl orphaned. Then you have the danger infinitely multiplied. There would have been no one in all the land of Egypt to redress the wrongs done to a Hebrew maiden. There are men in this world to whom, putting religion out of the question even, the very fact of wanting protection is cause sufficient for them to render protection. There are men to whom defencelessness is its own all-sufficient plea:—there are men in whose presence the woman and the orphan, just because they are unshielded by any care, are protected more than they could be by any laws.

But remember, I pray you, that there is another spirit in the world—the spirit of oppression, and even worse; the spirit against which Jewish prophets rose to the height of a divine eloquence when they pleaded the cause of the fatherless and the widow; that spirit which in our own day makes the daughter of the poor man less safe than the daughter of the rich; that spirit of seduction, than which there is nothing more cowardly, more selfish, more damnable. For alas! it is true that to say that a girl is unprotected, fatherless, and poor, is almost equivalent to saying that she will fall into sin.

II. We pass on now to consider the orphan's education; and first I notice that it was a suggestion from another.

The princess felt compassion, and so far was in the state of one who has warm feelings, but does not know how to do good. Brought up in a court, born to be waited on, nursed in luxury, ignorant of life and how the poor lived, those feelings might have remained helpless feelings.

Then, in the providence of God, one stood by who offered a suggestion how she might benefit the child, "Shall I go and call a nurse?" In other words, she suggested that it would be a princely and noble thing for Pharaoh's daughter to adopt and educate it.

And now observe the value of such a suggestion :—what we want is not feeling—emotions are common, feelings super-abound. In the educated classes, feeling is extremely refined, but is much occupied with imaginary and unreal troubles : and the reason why, with such warm feelings so little good is done, is that we want the suggestion how to do it.

Observe how differently the Bible treats this from what the painter or the novelist would have done. A painter would have shown the majesty and beauty of the royal actor. A romance would have given a touching history of womanly sentiment. But the Bible, being a real book, says little of the emotion—merely mentions it—and passes on to the act to which the feeling was meant to lead.

Brethren, we often make a mistake here ; we are proud of our emotions, of our refined feeling, of our quick sensibilities ; but remember, I pray you, feeling by itself is worthless—it is meant to lead to action, and if it fails to do this, it is a danger rather than a blessing ; for excited feeling that stops short of deeds is the precursor of callousness and hardness of heart. Your sensibility is well—but what has it *done ?*

We feel the orphans' claims, and now comes the question, how shall we do them good ?

Let us observe that Moses was nursed by a Hebrew matron. She was one of his own grade. It would have been a capital error to have given him to an Egyptian nurse. Probably, the princess left to herself would have done so.

But then he would have been weaned from his own race. In heart, sympathies, feelings, he would have been an Egyptian. Nay, he would have been more exclusive; for the hardest are almost always those who have been raised above their former position. The slave's hardest taskmaster is a negro. The one who is most exclusive in his sympathies is usually the raised merchant, or the one recently ennobled.

The great thing is to emancipate the degraded through their own class. Only through their own class can they be effectually delivered; the mere patronage of the great and rich injures character.

So it was with Judaism; so it was with Christianity. The Redeemer was made of a woman—"born under the law to redeem them that were under the law." He Who came to preach the Gospel to the poor, was born of a poor woman.

But it was not only a Hebrew nurse to whom Moses was given, it was a mother—his own mother—who nursed him; and from her he heard the story of his people's history. From her he learned to feel his country's wrongs to be his own. In the splendour of Pharaoh's court he never could forget that his mother was a slave, and that his father was working in brick and mortar, under cruel taskmasters.

From the princess he gained the wisdom of Egypt—he was taught legislative science. From hardship, he learned endurance and patience. Instruction ends in the school-room, but education ends only with life. A child is given to the universe to educate.

Now let us see the results of this training on his intellectual and moral nature.

1. Intellectually. We will only notice the spirit of

inquiry and habit of observation. To ask "Why?" is the best Christian lesson for a child. Not the "*why*" which is the language of disobedience, but that "*why*" which demands for all phenomena a cause. It was this which led Moses on Mount Horeb to say, "I will turn aside and see this great sight, why the bush is not burned." So it was that Moses found out God.

2. In the moral part of his character we note his hatred of injustice and cruelty; ever was he found ranged against oppression in whatever form it might appear. He stood ever on the side of Right against Might, whether it was to avenge the wrong done by the Egyptian to one of his Hebrew brethren, or to rescue the daughter of the priest of Midian from the oppressing shepherds. He became, too, a peacemaker. Thus we get a glimpse of the moral and intellectual nature of the man who afterwards led Israel out of Egyptian bondage, and who, but for the education he had received, might have become as degraded as any of the nation he freed from slavery.

At the present day, that child who might have become so degraded, stands second but to One in dignity and influence in the annals of the human race. Take for one example the Jewish Sabbath. Thousands upon thousands of that nation, fond of gain and mammon as they proverbially are said to be, yet gave up their gains yesterday, and voluntarily surrendered that one day in addition to this day which, by the law of the land, they are obliged to keep holy. And all this in obedience to the enactments of that orphan child, who three thousand years ago commanded the Sabbath-day to be kept holy. In those days the Pharaohs of Egypt raised their memorials in the enduring stone of the Pyramids, which still remain almost untouched by time.

A princess of Egypt raised her memorial in a human spirit, and just so far as spirit is more enduring than stone, just so far is the work of that princess more enduring than the work of the Pharaohs; for when the day comes when those Pyramids shall have crumbled into nothingness and ruin, then shall the spirit of the laws of Moses still remain interwoven with the most hallowed of human institutions. So long as the spirit of Moses influences this world, so long shall her work endure, the work of that royal-hearted lady who adopted this Hebrew orphan child.

It now only remains for me to say a word on the claims of that institution for which I am to plead to-day—the Female Orphan Asylum in this town. It was established in 1823, and for years its funds flourished; lately they have fallen off considerably, and that not in consequence of fault in the institution itself, but simply for this cause, that of those who took it up warmly once, many have been removed by death, and many have altered their place of residence, and also because many fresh calls and institutions have come forward, and thus have excluded this one. The consequence has been a sad falling off of funds. Last year the expenditure exceeded the receipts by one hundred pounds.

Within the walls of that institution, now almost dilapidated and falling into decay, there are twenty-four female orphan children, received from the age of six to sixteen; not educated above their station, but educated simply to enable them "to do their duty in that state of life to which it has pleased God to call them."

And now I earnestly desire to appeal to you for this object by the thoughts that have to-day been brought before you. Because they are children, I make an appeal to every mother's and woman's heart; because they are females, young and unprotected, I make an appeal to the heart of every man who knows and feels the evils of society; because they belong to the lowest class, I make an appeal to all who have ever felt the infinite preciousness of the fact that the Saviour of this world was born a poor man's child.

My beloved Christian brethren, let us not be content with feeling; give, I pray you, as God has prospered you.

XXIV.

CHRISTIANITY AND HINDOOISM.

(A Fragment of an Advent Lecture.)

" Hear, O Israel : The Lord our God is one Lord.—And thou shalt love the Lord thy God with all thine heart, and with all thy soul, and with all thy might."—Deuteronomy vi. 4, 5.

IT is my intention, in giving the present course of lectures, to consider the Advent of our Lord in connection with the cause of missionary labours. This connection is clear. His Advent is the reign of God in the hearts of men ; and it is the aim of the missionary to set up that kingdom in men's hearts. There is also a more indirect connection between the two, because at this time, the Church Missionary Society is celebrating its jubilee. It is now fifty years since the first mission was established at Sierra Leone, where, although they who composed that little band were swept off one after another by jungle fever—their groans unheard, themselves unwept, and almost unhonoured—yet there rose up other labourers after them ; and a firm footing was at length gained in that dark heathen land.

On the Epiphany of next year we are to celebrate this jubilee in Brighton ; and it has seemed to me a good preparation, that we should occupy, in thought, some field of missionary exertion, and look at the difficulties which those have had to contend against, who have gone out in that work. There can be no doubt as to which shall be first chosen for our contemplation. India, with its vast territories and millions of people, comes first, both as being one of our own possessions, and by the heavy responsibilities attaching to us on account of it.

We propose therefore, to give some account of Hindoo superstition ; and here I would remark, there are three ways of looking at idolatry.

I. There is the way of the mere *scholar*—that of men who read about it as the schoolboy does, as a thing past —a curious but worn-out system. This scholastic spirit is the worst ; for it treats the question of religious worship as a piece of antiquarianism, of no vital consequence, but just curious and amusing.

II. There is the view taken by the religious *partisan*. There are some men who, thinking their religion right, determine, therefore, that every one who differs from them is wrong. They look with scorn and contempt on the religion of the Hindoo, and only think how they may force theirs upon him. In this spirit, the world can never be evangelized. A man may say to another, " I cannot understand your believing such folly," but he will not convince him so of his error. It is only by entering into the mind and difficulties of the heathen that we can learn how to meet them and treat them effectually.

III. There is the way of enlightened Christianity. In this spirit stood St. Paul on the Hill at Athens. The beauty of Greek worship was nothing to him. To him it was still idolatry, though it was enlightened ; but he was not hard enough not to be able to feel for them. He did not denounce it to them as damnable ; he showed them that they were feeling after God, but blindly, ignorantly, wrongly. "Whom ye ignorantly worship, Him declare I unto you."

The religion on which we are going to dwell to-day is one of the most subtle the world has ever received. It has stood the test of long ages and of great changes. The Land has in turn submitted to the Macedonian, the Saracen, the Mahomedan conqueror ; yet its civilization, and its ways of thinking, have remained always the same,—in stagnation. We marvel how it has happened that their religion has remained sufficient for them. Let us look at it.

I. We take, as the first branch of our subject,—The Hindoo conception of Divinity. We start with the assertion, that the god whom a man worships is but the reflection of himself. Tell us what a man's mind is, and we will tell you what his god is. Thus amongst the Africans, the lowest and most degraded of mankind, forms of horror are reverenced. The frightful, black, shapeless god, who can be frightened by the noise of a drum, is their object of worship.

Our Scandinavian forefathers, whose delight was in the battle and the sea-fight, worshipped warlike gods, whose names still descend to us in the names given to the days of the week ; they expected after death the conqueror's feast in Walhalla, the flowing cup, and the victor's wreath.

Look at Christianity itself. We profess to worship the Father of our Lord Jesus Christ, but we do not all worship the same God. The God of the child is not the God of the man. He is a beneficent being—an enlarged representation (to him) of his own father. The man whose mind is cast in a stern mould worships a God, who sits above to administer justice and punishment. The man who shrinks from the idea of suffering, worships a placable God, who combines the greatest possible amount of happiness for the race with the least possible amount of pain.

[Now, consider the man who worships God as He appears in Jesus Christ.]

There are two things distinctly marked in the Hindoo religion :—The love of physical repose ; and mental activity, restlessness, and subtlety. Theirs are ideas passing through trains of thought which leave our European minds marvelling in astonishment.

Their first principle is that of God's unity. We are told by some that they have many gods, but all those who have deeply studied the subject agree in this—that they really have but *one*. This Hindoo deity is capable of two states— 1. Inaction ; 2. Action. The first state is that of a dream-less sleep, unconscious of its own existence ; all attributes have passed away—it is infinite nothing. We remark in men generally a desire for *rest;* in the Hindoo it is a desire merely for indolence. Far deeper lodged in the human breast than the desire of honour or riches, is seated the desire for rest : there are, doubtless, eager, earnest spirits, who may scorn pleasure, but, nevertheless, they long for rest. Well and rightly has the Hindoo thrown this idea on God ; but he has erred in the character of that repose.

There are two kinds of rest :—1st. There is the rest desired by the world. 2nd. There is the rest we find in Christ. The active mind, if out of its proper sphere, corrodes itself, and frets itself with plans and projects, finding no rest. The rest of Christ is not that of torpor, but harmony; it is not refusing the struggle, but conquering *in it;* not resting *from* duty, but finding rest *in* duty.

The Sabbaths of Eternity have kept the Supreme Mind in infinite blessedness : on our restless, unquiet, throbbing hearts, God has been looking down, serene and calm. When chaos took lovely form and shape, then that Rest began— not in the torpor of inaction, but in harmonious work. " My Father worketh hitherto." God works in all the smallest objects of creation, as well as in the largest. Even in midnight stillness harmonious action is the law ; when everything seems to slumber, all is really at work, for the spirit of life and the spirit of death are weaving and unweaving for ever.

We remark that to this god of Hindostan there rises no temple throughout the length and breadth of the land. If you ask in astonishment, why is this ? the Hindoo replies, " Pure, unmixed Deity is *mind*, and cannot be confined to place ; " and well does he here teach us that God is a Spirit : but in his idea there is an exhibition of a god without qualities—a deity whom man may meditate on, and be absorbed in, but not one to be loved or adored.

Here is his first error ; here we can teach him something—that God is a Personal Being.

Personality is made up of three attributes—Conscious-ness, Character, Will. Without the union of these three, the idea is imperfect. Personality the Hindoo Deity has none ; therefore he cannot be loved.

Now when we look at God as revealed in Jesus Christ, He appears to us as having a mind like ours ; the ideas of number, of right and wrong, of sanctity, are to God precisely what they are to man. Conceive a mind without these, and it may be a high and lofty one, but there can be no communion with it. But when Christ speaks of love, of purity, of holiness, we feel that it is no abstraction we worship.

II. We shall consider as the second branch of our subject the Hindoo theory of creation.

We have spoken of the Hindoo Deity as capable of two states—that of perfection, or rest ; that of imperfection, or unrest. The Hindoo thinks that a time arrives when rest becomes action, and slumber becomes life ; and when, not willing to be alone, feeling solitary in his awaking, God wishes to impart life ; therefore He creates.

Here again, we recognize a partial truth. In the Scriptures we never read of a time when God was alone. What is love but this, to find ourselves again in another? The "Word," we read, "was with God" before the world began. What the word is to the thought, that is Christ to God. Creation was one expression of this—of His inmost feelings of beauty and loveliness ; whether it be the doleful sighings of the night-wind, or the flower that nestles in the grass, they tell alike of Love. So has He also shown that Love on earth, in the outward manifestation of the Life of Christ— not only in the translated Word which we have—beautiful as it is, but in the living Word. Read without *this*, history is a dark, tangled web, philosophy a disappointing thing. Without *this* light, society is imperfect, and the greatest men, small and insignificant. From all these we turn to Christ ; *here* is that perfect Word to which our hearts echo, where no one syllable is wrong.

There are two Hindoo theories of creation—the gross view held by the many ; the refined one held by the philosopher and the Brahmin. Yet these two so mix and intermingle that it is difficult to give to European minds a clear notion of either of them separately. We will leave the popular view for another time, and we will try to deal now with the metaphysical and transcendental one. It is this—creation is illusion—the Deity awaking from sleep. The universe is God : God is the universe : therefore He cannot create. The Hindoo says, you, and I, and all men, are but gods— ourselves in a wretched state of dream and illusion. We must try to explain this in part by our own records of times which we can all remember, when we have lain in a state between dreaming and waking—a phantasmagoric state, changing, combining, altering, like the kaleidoscope, so that we hardly knew realities from unrealities. "Such," says the Hindoo, "is your life—a delusion." I merely tell of this because it colours all Hindoo existence ; the practical results we shall consider another time. For this the visionary contemplator of Brahm, and the Fakeer, sit beneath the tree, scarcely eating, speaking, or thinking ; hoping at length to become absorbed into that calm, dreamless, passive state, which to them represents perfection.

One truth we find acknowledged in this theory is the unreality of this world. Nobly has the Hindoo set forth the truth that the world is less real than the spirit. "What is your life? it is even a vapour." Ask you what we are to live for? The child, on whose young face the mother now gazes so tenderly, changes with years into the man with furrowed brow and silvered hair ; Constitutions are formed and broken, friendships pass, love decays, who can say he possesses the same now that blessed him in his early life? All passes whilst we look upon it. A most unreal, imaginative life. The spirit of life ever weaving—the spirit of death ever unweaving ; all things putting on change.

In conclusion—

We observe here a great truth—the evil of self-conscious-

ness.   This self-consciousness is all evil.   He who can dwel
on this and that symptom of his moral nature is already
diseased.   We are too much haunted by ourselves; we
project the spectral shadow of ourselves on everything
around us.   And then comes in the Gospel to rescue us
from this selfishness.   Redemption is this, to forget self in
God.   Does not the mother forget herself for a time in the
child; the loyal man in his strong feelings of devotion for
his sovereign?   So does the Christian forget himself in the
feeling that he has to live here for the performance of the
Will of God.

[And now contrast the Hindoo religion with the
Christian.]

The Hindoo tells us the remedy for this unreality is to
be found in the long unbroken sleep.   The Christian tells
us the remedy is this, that this broken dream of life shall
end in a higher life.   Life is but a sleep, a dream, and death
is the real awaking.

XXV.

REST.

"Come unto me, all ye that labour and are heavy laden, and I will give you rest.—Take my yoke upon you, and learn of me; for I am meek and lowly in heart : and ye shall find rest unto your souls."—Matthew xi. 28, 29.

NO one perhaps ever read these words of Christ without being struck with their singular adaptation to the necessities of our nature. We have read them again and again, and we have found them ever fresh, beautiful, and new. No man could ever read them without being conscious that they realized the very deepest and inmost want of his being. We feel it is a convincing proof of His Divine mission that He has thus struck the key-note of our nature, in offering us Rest.

Ancient systems were busy in the pursuit after happiness. Our modern systems of philosophy, science, ay, even of theology, occupy themselves with the same thought; telling us alike that " happiness is our being's end and aim." But it is not so that the Redeemer teaches. His doctrine is in words such as these : " In the world ye shall have "—not happiness, but—" tribulation ; but be of good cheer, I have overcome the world." " In Me ye shall have peace." Not happiness—the outward well-being so called in the world— but the inward rest which cometh from above. And He alone who made this promise had a right to say, "Take my yoke upon you, and learn of Me, for I am meek and lowly in heart; and ye shall find Rest unto your souls." He had that Rest in Himself, and therefore could impart it; but it is often offered by men who have it not themselves. There are some, high professors of religion too, who have never known this real rest, and who at fifty, sixty, seventy years of age, are as much slaves of the world as when they began, desiring still the honours, the riches, or the pleasures it has to give, and utterly neglecting the Life which is to come.

When we turn to the history of Christ we find this repose characterizing His whole existence. For example, first, in the marriage feast at Cana, in Galilee. He looked not upon that festivity with cynical asperity; He frowned not upon the innocent joys of life: He made the wine to give enjoyment, and yet singularly contrasted was His Human and His Divine joy. His mother came to Him full of consternation, and said, "They have no wine;" and the Redeemer, with calm self-possession, replied, "Woman, what have I to do with thee? mine hour is not yet come." He felt not the deficiency which He supplied.

We pass from the marriage feast to the scene of grief at Bethany, and still there we find that singular repose. Those words which we have seen to possess an almost magical charm in soothing the grief of mourners congregated round the coffin of the dead—"I am the resurrection and the life: he that believeth in Me, though he were dead, yet shall he live; and whosoever liveth and believeth in Me shall never die,"—speak they not of repose? But in the requirements of these great matters many men are not found wanting; it is when we come to the domesticities of their existence that we see fretting anxiety comes upon their soul. Therefore it is that we gladly turn to that home at Bethany where He had gone for quiet rest. Let us hear His words on the subject of every-day cares: " Martha, Martha, thou art careful and troubled about many things; but one thing is needful."

We pass on from that, to the state in which a man is tried the most : and if ever we can pardon words of restlessness and petulance, it is when friends are unfaithful. Yet even here there is perfect calmness. Looking steadfastly into the future, He says, " Do ye now believe ? Behold, the hour cometh, yea, is now come, that ye shall be scattered, every man to his own, and shall leave Me alone : and yet I am not alone, because the Father is with Me."

Once more, we turn to the Redeemer's prayers. They are characterized by a calmness singularly contrasted with the vehemence which we sometimes see endeavouring to lash itself into a greater fervour of devotion. The model prayer has no eloquence in it ; it is calm, simple, full of repose.

We find this again in the 17th chapter of St. John. If a man feels himself artificial and worldly, if a man feels restless, we would recommend him to take up that chapter as his best cure. For at least one moment, as he read it, he would feel in his soul calmness and repose ; it would seem almost as if he were listening to the grave and solemn words of a divine soliloquy. This was the Mind of Him who gave this gracious promise, " Come unto Me all ye that labour and are heavy laden, and I will give you rest." We repeat these words as a matter of course ; but I ask, Has that repose been found ? —has this peace come to us ? for it is not by merely repeating them over and over again that we can enter into the deep Rest of Christ.

Our subject this day will be to consider, in the first place, the false systems of rest which the world holds out, and to contrast them with the true Rest of Christ. The first false system proposed is the expectation of repose in the grave. When the spirit has parted from the body after long-protracted sufferings, we often hear it said that the release was a happy one ; that there is a repose in the grave; that there "the wicked cease from troubling and the weary are at rest." Nay, at times, perhaps, we find ourselves hazarding a wish that our own particular current of existence had come to that point, when it should mingle with the vast ocean of eternity.

There is in all this a kind of spurious Pantheism, a sort of feeling that God is alike in every heart, that every man is to be blessed at last, that death is but a mere transition to a blessed sleep, that in the grave there is nothing but quiet, and that there is no misery beyond it. And yet one of the deepest thinkers of our nation suggests that there *may be* dreams even in the sleep of death. There is an illusion often in the way in which we think of death. The countenance, after the spirit has departed, is so strangely calm and meek that it produces the feeling of repose within us, and we transfer our feelings to that of the departed spirit, and we fancy that body no longer convulsed with pain, those features so serene and full of peace, do but figure the rest which the spirit is enjoying; and yet, perhaps that soul, a few hours ago, was full of worldliness, full of pride, full of self-love. Think you that now that spirit is at rest—that it has entered into the Rest of Christ? The repose that belongs to the grave is not even a rest of the atoms composing our material form.

There is another fallacious system of rest which would place it in the absence of outward trial. This is the world's peace. The world's peace ever consists in plans for the removal of outward trials. There lies at the bottom of all false systems of peace, the fallacy that if we can but produce a perfect set of circumstances, then we shall have the perfect man ; if we remove temptation, we shall have a holy being : and so the world's rest comes to this—merely happiness and outward enjoyment. Ay, my Christian brethren, we carry these anticipations beyond the grave, and we think the Heaven of God is but like the Mahometan paradise—a place in which the rain shall beat on us no longer, and the sun pour his burning rays upon us no more. Very often it is only a little less sensual, but quite as ignoble as that fabled by Mahomet.

The Redeemer throws all this aside at once as mere illusion. He teaches just the contrary. He says, " Not as the world giveth, give I unto you." The world proposes a rest by the removal of a burden. The Redeemer gives Rest by giving us the spirit and power to bear the burden. " Take my yoke upon you, and learn of Me, and ye shall find rest unto your souls." Christ does not promise a rest of inaction, neither that the thorns shall be converted into roses, nor that the trials of life shall be removed.

To the man who takes this yoke up in Christ's spirit, labour becomes blessedness—rest of soul and rest of body.

It matters not in what circumstances men are, whether high or low, never shall the Rest of Christ be found in ease and self-gratification ; never, throughout eternity, will there be rest found in a life of freedom from duty :—the paradise of the sluggard, where there is no exertion ; the heaven of the coward, where there is no difficulty to be opposed, is not the Rest of Christ. " Take my yoke upon you." Nay, more—if God could give us a heaven like that, it would be but misery ; there can be no joy in indolent inaction. The curse on this world is labour; but to him who labours earnestly and truly it turns to blessedness. It is a curse only to him who tries to escape from the work allotted to him, who endeavours to make a compromise with duty. To him who takes Christ's yoke, not in a spirit of selfish ease and acquiescence in evil, but in strife and stern battle with it, the Rest of Christ streams in upon his soul.

Many of us are drifting away from our moorings; we are quitting the old forms of thought, and faith, and life, and are seeking for something other than what satisfied the last generation: and this in a vain search for rest.

Many are the different systems of repose offered to us, and foremost is that proposed by the Church of Rome. Let us do her the justice, at all events, to allow that she follows the Redeemer in this—it is not happiness she promises, she promises rest. The great strength of Romanism lies in this, that she professes to answer and satisfy the deep want of human nature for rest. She speaks of an infallibility on which she would persuade men, weary of the strain of doubt, to rest. It is not to the tales of miracles, and of the personal interference of God Himself; but to the promise of an impossibility of error to those within her pale, that she owes her influence. And we say, better far to face doubt and perplexity manfully; to bear any yoke of Christ's than be content with the rest of a Church's infallibility.

There is another error among many Dissenters; in a different form, we find the same promise held out. One says that if we will but rely on God's promise of election, our soul must find repose. Another system tells us that the penalty has fallen upon Christ, and that if we believe, we shall no longer suffer. Narrowing their doctrines into one, as if all the want of the soul was to escape from punishment, they place before us this doctrine, and say, believe that, and your soul shall find repose.

We have seen earnest men anxiously turning from view to view, and yet finding their souls as far from rest as ever. They remind us of the struggles of a man in fever, finding no rest, tossing from side to side, in vain seeking a cool spot on his pillow, and forgetting that the fever is within himself. And so it is with us; the unrest is within us: we foolishly expect to find that tranquillity in outward doctrine, which alone can come from the calmness of the soul.

We will not deny that there is a *kind* of rest to be found in doctrine for a time : for instance, when a man, whose only idea of evil is its penalty, has received the consoling doctrine that there is no suffering for him to bear : but the unrest comes again. Doubtless, the Pharisees and Sadducees, when they went to the baptism of John, found something of repose there; but think you that they went back to their daily life with the Rest of Christ? We expect some outward change will do that which nothing but the inward life can do—it is the life of Christ within the soul which alone can give repose. There have been men in the Church of Rome and in the ranks of Dissent who have indeed erred grievously, but yet have lived a life of godliness. There have been men in the true Church—as Judas, who was a member of the true Church—who yet, step by step, have formed in themselves the devil's nature : the Rest of Christ pertains not to any one outward communion.

Before we go farther, let us understand what is meant by this Rest ; let us look to those symbols about us in the world of nature by which it is suggested. It is not the lake locked in ice that suggests repose, but the river moving on calmly and rapidly in silent majesty and strength. It is not the cattle lying in the sun, but the eagle cleaving the air with fixed pinions, that gives you the idea of repose combined with strength and motion. In creation, the Rest of God is exhibited as a sense of Power which nothing wearies. When chaos burst into harmony, so to speak, God had Rest.

There are two deep principles in Nature in apparent contradiction—one, the aspiration after perfection ; the other, the longing after repose. In the harmony of these lies the rest of the soul of man. There have been times when we have experienced this. Then the winds have been hushed, and the throb and the tumult of the passions have been blotted out of our bosoms. That was a moment when we were in harmony with all around, reconciled to ourselves and to our God ; when we sympathised with all that was pure, all that was beautiful, all that was lovely.

This was not stagnation, it was fulness of life—life in its most expanded form, such as nature witnessed in her first hour. This is life in that form of benevolence which expands into the mind of Christ. And when this is working in the soul, it is marvellous how it distils into a man's words and countenance. Strange and magical is the power of that collect wherein we pray to God, " Who alone can order the unruly wills and affections of sinful men, to grant unto His people that they may love the thing which he commands, and desire that which He promises ; that so among the sundry and manifold changes of the world, our hearts may surely there be fixed where true joys are to be found." There is a wondrous melody in that rhythm ; the words are the echoes of the thought. The mind of the man who wrote them was in repose—all is ringing of rest. We do not wonder when Moses came down from the mount on which he had been bowing in adoration before the harmony of God, that his face was shining with a brightness too dazzling to look upon.

Our blessed Redeemer refers this Rest to meekness and lowliness. There are three causes in men producing unrest:—1. Suspicion of God. 2. Inward discord. 3. Dissatisfaction with outward circumstances. For all these Meekness is the cure. For the difficulty of understanding this world, the secret is in meekness. There is no mystery in God's dealings to the meek man, for "the secret of the Lord is with them that fear Him, and He will show them His covenant;" there is no dread of God's judgments when our souls are meek.

The second cause of unrest is inward discord. We are going on in our selfishness. We stand, as Balaam stood, against the angel of the Lord, pressing on whilst the angel of Love stands against us. Just as the dove struggling against the storm, feeble and tired, is almost spent, until gradually, as if by inspiration, it has descended to the lower atmosphere, and so avoided the buffeting of the tempests above, and is then borne on by the wind of heaven in entire repose: like that is the rest of the soul. While we are unreconciled, the Love of God stands against us, and, by His Will, as long as man refuses to take up that yoke of His, he is full of discord; he is like the dove struggling with the elements aloft, as yet unconscious of the calm there is below. And you must make no compromise in taking up the burden of the Lord.

Lastly, unrest comes from dissatisfaction with outward circumstances. Part, perhaps the greater part, of our misery here, comes from over-estimation of ourselves. We are slaves to vanity and pride. We think we are not in the right station ; our genius has been misunderstood ; we have been slighted, we have been passed by, we have not been rewarded as we ought to have been. So long as we have this false opinion of ourselves, it is impossible for us to realize true rest.

Sinners in a world of love, encircling you round on every side, with blessings infinite upon infinite, and that again multiplied by infinity : God loves you : God fills you with enjoyment ! Unjustly, unfairly treated in this world of love ! Once let a man know for himself what God is, and then in that he will find peace. It will be the dawn of an everlasting day of calmness and serenity. I speak to some who have felt the darkness, the clouds, and the dreariness of life, whose affections have been blighted, who feel a discord and confusion in their being. To some to whom the world, lovely though it be, is such that they are obliged to say, " I see, I do not feel, how beautiful it is."

Brother men, there is Rest in Christ, because He is Love ; because His are the everlasting Verities of Humanity. God does not cease to be the God of Love because men are low, sad, and desponding. In the performance of duty, in meekness, in trust in God, is our rest—our only rest. It is not in understanding a set of doctrines ; not in an outward comprehension of the " scheme of salvation," that rest and peace are to be found, but in taking up in all lowliness and meekness, the yoke of the Lord Jesus Christ.

" For thus saith the high and lofty One that inhabiteth eternity, whose name is Holy ; I dwell in the high and holy place, with him also that is of a contrite and humble spirit, to revive the spirit of the humble, and to revive the heart of the contrite ones."

XXVI.

THE HUMANE SOCIETY.

(*A Sermon preached on its Behalf.*)

"While he yet spake, there came from the ruler of the synagogue's house certain which said, Thy daughter is dead: why troublest thou the Master any further?—As soon as Jesus heard the word that was spoken, he saith unto the ruler of the synagogue, Be not afraid, only believe.—— And he suffered no man to follow him, save Peter, and James, and John the brother of James.—And he cometh to the house of the ruler of the synagogue, and seeth the tumult, and them that wept and wailed greatly.—And when he was come in, he saith unto them, Why make ye this ado, and weep? the damsel is not dead, but sleepeth.—And they laughed him to scorn. But when he had put them all out, he taketh the father and the mother of the damsel, and them that were with him, and entereth in where the damsel was lying.—And he took the damsel by the hand, and said unto her, Talitha cumi; which is, being interpreted, Damsel, I say unto thee, arise.—And straightway the damsel arose, and walked; for she was of the age of twelve years. And they were astonished with a great astonishment.—And he charged them straitly that no man should know it; and commanded that something should be given her to eat."—Mark v. 35—43.

I PLEAD to-day for a society whose cause has not been advocated in this chapel for many years. It is now exactly ten years since a collection was made in Trinity Chapel for the Humane Society.

Its general objects, as everybody knows, are the preservation of the life of drowning persons, by precautions previously taken, and by subsequent remedies. But this vague statement being insufficient to awaken the interest which the Society deserves, I propose to consider it in its details, and to view these—as in the pulpit we are bound to do—from the peculiar Christian point of view.

It is remarkable that there is a Scripture passage which, point by point, offers a parallel to the work of this Society, and a special sanction and a precedent, both for its peculiar work and the spirit in which it is to be done. I shall consider—

I. This particular form of the Redeemer's work.
II. The spirit of the Redeemer's work.

I. We find among the many forms of His work—

1. Restoration from a special form of death—I cannot class this case with that of Lazarus.

The narrative seems to distinguish this from the other miracle. Christ says, "She is not dead, but sleepeth." Hence this particular case was one of restoration from apparent death. The other case was that of restoration from real death.

Here then is our first point of resemblance.

Before this Society was formed, persons apparently suffocated were left to perish. Myriads, doubtless, have died who might have been saved. But the idea of restoration was as far from them as from the friends of Jairus. They would have laughed the proposer "to scorn." But, Christlike, this Society came into the world with a strange message—revealed by science, but vitalized by love—a Christ-like message: "Be not afraid; he is not dead, but sleepeth."

Now the sphere of the Society's operations is thus defined :—" To preserve from premature death persons apparently dead from either drowning, hanging, lightning, cold, heat, noxious vapours, apoplexy, or intoxication." They are, consequently, large, taking cognizance not merely of cases of drowning only, but all of the same generic character —suspended animation, apparent death, asphyxia.

[Causes—foul air, in drains and brewers' vats, accidental hanging, mines, cellars, wells.]

In England their causes are more peculiarly extensive, because of our sea-girt shores, and because of the variable climate, which to-day leaves the ice firm, and to-morrow has made it rotten and unsafe.

2. Here was the recognition of the value of life. The force of the whole petition lay in one single consideration— " she shall live."

It has been often said that Christianity has enhanced the value of life, and our charitable societies are alleged in evidence ; our hospitals ; the increased average of human life, which has been the result of sanitary regulations and improvements in medical treatment. But this statement needs some qualification.

The value attached to life by the ancient Egyptian was quite as great as that attributed to it by the modern Englishman. When Abraham went into Egypt he found a people whose feeling of the sacredness of life was so great that they saw God wherever life was; and venerated the bull, and the fish, and the crocodile. To slay one of them was like murder.

And again : it could not be said that we owe to Christianity the recognition of the honour due to one who saves life. The most honourable of crowns was that presented to one who had saved the life of a Roman citizen.

Nay more : instead of peculiarly exalting the value of life, there is a sense in which Christianity depreciates it. " If a man hate not his own life he cannot be my disciple." The Son of Man came to be a sacrifice ; and it is the peculiar dignity of the Christian that he has a life to *give.*

Therefore we must distinguish.

It is not mere life on which Christianity has shed a richer value. It is by ennobling the purpose to which life is to be dedicated that it has made life more precious. A crowded metropolis, looked at merely as a mass of living beings, is no more dignified, and far more disgusting, than an ant-hill with its innumerable creeping lives. Looked on as a place in which each individual is a temple of the Holy Ghost, and every pang and joy of whom has in it something of infinitude, it becomes almost priceless in its value.

And again : Christianity differs from heathenism in this, that it has declared the dignity of the life of man—not merely that of certain classes. It has not "saved citizens," but saved *men.*

[Consider the worth of a single soul.]

Hence this is appropriately called the *Humane* Society, that word originally meaning human. It is no Brahminical association, abstaining from shedding animal blood and living on no animal food, but it recognizes the worth of a life in which God moves, and which Christ has redeemed.

It is human life, not animal, that it cares for. The life of man as man, not of some peculiar class of men.

3. We consider the Saviour's direction respecting the means of effecting complete recovery. He " commanded that something should be given her to eat."

Observe His reverential submission to the laws of nature. He did not suspend those laws. It did not seem to Him that where law was, God was not; or that the proof of God's agency was to be found only in the abrogation of law. He recognized the sanctity of those laws which make certain remedies and certain treatment indispensable to health.

[Sanitary regulations are as religious as a miracle.]

And in doing this He furnished a precedent singularly close for the operations of this Society. It is one great part of the object of its existence to spread a knowledge of the right methods of treatment in case of suspended animation. It has compiled and published rules for the treatment of the drowned, the apparently suffocated, and those struck by sudden apoplexy.

And consider the indirect results of this, as well as the direct.

Such cases occur unexpectedly. No medical aid is near. Friends are alarmed. Presence of mind is lost. The vulgar means resorted to from superstition and ignorance are almost incredible. But gradually the knowledge is spread through the country of what to do in cases of emergency. Many here would be prepared to act if a need arose. I have been present at such a case, and have seen life saved by arresting the rough treatment of ignorance acting traditionally. But in that and most cases, the knowledge had been gained from the publications of this Society.

An immense step is gained by the systematic direction of

attention to these matters. Every one ought to know what to do on a sudden emergency, a case of strangulation, of suffocation, or of apoplexy; and yet, this forming no definite part of the general plan of education, there are comparatively few who have the least idea what should be done before medical aid can be obtained. Probably, thousands would be helpless as a child, and human life would be sacrificed.

II. We consider the spirit of the Redeemer's work.

1. It was Love.

It was not reward—not even the reward of applause—which was the spring of beneficence in the Son of Man. He desired that it should be unknown. He did good because it was good. He relieved because it was the expression of His own exuberant loving-kindness.

2. It was a spirit of retiring modesty.

He did not wish that it should be known. But His disciples have made it known to the world.

Now observe first, the evidence here afforded of His real Humanity. Why did Christ wish to conceal, and the Apostles wish to publish abroad his miracles? Take the simple view, and all is plain. Christ, the *man*, with unaffected modesty, shrank from publicity and applause. The Apostles, with genuine human admiration, record the deed. But seek for some deeper and more mysterious reason, and at once the whole becomes a pantomime, an unreal transaction acted on this world's stage for effect, as though we should say that He was wishing to have it known, but for certain reasons He made as if He wished it to be concealed. Here, as usual, the simple is the sublime and true.

Observe, however, secondly :—

That publication by the Apostles sanctions and explains another part of this Society's operations. Its office is to observe, to record, and to reward acts of self-devotion. Certain scales of reward are given to one who risks his life to save life, to the surgeon whose skill restores life, to the publican who opens his house to receive the apparently dead body. And every year lists of names are published of those who have been thus distinguished by their humanity. The eyes of the Society are over all England, and no heroic act can pass unnoticed or unhonoured by them.

Now distinctly understand on what principle this is done. It is an apostolic office. It is precisely the principle on which the Apostles were appointed by God to record the acts and life of Christ. Was this for Christ's sake? Nay, it was for the world's good. That Sacrifice of Christ recorded, pronounced Divine, has been the spring and life of innumerable sacrifices and unknown self-devotion. ·

And so the rewards given by this Society are not given as recompense. Think you that a medal can pay self-devotion? or a few pounds liquidate the debt due to generosity? or even, that the thought of the reward would lead a man to plunge into the water to save life, who would not have plunged in without any hope of reward? No! —But it is good for the world to hear of what is generous and good. It is good to appropriate rewards to such acts, in order to set the standard. It is right that, in a country where enormous subscriptions are collected, and monuments are erected to men who have made fortunes by speculation, there should be some visible, tangible recognition of the worth and value of more generous deeds.

The medal over the fire-place of the poor fisherman is

to him a *title;* and, truer than most titles, it tells what has been *done.* It descends an heirloom to the family, saying to the children, Be brave, self-sacrificing, as your father was.

3. It was a spirit of perseverance.

They laughed Him to scorn, yet He persisted. Slow calm perseverance amidst ridicule.

In the progress of this Society we find again a parallel. When the idea of resuscitation was first promulgated, it was met with incredulity and ridicule. Even in 1773, when Dr. Hawes laid the first foundation of the Humane Society, it was with difficulty he could overcome the prejudice which existed against the idea, and he had to bear the whole cost of demonstrating the practicability of his theory. For one whole year he paid all the rewards and expenses himself, and then, attracted by the self-sacrificing ardour with which he had given himself up to the idea of rescuing human life, thirty-two gentlemen, his own and Dr. Cogan's friends, united together in furtherance of this benevolent design, and thus laid the foundation of the Humane Society.

Here note the attractive power of self-denying work : the Redeemer's Life and Death has been the living power of the world's work, of the world's life.

XXVII.

THREE TIMES IN A NATION'S HISTORY.

"And when he was come near, he beheld the city, and wept over it,
—Saying, If thou hadst known, even thou, at least in this thy day, the
things which belong unto thy peace! but now they are hid from thine
eyes.—For the days shall come upon thee, that thine enemies shall cast
a trench about thee, and compass thee round, and keep thee in on every
side,—And shall lay thee even with the ground, and thy children within
thee; and they shall not leave in thee one stone upon another; because
thou knewest not the time of thy visitation."—Luke xix. 41—44.

THE event of which we have just read took place in the
last year of our Redeemer's life. For nearly four years
He had been preaching the Gospel. His pilgrim life was
drawing to a close ; yet no one looking at the outward
circumstances of that journey would have imagined that He
was on His way to die. It was far more like a triumphal
journey, for a rejoicing multitude heralded His way to
Jerusalem with shouts—" Hosanna to the Son of David."
He trod, too, a road green with palm branches, and strewn
with their garments ; and yet in the midst of all this joy,
as if rejoicing were not for Him, the Man of Sorrows paused
to weep.

There is something significant and characteristic in that
peculiar tone of melancholy which pervaded the Redeemer's
intercourse with man. We read of but one occasion on
which he rejoiced, and then only in spirit. He did not

shrink from occasions of human joy, for he attended the marriage feast; yet even there the solemn remark, apparently out of place, was heard—" Mine hour is not yet come." There was in Him that peculiarity which we find more or less in all the purest, most thoughtful minds—a shade of melancholy; much of sadness; though none of austerity. For, after all, when we come to look at this life of ours, whatever may be its outward appearance, in the depths of it there is great seriousness; the externalities of it may seem to be joy and brightness, but in the deep beneath there is a strange, stern aspect. It may be that the human race is on its way to good, but the victory hitherto gained is so small that we can scarcely rejoice over it. It may be that human nature is progressing, but that progress has been but slowly making, through years and centuries of blood. And therefore contemplating all this, and penetrating beyond the time of the present joy, the Redeemer wept, not for Himself, but for that devoted city.

He was then on the Mount of Olives; beneath Him there lay the metropolis of Judea, with the Temple in full sight; the towers and the walls of Jerusalem flashing back the brightness of an Oriental sky. The Redeemer knew that she was doomed, and therefore with tears He pronounced her coming fate: " The days shall come that thine enemies shall cast a trench about thee, and shall not leave in thee one stone upon another." These words, which rang the funeral knell of Jerusalem, tell out in our ears this day a solemn lesson; they tell us that in the history of nations, and also, it may be, in the personal history of individuals, there are Three Times,—a time of grace, a time of blindness, and a time of judgment.

This then, is our subject,—the Three Times in a Nation's

history. When the Redeemer spake, it was for Jerusalem the time of blindness ; the time of grace was past ; that of judgment was to come.

We take these three in order : first, the time of grace. We find it expressed here in three different modes : first, "in this thy day ;" then, "the things which belong to thy peace ;" and thirdly, "the time of thy visitation." And from this we understand the meaning of a time of grace ; it was Jerusalem's time of opportunity. The time in which the Redeemer appeared was that in which faith was almost worn out. He found men with their faces turned backward to the past, instead of forward to the future. They were as children clinging to the garments of a relation they have lost ; life there was not, faith there was not—only the garments of a past belief. He found them groaning under the dominion of Rome ; rising up against it, and thinking it their worst evil.

The coldest hour of all the night is that which immediately precedes the dawn, and in that darkest hour of Jerusalem's night her Light beamed forth ; her Wisest and Greatest came in the midst of her, almost unknown, born under the law, to emancipate those who were groaning under the law. His Life, the day of His preaching, was Jerusalem's time of grace. During that time the Redeemer spake the things which belonged to her peace : those things were few and simple. He found her people mourning under political degradation. He told them that political degradation does not degrade the man ; the only thing that can degrade a man is slavery to sin. He told men who were looking merely to the past, no longer to look thither and say that Abraham was their father, for that God could raise up out of those stones children to Abraham, and a greater than Abraham was there. He told them also not to look for some future deliverer, for deliverance was already come. They asked Him when the Kingdom of God should come; He told them they were not to cry, Lo here! or, lo there! for the Kingdom of God was within;—that they were to begin the Kingdom of God now, by each man becoming individually more holy, that if each man so reformed his own soul, the reformation of the kingdom would soon spread around them. They came to Him complaining of the Roman tribute; He asked for a piece of money, and said, " Render unto Cæsar the things that be Cæsar's, and to God the things that be God's; "—plainly telling them that the bondage from which men were to be delivered was not an earthly, but a spiritual bondage. He drew the distinction sharply between happiness and blessedness—the two things are opposite, although not necessarily contrary—He told them, " Blessed are the meek! Blessed are the poor in spirit!" The mourning man, and the poor man, and the persecuted man,—these were not happy, if happiness consists in the gratification of all our desires; but they were blessed beyond all earthly blessedness, for happiness is but the contentment of desire, while blessedness is the satisfaction of those aspirations which have God alone for their end and aim.

All these things were rejected by the nation. They were rejected first by the priests. They knew not that the mind of the age in which they lived was in advance of the traditional Judaism, and, therefore, they looked upon the Redeemer as an irreverent, ungodly man, a Sabbath-breaker. He was rejected by the rulers, who did not understand that in righteousness alone are governments to subsist, and, therefore, when He demanded of them justice, mercy, truth, they

looked upon Him as a revolutionizer. He was rejected likewise by the people—that people ever ready to listen to any
demagogue promising them earthly grandeur. They who on
this occasion called out, " Hosanna to the Son of David,"
and were content to do so, so long as they believed He
intended to lead them to personal comfort and enjoyment,
afterwards cried out, " Crucify Him ! crucify him ! " " His
blood be on us, and on our children; " so that His rejection
was the act of the whole nation. Now, respecting this day of
grace we have two remarks to make.

First : In this Advent of the Redeemer there was
nothing outwardly remarkable to the men of that day. It
was almost nothing. Of all the historians of that period few,
indeed, are found to mention it. This is a thing which we
at this day can scarcely understand ; for to us the blessed
Advent of our Lord is the brightest page in the world's
history : but to them it was far otherwise. Remember for
one moment, what the Advent of our Lord was to all outward
appearance. He seemed, let it be said reverently, to the
rulers of those days, a fanatical freethinker. They heard of
His miracles, but they appeared nothing remarkable to
them ; there was nothing there on which to fasten their
attention. They heard that some of the populace had been
led away, and now and then, it may be, some of His words
reached their ears, but to them they were hard to be understood—full of mystery, or else they roused every evil passion
in their hearts, so stern and uncompromising was the morality
they taught. They put aside these words in that brief period,
and the day of grace passed.

And just such as this is God's visitation to us. Generally,
the day of God's visitation is not a day very remarkable outwardly. Bereavements, sorrows—no doubt, in these God

speaks; but there are other occasions far more quiet and unobtrusive, but which are yet plainly days of grace. A scruple which others do not see, a doubt coming into the mind respecting some views held sacred by the popular creed; a sense of heart loneliness and solitariness, a feeling of awful misgiving when the Future lies open before us, the dread feeling of an eternal godlessness, for men who are living godless lives now,—these silent moments unmarked, these are the moments in which the Eternal is speaking to our souls.

Once more, that day of Jerusalem's visitation—her day of grace—was short. It was narrowed up into the short space of three years and a half. After that, God still pleaded with individuals; but the national cause, as a cause, was gone. Jerusalem's doom was sealed when He pronounced those words. Again there is a lesson, a principle for us: God's day of visitation is frequently short. A few actions often decide the destiny of individuals, because they give a destination and form to habits; they settle the tone and form of the mind from which there will be in this life no alteration. So it is in the earliest history of our species. In those mysterious chapters at the commencement of the book of Genesis, we are told that it was one act which sealed the destiny of Adam and of all the human race. What was it but a very few actions, done in a very short time, that settled the destiny of those nations through which the children of Israel passed on their way to Canaan? The question for them was simply, whether they would show Israel mercy or not; this was all.

Once more, we see it again in the case of Saul. One circumstance, or at the most, two, marked out his destiny. Then came those solemn words, "The strength of Israel cannot lie nor repent. The Lord hath rent the kingdom from thee this day." From that hour his course was downwards, his day of grace was past.

Brethren, the truth is plain. The day of visitation is awfully short. We say not that God *never* pleads a long time, but we say this, that sometimes God speaks to a nation or to a man but once. If not heard then, His Voice is heard no more.

We pass on now to consider Israel's day of blindness. Judicial blindness is of a twofold character. It may be produced by removing the light, or by incapacitating the eye to receive that light. Sometimes men do not see because there is no light for them to see; and this was what was done to Israel—the Saviour was taken away from her. The voice of the Apostles declared this truth : " It was necessary that the word should first have been spoken to you ; but seeing ye put it from you, and judge yourselves unworthy of everlasting life, lo, we turn to the Gentiles."

There is a way of blindness by hardening the heart. Let us not conceal this truth from ourselves. God blinds the eye, but it is in the appointed course of His providential dealings. If a man *will not* see, the law is he *shall* not see ; if he will not *do* what is right when he knows the right, then right shall become to him wrong, and wrong shall seem to be right. We read that God hardened Pharaoh's heart; that He blinded Israel. It is impossible to look at these cases of blindness without perceiving in them something of Divine action. Even at the moment when the Romans were at their gates, Jerusalem still dreamed of security ; and when the battering-ram was at the tower of Antonia, the priests were celebrating, in fancied safety, their daily sacrifices. From the moment when our Master spake, there was deep stillness over her until her destruction; like the strange and unnatural stillness before the thunder-storm, when every breath seems hushed, and every leaf may be almost heard moving in the motionless air ; and all this calm and stillness is but the prelude to the moment when the east and west are lighted up with the red flashes, and the whole creation seems to reel. Such was the blindness of that nation which would not know the day of her visitation.

We pass on now to consider lastly, her day of judgment. Her beautiful morning was clouded, her sun had gone down in gloom, and she was left in darkness. The account of the siege is one of the darkest passages in Roman history. In the providence of God, the history of that belongs, not to a Christian, but to a Jew. We all know the account that he has given us of the eleven hundred thousand who perished in that siege, of the thousands crucified along the sea-shore. We have all heard of the two factions that divided the city, of the intense hatred that made the cruelty of Jew towards Jew more terrible than even the vengeance of the Romans. This was the destruction of Jerusalem— the day of her ruin.

And now brethren, let us observe, this judgment came in the way of natural consequences. We make a great mistake respecting judgments. God's judgments are not arbitrary, but the results of natural laws. The historians tell us that Jerusalem owed her ruin to the fanaticism and obstinate blindness of her citizens; from all of which her Redeemer came to emancipate her. Had they understood, " Blessed are the poor in spirit," "Blessed are the meek," and "Blessed are the peace-makers ;" had they understood that, Jerusalem's day of ruin might never have come.

Now let us apply this to the day we are at present celebrating. We all know that this destruction of Jerusalem is connected with the second coming of Christ. In St. Matthew the two advents are so blended together, that it is hard to separate one from the other; nay rather, it is impossible, because we have our Master's words, "Verily, I say unto you, this generation shall not pass till all be fulfilled." Therefore this prophecy, in all its fulness, came to pass in the destruction of Jerusalem. But it is impossible to look at it without perceiving there is also something farther included; we shall understand it by turning to the elucidation given by our Lord Himself. When the Apostles asked, Where shall all these things be? His reply was, in effect, this: Ask you where? I tell you nowhere in particular, or rather, everywhere; for wheresoever there is corruption, there will be destruction—"where the carcase is, thither will the eagles be gathered together." So that this first coming of the Son of Man to judgment was the type, the specimen of what shall be hereafter.

And now brethren, let us apply this subject still more home. Is there no such thing as blindness among ourselves? May not this be *our* day of visitation? First, there is among us priestly blindness; the blindness of men who know not that the demands of this age are in advance of those that have gone before. There is no blindness greater than that of those who think that the panacea for the evils of a country is to be found in ecclesiastical union. But let us not be mistaken: it is not here, we think, that the great danger lies. We dread not Rome. No man can understand the signs of the times, who does not feel that the day of Rome is passing away, as that of Jerusalem once did. But the danger lies in this consideration,—we find that where the doctrines of Rome have been at all successful, it has been among the clergy and upper classes; while, when presented to the middle and lower classes, they have been at once rejected. There is then, apparently, a gulf between the two. If there be added to the difference of position a still further and deeper difference of religion, then who shall dare to say what the end shall be?

Once more, we look at the blindness of men talking of intellectual enlightenment. It is true that we have more enlightened civilization and comfort. What then? will that retard our day of judgment? Jerusalem was becoming more enlightened, and Rome was at its most civilized point, when the destroyer was at their gates.

Therefore, let us know the day of our visitation. It is not the day of refinement, nor of political liberty, nor of advancing intellect. We must go again in the old, old way; we must return to simpler manners and to a purer life. We want more faith, more love. The Life of Christ and the Death of Christ must be made the law of our life. Reject that, and we reject our own salvation; and, in rejecting that, we bring on in rapid steps, for the nation and for ourselves, the day of judgment and of ruin.

XXVIII

INSPIRATION.

"We then that are strong ought to bear the infirmities of the weak, and not to please ourselves.—Let every one of us please his neighbour for his good to edification.—For even Christ pleased not himself; but, as it is written, The reproaches of them that reproached thee fell on me. —For whatsoever things were written aforetime were written for our learning, that we through patience and comfort of the Scriptures might have hope."—Romans xv. 1—4.

WE will endeavour, brethren, to search the connection between the different parts of these verses.

First, the Apostle lays down a Christian's duty—"Let every one of us please his neighbour for his good to edification." After that he brings forward as the sanction of that duty, the spirit of the Life of Christ—"For even Christ pleased not Himself." Next, he adds an illustration of that principle by a quotation from Psalm lxix. :—"It is written, The reproaches of them that reproached thee fell on me." Lastly, he explains and defends that application of the psalm, as if he had said, "I am perfectly justified in applying that passage to Christ, for 'whatsoever things were written aforetime were written for our learning.'"

So that in this quotation, and the defence of it as contained in these verses, we have the principle of Apostolical interpretation; we have the principle upon which the Apostles used the Old Testament Scriptures, and we are enabled to understand their view of inspiration. This is one of the most important considerations upon which we can be at this moment engaged. It is the deepest question of our day; the one which lies beneath all others, and in comparison of which the questions just now agitating the popular mind—whether of Papal jurisdiction or varieties of Church doctrine in our own communion—are but super-ficial : it is this grand question of Inspiration which is given to this age to solve.

Our subject will break itself up into questions such as these—What the Bible is, and what the Bible is not? What is meant by inspiration? Whether inspiration is the same thing as infallibility? When God inspired the minds, did He dictate the words? Does the inspiration of men mean the infallibility of their words? Is inspiration the same as dicta-tion? Whether, granting that we have the Word of God, we have also the words of God? Are the operations of the Holy Spirit inspiring men, compatible with partial error, as His operations in sanctifying them are compatible with partial evil? How are we to interpret and apply the Scrip-tures? Is Scripture, as the Romanists say, so unintelligible and obscure that we cannot understand it without having the guidance of an infallible Church? Or is it, as some fanciful Protestants will tell us, a book upon which all ingenuity may be used to find Christ in every sentence? Upon these things there are many views, some of them false, some superstitious ; but it is not our business now to deal with these ; our way is rather to teach positively than negatively : we will try to set up the truth, and error may fall before it.

The Collect for this day leads us to the special considera-tion of Holy Scripture ; we shall therefore take this for our subject, and endeavour to understand what was the Apostolical principle of Interpretation.

In the text we find two principles : first, that Scripture is of universal application ;

And second, that all the lines of Scripture converge towards Jesus Christ.

First, then, there is here an universal application of Scripture. This passage quoted by the Apostle is from the sixtyninth Psalm. That was evidently spoken by David of himself. From first to last, no unprejudiced mind can detect a conception in the writer's mind of an application to Christ, or to any other person after him ; the psalmist is there full of himself and his own sorrows. It is a natural and touching exposition of human grief and a good man's trust. Nevertheless, you will observe that St. Paul extends the use of these words, and applies them to Jesus Christ. Nay, more than that, he uses them as belonging to all Christians; for, he says, " whatsoever things were written aforetime, were written for our learning." Now this principle will be more evident if we state it in the words of Scripture, " Knowing that no prophecy of Scripture is of any private interpretation:" those holy men spake not their own limited individual feelings, but as feeling that they were inspired by the Spirit of God. Their words belonged to the whole of our common Humanity. No prophecy of the Scriptures is of any private interpretation. Bear in mind that the word prophecy does not mean what we now understand by it—merely prediction of future events—in the Scriptures it signifies inspired teaching. The teaching of the prophets was by no means always prediction. Bearing this in mind, let us remember that the Apostle says it is of no private interpretation. Had the Psalm applied only to David, then it would have been of private interpretation

—it would have been special, limited, particular; it would have belonged to an individual ; instead of which, it belongs to Humanity. Take again the subject of which we spoke last Sunday—the prophecy of the destruction of Jerusalem. Manifestly that was spoken originally at Jerusalem ; in a manner it seemed limited to Jerusalem, for its very name was mentioned ; and besides, as we read this morning, our Saviour says, "This generation shall not pass until all be fulfilled."

But had the prophecy ended there, then you would still have had prophecy, but it would have been of private—that is, peculiar, limited—interpretation; whereas our Redeemer's principle was this : that this doom pronounced on Jerusalem was universally applicable, that it was but a style and specimen of God's judgments. The judgment coming of the Son of Man takes place wherever there is evil grown ripe, whenever corruption is complete. And the gathering of the Roman eagles is but a specimen of the way in which judgment at last overtakes every city, every country and every man in whom evil has reached the point where there is no possibility of cure.

So that the prophecy belongs to all ages, from the destruction of Jerusalem to the end of the world. The words of St. Matthew are universally applicable. For Scripture deals with principles; not with individuals, but rather with states of humanity. Promises and threatenings are made to individuals, because they are in a particular state of character ; but they belong to all who are in that state, for "God is no respecter of persons."

First, we will take an instance of the state of blessing.

There was blessing pronounced to Abraham, in which it will be seen how large a grasp on Humanity this view of

Scripture gave to St. Paul. The whole argument in the Epistle to the Romans is, that the promises made to Abraham were not to his person, but to his faith ; and thus the Apostle says, " They who are of faith, are blessed with faithful Abraham."

We will now take the case of curse or threatening. Jonah, by Divine command, went through Nineveh, proclaiming its destruction ; but that prophecy belonged to the state in which Nineveh was ; it was true only while it remained in that state ; and therefore, as they repented, and their state was thus changed, the prophecy was left unfulfilled. From this we perceive the largeness and grandeur of Scripture interpretation. In the Epistle to the Corinthians, we find the Apostle telling of the state of the Jews in their passage towards the Promised Land, their state of idolatry and gluttony, and then he proceeds to pronounce the judgments that fell upon them, adding that he tells us this not merely as a matter of history, but rather as an illustration of a principle. They are specimens of eternal, unalterable Law. So that whosoever shall be in the state of these Jews, whosoever shall imitate them, the same judgments must fall upon them, the same satiety and weariness, the same creeping of the inward serpent polluting all their feelings ; and therefore he says, " All these things happened unto them for ensamples." Again he uses the same principle, not as a private, but a general application ; for, he says, " There hath no temptation taken you but such as is common to man."

We will take now another case, applied not to nations, but to individuals. In Hebrews xiii. we find these words from the Old Testament, " I will never leave thee, nor forsake thee ; " and there the Apostle's inference is that we may boldly say, "The Lord is my helper, I will not fear what men shall do unto me." Now, when we refer to Scripture, we shall find that this was a promise originally made to Jacob. The Apostle does not hesitate to take that promise and appropriate it to all Christians; for it was made, not to Jacob as a person, but to the state in which Jacob was; it was made to all who, like Jacob, are wanderers and pilgrims in the world; it was made to all whom sin has rendered outcasts and who are longing to return. The promises made to the meek belong to Meekness; the promises made to the humble belong to Humility.

And this it is which makes this Bible, not only a blessed Book, but *our* Book. It is this universal applicability of Scripture which has made the influence of the Bible universal: this book has held spell-bound the hearts of nations, in a way in which no single book has ever held men before. Remember too, in order to enhance the marvellousness of this, that the nation from which it emanated was a despised people. For the last eighteen hundred years the Jews have been proverbially a by-word and a reproach. But that contempt for Israel is nothing new to the world, for before even the Roman despised them, the Assyrian and Egyptian regarded them with scorn. Yet the words which came from Israel's prophets have been the life-blood of the world's devotions. And the teachers, the psalmists, the prophets, and the lawgivers of this despised nation spoke out truths that have struck the key-note of the heart of man; and this, not because they were of Jewish, but just because they were of universal application.

This collection of books has been to the world what no other book has ever been to a nation. States have been founded on its principles. Kings rule by a compact based on it. Men hold the Bible in their hands when they prepare to give solemn evidence affecting life, death, or property; the sick man is almost afraid to die unless the Book be within reach of his hands; the battle-ship goes into action with one on board whose office is to expound it; its prayers, its psalms are the language which we use when we speak to God; eighteen centuries have found no holier, no diviner language. If ever there has been a prayer or a hymn enshrined in the heart of a nation, you are sure to find its basis in the Bible. There is no new religious idea given to the world, but it is merely the development of something given in the Bible. The very translation of it has fixed language and settled the idioms of speech. Germany and England speak as they speak because the Bible was translated. It has made the most illiterate peasant more familiar with the history, customs, and geography of ancient Palestine than with the localities of his own country. Men who know nothing of the Grampians, of Snowdon, or of Skiddaw, are at home in Zion, the lake of Gennesareth, or among the rills of Carmel. People who know little about London, know by heart the places in Jerusalem where those blessed feet trod which were nailed to the Cross. Men who know nothing of the architecture of a Christian cathedral can yet tell you all about the pattern of the Holy Temple. Even this shows us the influence of the Bible. The orator holds a thousand men for half an hour breathless—a thousand men as one, listening to his single word. But this Word of God has held a thousand nations for thrice a thousand years spell-bound; held them by an abiding power, even the universality of its truth; and we feel it to be no more a collection of books, but *the* Book.

We pass on now to consider the second principle contained in these words, which is, that all Scripture bears towards Jesus Christ. St. Paul quotes these Jewish words as fulfilled in Christ. Jesus of Nazareth is the central point in which all the converging lines of Scripture meet. Again we state this principle in Scripture language : in the book of Revelation we find it written, " The testimony of Jesus is the spirit of prophecy," that is, the sum and substance of prophecy; the very spirit of Scripture is to bear testimony to Jesus Christ. We must often have been surprised and perplexed at the way in which the Apostles quote passages in reference to Christ, which originally had no reference to Him. In our text, for instance, David speaks only of himself, and yet St. Paul refers it to Christ. Let us understand this. We have already said that Scripture deals not with individuals, but with states and principles. Promises belong to persons only so far as they are what they are taken to be ; and consequently all unlimited promises made to individuals so far as they are referred merely to those individuals, are necessarily exaggerated and hyperbolical. They can only be true of One in whom that is fulfilled which was unfulfilled in them.

We will take an instance. We are all familiar with the well-known prophecy of Balaam. We all remember the magnificent destinies he promised to the people whom he was called to curse. Those promises have never been fulfilled, neither from the whole appearance of things does it seem likely that they ever will be fulfilled in their literal sense. To whom then, are they made ? To Israel ? Yes ; so far as they developed God's own conception. Balaam says, " God hath not beheld iniquity in Jacob, neither hath He seen perverseness in Israel." Is this the character of

Israel, an idolatrous and rebellious nation? Spoken of the literal Israel, this prophecy is false; but it was not false of that spotlessness and purity of which Israel was the temporal and imperfect type. If one can be found of whom that description is true, of whom we can say the Lord hath not beheld iniquity in him, to him then that prophecy belongs.

Brethren, Jesus of Nazareth is that pure and spotless One. Christ is perfectly, all that every saint was partially. To Him belongs all: all that description of a perfect character, which would be exaggeration if spoken of others, and to this character the blessing belongs; hence it is that all the fragmentary representations of character collect and centre in Him alone. Therefore, the Apostle says, "It was added until the seed should come to whom the promise was made." Consequently St. Paul would not read the Psalm as spoken only of David. Were the lofty aspirations, the purity and humbleness expressed in the text, true of him, poor, sinful, erring David? These were the expressions of the Christ within his heart—the longing of the Spirit of God within Him; but they were no proper representation of the spirit of his life, for there is a marvellous difference between a man's ideal and his actual—between the man and the book he writes—a difference between the aspirations within the man and the character which is realized by his daily life. The promises are to the Christ within David; therefore they are applied to the Christ when He comes. Now, let us extract from that this application.

Brethren, Scripture is full of Christ. From Genesis to Revelation everything breathes of Him, not every letter of every sentence, but the spirit of every chapter. It is full of Christ, but not in the way that some suppose; for there is nothing more miserable, as specimens of perverted ingenuity, than the attempts of certain commentators and preachers, to find remote, and recondite, and intended allusions to Christ everywhere. For example, they chance to find in the construction of the temple the fusion of two metals, and this they conceive is meant to show the union of Divinity with Humanity in Christ. If they read of coverings to the tabernacle, they find implied the doctrine of imputed righteousness. If it chance that one of the curtains of the tabernacle be red, they see in that a prophecy of the blood of Christ. If they are told that the Kingdom of Heaven is a pearl of great price, they will see in it the allusion—that, as a pearl is the production of animal suffering, so the Kingdom of Heaven is produced by the sufferings of the Redeemer. I mention this perverted mode of comment, because it is not merely harmless, idle, and useless ; it is positively dangerous. This is to make the Holy Spirit speak riddles and conundrums, and the interpretation of Scripture but clever riddle-guessing. Putting aside all this childishness, we say that the Bible is full of Christ. Every unfulfilled aspiration of Humanity in the past ; all partial representation of perfect character ; all sacrifices, nay even those of idolatry, point to the fulfilment of what we want, the answer to every longing—the type of perfect Humanity, the Lord Jesus Christ.

Get the habit—a glorious one—of referring all to Christ. How did He feel?—think?—act? So then must I feel, and think, and act. Observe how Christ was a living reality in St. Paul's mind. "Should I please myself?" "For even Christ pleased not Himself." "It is more blessed to give than to receive."

XXIX

THE LAST UTTERANCES OF CHRIST.

"When Jesus therefore had received the vinegar, he said, It is finished: and he bowed his head, and gave up the ghost."—John xix. 30.

THERE are seven dying sentences of our Lord's recorded in the Gospels; one recorded conjointly by St. Matthew and St. Mark, three recorded by St. Luke, and three by St. John. That recorded by the first two Evangelists is, "My God, my God, why hast thou forsaken me?" Those preserved by St. Luke only are, "Verily, I say unto thee, to-day shalt thou be with me in Paradise;" "Father, forgive them, for they know not what they do;" and, "Father, into Thy hands I commend my spirit." The three recorded by St. John are these—"I thirst;" "Behold thy mother; behold thy son;" and lastly, "It is finished." And these seven group themselves into two divisions: we perceive that some of them are the utterances of personal feeling, and others are the utterances of sympathy for others.

These are therefore, the two divisions of our subject to-day—First. The natural exclamations of the Man. Secondly. The utterances of the Saviour.

The first of those which we class under the exclamations of the Man, referring to His personal feelings, is, "I thirst;" in answer to which they gave Him vinegar to drink. Now upon first reading this, we are often tempted to suppose, from the unnatural character of the draught, that an insult was intended; and therefore we rank this among the taunts and fearful sufferings which he endured at His crucifixion. But as we become acquainted with Oriental history, we discover that this vinegar was the common drink of the Roman army, their wine, and therefore was the most likely to be at hand when in the company of soldiers, as He then was. Let it be borne in mind that a draught was twice offered to him; once it was accepted, once it was refused. That which was refused was the medicated potion—wine mingled with myrrh—the intention of which was to deaden pain, and therefore when it was presented to the Saviour it was rejected. And the reason commonly assigned for that seems to be the true one: the Son of Man would not meet death in a state of stupefaction, He chose to meet His God awake.

There are two modes in which pain may be struggled with—through the flesh, and through the spirit; the one is the office of the physician, the other that of the Christian. The physician's care is at once to deaden pain either by insensibility or specifics; the Christian's object is to deaden pain by patience. We dispute not the value of the physician's remedies, in their way they are permissible and valuable; but yet let it be observed that in these there is nothing moral; they may take away the venom of the serpent's sting, but they do not give the courage to plant the foot upon the serpent's head, and to bear the pain without flinching. Therefore the Redeemer refused, because it was not through the flesh, but through the Spirit, that He would conquer; to have accepted the anodyne would have been to escape from suffering, but not to conquer it. But the vinegar or sour wine was accepted as a refreshing draught, for it would seem that He did not look upon the value of the suffering as consisting in this, that He should make it as exquisite as possible, but rather that he should not suffer one drop of the cup of agony which His Father had put into His hand to trickle down the side untasted. Neither would He make to Himself one drop more of suffering than His Father had given.

There are books on the value of pain; they tell us that if of two kinds of food the one is pleasant and the other nauseous, we are to choose the nauseous one. Let a lesson on this subject be learnt from the divine example of our Master.

To suffer pain for others without flinching, that is our Master's example; but pain for the mere sake of pain, that is not Christian; to accept poverty in order to do good for others, that is our Saviour's principle; but to become poor for the sake and the merit of being poor, is but selfishness after all. Our Lord refused the anodyne that would have made the cup untasted which His Father had put into His hand to drink, but He would not taste one drop more than His Father gave Him. Yet He did not refuse the natural solace which His Father's hand had placed before Him.

There are some who urge most erroneously the doctrine of discipline and self-denial. If of two ways one is disagreeable, they will choose it, just because it is disagreeable; because food is pleasant and needful, they will fast. There is in this a great mistake. To deny self for the sake of duty is right—to sacrifice life and interests rather than principle is right; but self-denial for the mere sake of self-denial, torture for torture's sake, is neither good nor Christ-like. Remember, He drank the cooling beverage in the very moment of the Sacrifice; the value of which did not consist in its being made as intensely painful as possible, but in His not flinching from the pain, when Love and Duty said, Endure.

His second exclamation was, " My God, my God, why hast Thou forsaken me ? " We will not dive into the deep mysteries of that expression—we will not pretend to be wiser than what is written, endeavouring to comprehend where the Human is mingled with the Divine—we will take the matter simply as it stands. It is plain from this expression that the Son of God *felt* as if He had been deserted by His Father. We know that He was not deserted by Him, or else God had denied Himself, after saying, " This is my beloved Son, in whom I am well pleased." And they who maintain that this was real desertion, attribute that to the Lord of Love which can alone belong to Judas—the desertion of innocence— therefore we conclude that it arose from the infirmities of our Master's innocent human nature. It was the darkening of His human soul, not the hiding of God's countenance. He was worn, faint, and exhausted ; His body was hanging from four lacerated wounds ; and more than that, there was much to perplex the Redeemer's human feelings, for He was suffering there, the innocent for the guilty. For once God's law seemed reversed ; and then came the human cry, " My God, my God, why hast Thou forsaken me ? "

And now brethren, observe in this, that it arose apparently from the connection of the Redeemer's death with sin. When the death-struggle of the flesh begins, and we first become aware of the frailty of our Humanity, then the controversy of God with the soul is felt to be real by reason of our consciousness of sin ; then is felt, as it were, the immense gulf that separates between the pure and the impure. In the case of the Son of Man this was, of course, impossible ; consciousness of sin He had none, for He had no sin ; but there was a connection, so to speak, between the death of Christ and sin, for the Apostle says, " In that He died, He died unto sin once." "He died unto sin ;" there was a connection between His death and sin, though it was not His own sin, but the sin of the whole world. In that moment of the apparent victory of evil, the Redeemer's spirit, as it would appear, felt a darkness similar to ours when sin has hidden our consciousness of God. When death is merely natural, we can feel that the hand of God is there ; but when man interferes, and the hand of God is invisible, and that of man is alone seen, then all seems dark and uncertain. The despondency of the Redeemer was not supernatural, but most natural darkness. The words He used were not His own, but David's words ; and this proclaims that suffering such as He was then bearing, had been borne before Him—the difference was in degree, not in kind. The idea of piety struggling with, and victorious over, evil had been exhibited on earth before. The idea was imperfectly exhibited in the sufferings of Israel regarded as typical of Christ. In Christ alone is it perfectly presented. So also that wondrous chapter, the fifty-third of Isaiah, justly describing both, belongs in its entireness to Christ : He therefore adopted these words as His own.

The last personal ejaculation of our Redeemer was, " Father, into Thy hands I commend my spirit." We take this in connection with the preceding ; for if we do not, the two will be unintelligible, but taking them together, it becomes plain that the darkness of the Redeemer's mind was but momentary. For a moment the Redeemer felt alone and deserted, and then, in the midst of it, He cried out, " Father, into Thy hands I commend my spirit." In that moment He realized His inseparable union with the Father.

And now I would observe, if I may do it without being misunderstood, that the Redeemer speaks as if not knowing where He was going—"Into Thy hands," that is sufficient. It is as well to look at these things as simply as possible. Do not confuse the mind with attempting to draw the distinction between the human and the Divine. He speaks here as if His human soul, like ours, entered into the dark unknown, not seeing what was to be in the Hereafter : and this is Faith, or, if it were not so, there arises an idea from which we shrink, as if He were speaking words He did not feel. We know nothing of the world beyond, we are like children ; even revelation has told us almost nothing concerning this, and an inspired Apostle says, "We know not yet what we shall be." Then rises Faith, and dares to say, "My Father, I know nothing, but, be where I may, still I am with Thee." "Into Thy hands I commend my spirit." Therefore, and only therefore, do we dare to die.

We pass on, secondly, to the consideration of those utterances which our Master spake as the Saviour of the world. The first is, "Father, forgive them, for they know not what they do." From this expression we infer two things : first, that sin needs forgiveness ; and, secondly, that forgiveness can be granted.

Sin needs forgiveness, or the Redeemer would not have so prayed. That it needs forgiveness we also prove, from the fact that it always connects itself with penalty. Years may separate the present from your past misconduct, but the remembrance of it remains ; nay more than that, even those errors which we did ignorantly, carry with them their retribution ; and from this we collect the fact that even errors, failures in judgment, need God's forgiveness. Another proof that sin needs pardon is from the testimony of conscience. In all men it speaks, in some in but a feeble whisper, in others with an irregular sound, now a lull, and then a storm of recollection; in others, conscience is as a low perpetual knell, ever sounding, telling of the death going on within, proclaiming that the past has been accursed, the present withered, and that the future is one vast terrible blank.

In these several forms, Conscience tells us also that the sin has been committed against our Father. The permanence of all our acts, the eternal consequences of every small thing done by man, all point to God as the One against whom the sin is committed; and, therefore, that Voice still speaks, though the thing we have done never can be undone. The other thing that we learn from that utterance of Christ is, that the pardon of sin is a thing possible, for the utterance of Christ was the expression of the Voice of God—it was but another form of the Father saying, "I can and I will forgive."

Remark here a condition imposed by Christ on the Divine forgiveness when He taught His disciples to pray. "If ye forgive men from your hearts, your Father will forgive you; but if ye do not forgive, neither will your Father which is in heaven forgive you." It is natural to forgive on a dying bed; yet that forgiveness is only making a merit of necessity, for we can revenge ourselves no more. There is abundance of good-natured charity abroad in the world; that charity which is indiscriminating. It may co-exist with the resentment of personal injury, but the spirit of forgiveness which we must have before we can be forgiven, can be ours only so far as our life is a representative of the life of Christ. Then it is possible for us to realize God's forgiveness.

The second utterance which our Lord spake for others rather than Himself was, "To-day shalt thou be with me in Paradise."

Now, what we have here to observe on is the law of personal influence; the dying hour of Christ had an influence over one thief, he became converted. The first thing we remark is, that indirect influence often succeeds where direct influence has failed. Thus, when the Redeemer selected His disciples, and endeavoured to teach them His truth, that was direct influence; but when He prayed for them, and those disciples heard Him, and then came to Him with this petition, "Lord, teach us to pray," that was indirect influence; and so in this instance, while praying for Himself, He did influence the mind of the dying thief, though that influence was indirect. Indirect influence is often far more successful than that which is direct; and for this reason—the direct aims that we make to convert others may be contradicted by our lives, while the indirect influence is our very life. What we really are, somehow or other, will ooze out, in tone, in look, in act, and this tells upon those who come in daily contact with us. The law of personal influence is mysterious. The influence of the Son of God told on the one thief, not on the other; it softened and touched the hearts of two of His hearers, but it only hardened others. There is much to be learnt from this, for some are disposed to write bitter things against themselves because their influence on earth has failed. Let all such remember that some are too pure to act universally on others. If our influence has failed, the Redeemer's was not universal.

The third utterance of our Master on the Cross, for others, not for Himself, was, "Behold thy mother." He who was dying on the Cross, whose name was Love, was the great Philanthropist, whose charity embraced the whole human race. His last dying act was an act of individual attachment, tenderness towards a mother, fidelity towards a friend. Now, some well-meaning persons seem to think that the larger charities are incompatible with the indulgence of particular affections ; and, therefore, all that they do, and aim at, is on a large scale, they occupy themselves with the desire to emancipate the whole mass of mankind. But, brethren, it not unfrequently happens that those who act in this manner are but selfish after all, and are quite inattentive to all the fidelities of friendship and the amenities of social life. It was not so, if we may venture to say it, that the spirit of the Redeemer grew, for as he progressed in wisdom and knowledge, He progressed also in love. First, we read of His tenderness and obedience to His parents, then the selection of twelve to be near Him from the rest of the disciples, and then the selection of one, more especially as a friend. It was through this that, apparently, His human soul grew in grace and in love. And if it were not so with Him, at all events it must be so with us. It is in vain for a man in his dying hour, who has loved no man individually, to attempt to love the human race ; everything here must be done by degrees. Love is a habit. God has given to us the love of relations and friends, the love of father and mother, brother, sister, friend, to prepare us gradually for the love of God ; if there be one stone of the foundation not securely laid, the superstructure will be imperfect. The domestic affections are the alphabet of Love.

Lastly, our Master said, "It is finished," partly for others, partly for Himself. In the earliest part of His life, we read that He said, "I have a baptism to be baptized with;" to Him as to every human soul, this life had its side of darkness and gloom, but all that was now accomplished: He has drunk His last earthly drop of anguish, He has to drink the wine no more till He drink it new in His Father's kingdom. It was finished; all was over; and with, as it were, a burst of subdued joy, He says, "It is finished."

There is another aspect in which we may regard these words, as spoken also for others. The way in which our Redeemer contemplated this life was altogether a peculiar one. He looked upon it, not as a place of rest or pleasure, but simply, solely, as a place of duty. He was here to do His Father's will, not His own; and therefore, now that life was closed, He looked upon it chiefly as a duty that was fulfilled. We have the meaning of this in the seventeenth chapter of this Gospel : "I have glorified Thee on earth, I have finished the work which Thou gavest me to do." The duty is done, the work is finished. Let us each apply this to ourselves. That hour is coming to us all; indeed it is, perhaps, *now* come. The dark night settles down on each day.

"It is finished." We are *ever* taking leave of something that will not come back again. We let go, with a pang, portion after portion of our existence. However dreary we may have felt life to be here, yet when that hour comes—the winding-up of all things, the last grand rush of darkness on our spirits, the hour of that awful sudden wrench from all we have ever known or loved, the long farewell to sun, moon, stars, and light—Brother men, I ask you this day, and I ask myself, humbly and fearfully, *What* will then be finished? When it is finished, what will it be? Will it be the butterfly existence of pleasure, the mere life of science, a life of uninterrupted sin, and selfish gratification; or will it be, "Father, I have finished the work which Thou gavest me to do?"

THE END.

LONDON : PRINTED BY
SPOTTISWOODE AND CO., NEW-STREET SQUARE
AND PARLIAMENT STREET

A SELECTION FROM THE NOTICES

OF

MR. ROBERTSON'S SERMONS,

AND OF THE

LIFE AND LETTERS OF F. W. ROBERTSON.

BY THE REV. STOPFORD A. BROOKE, M.A.

Chaplain in Ordinary to the Queen.

A SELECTION FROM THE NOTICES OF

MR. ROBERTSON'S SERMONS,

AND OF THE

LIFE AND LETTERS OF F. W. ROBERTSON,

BY THE REV. STOPFORD A. BROOKE, M.A.

Chaplain in Ordinary to the Queen.

[BLACKWOOD'S MAGAZINE, August, 1862.]

"For while hapless Englishmen complain in the papers, and in private, in many a varied wail, over the sermons they have to listen to, it is very apparent that the work of the preacher has not fallen in any respect out of estimation. Here is a book which has gone through as great a number of editions as the most popular novel. It bears Mudie's stamp upon its dingy boards, and has all those marks of arduous service which are only to be seen in books which belong to great public libraries. It is thumbed, dog's-eared, pencil-marked, worn by much perusal. Is it then a novel? On the contrary, it is a volume of sermons. A fine, tender, and lofty mind, full of thoughtfulness, full of devotion, has herein left his legacy to his country. It is not rhetoric or any vulgar excitement of eloquence that charms so many readers to the book, so many hearers to this preacher's feet. It is not with the action of a Demosthenes, with outstretched arms and countenance of flame, that he presses his gospel upon his audience. On the contrary, when we read those calm and lofty utterances, this preacher seems seated, like his Master, with the multitude palpitating round, but no agitation or passion in his own thoughtful, contemplative breast. The Sermons of Robertson, of Brighton, have few of the exciting qualities of oratory. Save for the charm of a singularly pure and lucid style, their almost sole attraction consists in their power of instruction, in their faculty of opening up the mysteries of life and truth. It is pure teaching, so far as that ever can be administered to a popular audience, which is offered to us in these volumes."

[EDINBURGH CHRISTIAN MAGAZINE.]

"They are Sermons of a bold, uncompromising thinker—of a man resolute for the truth of God, and determined in the strength of God's grace to make that truth clear, to brush away all the fine-spun sophistries and half-truths by which the cunning sins of men have hidden it. . . . There must be a great and true heart, where there is a great and true preacher. And in that, beyond everything else, lay the secret of Mr. Robertson's influence. His Sermons show evidence enough of acute logical power. His analysis is exquisite in its subtleness and delicacy. . . . With Mr. Robertson style is but the vehicle, not the substitute for thought. Eloquence, poetry, scholarship, originality—his Sermons show proof enough of these to put him on a level with the foremost men of his time. But, after all, their charm lies in the warm, loving, sympathetic heart, in the well-disciplined mind of the true Christian, in his noble scorn of all lies, of all things mean and crooked, in his brave battling for right, even when wrong seems crowned with success, in his honest simplicity and singleness of purpose, in the high and holy tone—as if, amid the discord of earth, he heard clear, though far off, the perfect harmony of heaven ; in the fiery earnestness of his love for Christ, the devotion of his whole being to the goodness and truth revealed in him."

[CHURCH OF ENGLAND MONTHLY REVIEW.]

"It is hardly too much to say, that had the Church of England produced no other fruit in the present century, this work alone would be amply sufficient to acquit her of the charge of barrenness. . . . The reputation of Mr. Robertson's Sermons is now so wide-spread, that any commendation of ours may seem superfluous. We will therefore simply, in conclusion, recommend such of our readers as have not yet made their acquaintance, to read them carefully and thoughtfully, and they will find in them more deeply suggestive matter than in almost any book published in the present century."

[MORNING POST.]

"They are distinguished by masterly exposition of Scriptural truths and the true spirit of Christian charity."

[BRITISH QUARTERLY.]

"These Sermons are full of thought and beauty, and admirable illustrations of the ease with which a gifted and disciplined mind can make the obscure transparent, the difficult plain. There is not a Sermon that does not furnish evidence of originality without extravagance, of discrimination without tediousness, and of piety without cant or conventionalism."

[ECLECTIC REVIEW.]

"We hail with unaffected delight the appearance of these volumes. The Sermons are altogether out of the common style. They are strong, free, and beautiful utterances of a gifted and cultivated mind. Occasionally, the expression of theological sentiment fails fully to represent our own thought, and we sometimes detect tendencies with which we cannot sympathize : but, taken as a whole, the discourses are fine specimens of a high order of preaching."

[GUARDIAN.]

"Very beautiful in feeling, and occasionally striking and forcible in conception to a remarkable degree. . . . . Even in the imperfect shape in which their deceased author left them, they are very remarkable compositions."

[CHRISTIAN REMEMBRANCER.]

"We should be glad if all preachers more united with ourselves, preached such Sermons as these."

[WESTMINSTER REVIEW.]

"To those who affectionately remember the author, they will recall, though imperfectly, his living eloquence and his living truthfulness."

[GLOBE.]

"Mr. Robertson, of Brighton, is a name familiar to most of us, and honoured by all to whom it is familiar. A true servant of Christ, a bold and heart-stirring preacher of the Gospel, his teaching was unlike the teaching of most clergymen, for it was beautified and intensified by genius. New truth, new light, streamed from each well-worn text when he handled it."

[BLACKWOOD'S MAGAZINE.]

"When teaching of this description keeps the popular ear and secures the general attention, it is unquestionable proof that the office of the preacher has, in no way, lost its hold on the mind of the people. The acceptance of a voice so unimpassioned and thoughtful, so independent of all vulgar auxiliaries, so intent upon bringing every theme it touches to the illustration and sanctifying of the living life of the hour, that which alone can be mended, and purified, and sanctified, is a better tribute to the undying office of the preacher than the success of a hundred Spurgeons. Attention and interest are as eager as ever where there is in reality any instruction to bestow."

[LITERARY GAZETTE.]

"In earnestness of practical appeal, and in eloquent and graceful diction, Mr. Robertson has few rivals, and these characteristics are sufficient to account for his unusual popularity."

[NATIONAL REVIEW.]

"A volume of very fine Sermons, quite equal to the previous series."

[BRIGHTON EXAMINER.]

"There is in the Sermons in this volume the same freshness, vigour of thought and felicity of expression, as characterised whatever Mr. Robertson said.

[ECONOMIST.]

"Mr. Robertson's Sermons have the great and rare merit of neutral-ising by a more charitable and affectionate spirit, and by a wider intelligence, all that may appear rigid and *doctrinaire* in the Church of England. The result seems to have been his special mission : it most fully explains the mind of the man. . . . . We recommend the Sermons to the perusal of our readers. They will find in them thought of so rare and beautiful a description, an earnestness of mind so steadfast in the search of truth, and a charity so pure and all-embracing, that we cannot venture to offer praise, which would be, in this case, almost as presumptuous as criticism."

[SATURDAY REVIEW.]

" When Mr. Robertson died, his name was scarcely known beyond the circle of his own private friends, and of those among whom he had laboured in his calling. Now, every word he wrote is eagerly sought for and affectionately treasured up, and meets with the most reverent and admiring welcome from men of all parties and all shades of opinion. . . . . To those that find in his writings what they themselves want, he is a teacher quite beyond comparison—his words having a meaning, his thoughts a truth and depth, which they cannot find elsewhere. And they never look to him in vain. . . . . He fixes himself upon the recollection as a most original and profound thinker, and as a man in whom excellence puts on a new form. . . . There are many persons, and the number increases every year, to whom Robertson's writings are the most stable, satisfactory, and exhaustless form of religious teaching which the nineteenth century has given—the most wise, suggestive, and practical."

[BRIGHTON HERALD.]

" To our thinking, no compositions of the same class, at least since the days of Jeremy Taylor, can be compared with these Sermons delivered to the congregation of Trinity Chapel, Brighton, by their late minister. They have that power over the mind which belongs only to the highest works of genius : they stir the soul to its inmost depths : they move the affections, raise the imagination, bring out the higher and spiritual part of our nature by the continual appeal that is made to it, and tend to make us, at the same time, humble and aspiring—merciful to others and doubtful of ourselves."

[From a SERMON preached at the CONSECRATION of the BISHOP of NORWICH, by the REV. J. H. GURNEY, late of MARYLEBONE.]

" I do not commit myself to all his theology ; I may differ from the preacher in some things, and listen doubtfully to others. But I know of no modern sermons at once so suggestive and so inspiriting, with reference to the whole range of Christian duty. He is fresh and original without being recondite : plain-spoken without severity ; and discusses some of the exciting topics of the day without provoking strife or lowering his tone as a Christian teacher. He delivers his message, in fact, like one who is commissioned to call men off from trifles and squabbles, and conventional sins and follies, to something higher and nobler than their common life : like a man in earnest, too, avoiding technicalities, speaking his honest mind in phrases that are his own, and with a directness from which there is no escape. O that a hundred like him were given us by God, and placed in prominent stations throughout our land ! "

[GUARDIAN.]

" Without anything of that artificial symmetry which the traditional division into heads was apt to display, they present each reflection in a distinct method of statement, clearly and briefly worked out ; the sentences are short and terse, as in all popular addresses they should be ; the thoughts are often very striking, and entirely out of the track of ordinary sermonising. In matters of doctrine such novelty is sometimes unsafe ; but the language is that of one who tries earnestly to penetrate into the very centre of the truth he has to expound, and differs as widely as possible from the sceptic's doubt or the controversialist's mistake. More frequently Mr. Robertson deals with questions of practical life, of public opinion, and of what we may call social casuistry—turning the light of Christian ethics upon this unnoticed though familiar ground. The use of a carriage on Sunday, the morality of feeing a railway porter against his employers' rules, are topics not too small for illustration or application of his lessons in divine truth."

[BRIGHTON GAZETTE.]

" As an author, Mr. Robertson was, in his lifetime, unknown ; for with the exception of one or two addresses, he never published, having a singular disinclination to bring his thoughts before the public in the form of published sermons. As a minister, he was beloved and esteemed for his unswerving fidelity to his principles and his fearless propagation of his religious views. As a townsman, he was held in the highest estimation ; his hand and voice being ever ready to do all in his power to advance the moral and social position of the working man. It was not till after his decease, which event created a sensation and demonstration such as Brighton never before or since witnessed, that his works were subjected to public criticism. It was then found that in the comparatively retired minister of Trinity Chapel there had existed a man possessed of consummate ability and intellect of the highest order ; that the sermons laid before his congregation were replete with the subtleties of intellect, and bore evidence of the keenest perception and most exalted catholicity. His teaching was of an extremely liberal character, and if fair to assign a man possessed of such a universality of sympathy to any party, we should say that he belonged to what is denominated the 'Broad Church.' We, with many others, cannot agree in the fullest extent of his teaching, but, at the same time, feel bound to accord the tribute due to his genius."

[MORNING CHRONICLE.]

"A volume of very excellent Sermons, by the late lamented Incumbent of Trinity Chapel, Brighton."

[TITAN.]

"But the Sermons now under notice are, we venture to say, taking all the circumstances into consideration, the most remarkable discourses of the age. . . . They are throughout vital with the rarest force, burning with an earnestness perhaps never surpassed, and luminous with the light of genius. . . . We suspect that even Brighton little knew what a man Providence had placed in its midst."

On the "*Analysis of Mr. Tennyson's In Memoriam :*"—

[GUARDIAN.]

"An endeavour to give, in a few weighty words, the key-note (so to speak) of each poem in the series. Those will best appreciate the amount of success attained by Mr. Robertson who try to do the same work better."

From a few of the Notices on Mr. Robertson's " *Lectures on the Epistles to the Corinthians :*"—

[MORNING POST.]

" It was Mr. Robertson's custom every Sunday afternoon, instead of preaching from one text, to expound an entire chapter of some book in the Scriptures. The present volume is made up from notes of fifty-six discourses of this kind. 'Some people were startled by the introduction of what they called secular subjects into the pulpit. But the lecturer in all his ministrations refused to recognize the distinction so drawn. He said that the whole life of a Christian was sacred—that common every-day doings, whether of a trade, or of a profession, or the minuter details of a woman's household life, were the arenas in which trial and temptation arose ; and that therefore it became the Christian minister's duty to enter into this family working life with his people, and help them to understand its meaning, its trials, and its compensations.' It is enough to add that the lectures now given to the public are written in this spirit."

[CRITIC.]

" Such discourses as these before us, so different from the shallow rhapsodies or tedious hair-splitting which are now so much in vogue, may well make us regret that Mr. Robertson can never be heard again in the pulpit. This single volume would in itself establish a reputation for its writer."

[BRIGHTON HERALD.]

" . . . . Were there no name on the title-page, the spirit which shines forth in these lectures could but be recognized as that of the earnest, true-hearted man, the deep thinker, the sympathizer with all kinds of human trouble, the aspirant for all things holy, and one who joined to these rare gifts, the faculty of speaking to his fellow-men in such a manner as to fix their attention and win their love. . . . . In whatever spirit the volume is read—of doubt, of criticism, or of full belief in the truths it teaches—it can but do good ; it can but leave behind the conviction that here was a genuine, true-hearted man, gifted with the highest intellect, inspired by the most disinterested motives and the purest love for his fellow-men, and that the fountain at which he warmed his heart and kindled his eloquence was that which flows from Christ."

[BRITISH QUARTERLY REVIEW.]

"This volume will be a welcome gift to many an intelligent and devout mind. There are few of our modern questions, theological or ecclesiastical, that do not come up for discussion in the course of these Epistles to the Christians at Corinth."

[MORNING HERALD.]

"No one can read these lectures without being charmed by their singular freshness and originality of thought, their earnest, simple eloquence, and their manly piety. There is no mawkish sentiment, no lukewarm, semi-religious twaddle, smacking of the *Record;* no proclamation of party views or party opinions, but a broad, healthy, living, and fervent exposition of one of the most difficult books in the Bible. Every page is full of personal earnestness and depth of feeling ; but every page is also free from the slightest trace of vanity and egotism. The words come home to the reader's heart as the utterance of a sincere man who felt every sentence which flowed from his lips."

[PRESS.]

"One of the most marked features of these lectures is the deep feeling which the preacher had of the emptiness and hollowness of the conventional religionism of the day. The clap-trap of popular ministers, the pride and uncharitableness of exclusive Evangelicalism, the pomp and pretension of ritualism and priestly affectation — the miserable Pharisaism which is lurking underneath them all—form the subject of many strikingly true and often cutting remarks. He has no patience with the unrealities of sectarian purism and pedantic orthodoxy. His constant cry, the constant struggle of his soul is for reality. Hence while his views of objective truth are at times deficient, or, at least, very imperfectly stated, he leaves a deep impress of subjective religion upon the mind, by a style of teaching which, far from uninstructive, is yet more eminently suggestive."

[THE SPECTATOR.]

"No book published since the 'Life of Dr. Arnold' has produced so strong an impression on the moral imagination and spiritual theology of England as we may expect from these volumes. Even for those who knew Mr. Robertson well, and for many who knew *him*, as they thought, better than his Sermons, the free and full discussion of the highest subjects in the familiar letters so admirably selected by the Editor of Mr. Robertson's *Life*, will give a far clearer insight into his remarkable character and inspire a deeper respect for his clear and manly intellect. Mr. Brooke has done his work as Dr. Stanley did his in writing the 'Life of Arnold,' and it is not possible to give higher praise. . . . . Everyone will talk of Mr. Robertson, and no one of Mr. Brooke, because Mr. Brooke has thought much of his subject, nothing of himself, and hence the figure which he wished to present comes out quite clear and keen, without any interposing haze of literary vapour."

[THE CHRISTIAN WORLD.]

"The Life of Robertson of Brighton supplies a very unique illustration of the way in which a man may attain his highest fame after he has passed away from earth. There are few who make any pretension to an acquaintance with modern literature who do not know something of Mr. Robertson's works. His sermons are indisputably ranked with the highest sacred classics. . . . . The publication of his 'Life and Letters' helps us to some information which is very precious, and explains much mystery that hangs around the name of the great Brighton preacher. It will be generally admitted that these two volumes will furnish means for estimating the character of Mr. Robertson which are not supplied in any or all of his published works. . . . . There was no artificiality or show about the pulpit production, no half-utterances or whispers of solemn belief; but there was the natural restraint which would be imposed by a true gentleman upon his words when speaking to mixed congregations. Many of us wanted to know how he talked and wrote when the restraint was removed. This privilege is granted to us in these volumes. . . . . There was no romance of scene and circumstance in the life of Frederick Robertson; but there was more than romance about the real life of the man. In some respects it was like the life of a new Elijah. . . . . A more thoughtful, suggestive, and beautiful preacher never entered a pulpit; a simpler and braver man never lived; a truer Christian never adorned any religious community. His life and death were *vicarious*, as he himself might have put it. He lived and died for others, for us all. The sorrows and agonies of his heart pressed rare music out of it, and the experience of a terribly bitter life leaves a wealth of thought and reflection never more than equalled in the history of men."

[The Guardian.]

"With all drawbacks of what seem to us imperfect taste, an imperfect standard of character, and an imperfect appreciation of what there is in the world beyond a given circle of interest, the book does what a biography ought to do—it shows us a remarkable man, and it gives us the means of forming our own judgment about him. It is not a tame panegyric or a fancy picture. The main portion of the book consists of Mr. Robertson's own letters, and his own account of himself, and we are allowed to see him, in a great degree at least, as he really was. . . . . It is the record of a genuine spontaneous character, seeking its way, its duty, its perfection, with much sincerity and elevation of purpose, many anxieties and sorrows, and not, we doubt not, without much of the fruits that come with real self-devotion; a record disclosing a man with great faults and conspicuous blanks in his nature.

[The Morning Post.]

"Mr. Brooke has done good service in giving to the world so faithful a sketch of so worthy a man. It would have been a reproach to the Church if this enduring and appropriate memorial had not been erected to one who was so entirely devoted to its service; and the labour of love, for such it evidently was, was committed to no unskilful hands. . . Mr. Robertson's epistolary writings—gathered in these valuable volumes—often unstudied, always necessarily from their nature free and unrestrained, but evidencing depth and vigour of thought, clear perception, varied knowledge, sound judgment, earnest piety, are doubtless destined to become as widely known and as largely beneficial as his published Sermons. It is impossible to peruse them without receiving impressions for good, and being persuaded that they are the offspring of no ordinary mind."

[THE MORNING HERALD.]

"Mr. Brooke has done his own work as a biographer with good sense, feeling, and taste. . . . . These volumes are of real value to all thoughtful readers. For many a year we have had no such picture of a pure and noble and well spent life."

[THE ATHENÆUM.]

"There is something here for all kinds of readers, but the higher a man's mind and the more general his sympathies, the keener will be his interest in the 'Life of Robertson.'"

[THE NONCONFORMIST.]

"As no English sermons of the century have been so widely read, and as few leaders of religious thought have exerted (especially by works in so much of an unperfected and fragmentary character) so penetrating and powerful an influence on the spiritual tendencies of the times, we can well believe that no biography since Arnold's will presently be possible to be compared with this, for the interest excited by it in the minds of readers who consciously live in the presence of the invisible and eternal, who feel the pressure of difficult questions and painful experiences, and who seek reality and depth, and freedom in the life and activity of the Church of Christ. . . . . Mr. Brooke has produced a 'Life of Robertson' which will not unworthily compare with Dean Stanley's 'Life of Arnold,' and which, with that, and Ryland's 'Life of Foster,' and the 'Life of Channing,' is likely to be prized as one of the most precious records of genuine manly and godly excellence."

[THE MORNING STAR.]

"The beautiful work which Mr. Brooke has written contains few, if any, romantic episodes. It is the life of a man who worked hard and died early. . . . . Mr. Brooke has acted wisely in allowing Mr. Robertson to speak so fully for himself, and in blending his letters with his narrative, and arranging them in chronological order. These letters are in themselves a mine of intellectual wealth. They contain little of table-talk or parlour gossip ; but they abound with many of his best and most ripened thoughts on multitudes of subjects, political, literary, and scientific, as well as theological. We wish we could present our readers

with extracts from them ; but even if we had space, it would be unfair
to the writer to quote disjointed fragments from a correspondence which
now belongs to the literature of the country. . . . . Mr. Brooke
has performed his responsible task as a biographer and an editor in
a spirit of just and discriminating appreciation, and with admirable
ability."

LONDON : PRINTED BY
SPOTTISWOODE AND CO., NEW-STREET SQUARE
AND PARLIAMENT STREET